THE LAST DAYS OF STALIN

JOSHUA RUBENSTEIN

THE LAST DAYS OF STALIN

YALE UNIVERSITY PRESS
NEW HAVEN AND LONDON

For information about this and other Yale University Press publications, please contact:
U.S. Office: sales.press@yale.edu   www.yalebooks.com
Europe Office: sales@yaleup.co.uk   www.yalebooks.co.uk

Typeset in Adobe Caslon Pro by IDSUK (DataConnection) Ltd
Printed in the United States of America

Library of Congress Cataloging-in-Publication Data

Rubenstein, Joshua, author.
Title: The last days of Stalin / Joshua Rubenstein.
Description: New Haven : Yale University Press, 2016. | Includes
    bibliographical references and index.
LCCN 2015047378 | ISBN 9780300192223 (hardback : alkaline paper)
LCSH: Stalin, Joseph, 1878-1953—Death and burial. | Stalin,
    Joseph, 1878-1953—Relations with Jews. | Stalin, Joseph,
    1878-1953—Political and social views. | Stalin, Joseph,
    1878-1953—Influence. | Heads of state—Soviet Union—Biography. | Soviet
    Union—Politics and government—1936-1953. | Social change—Soviet
    Union—History. | Soviet Union—Foreign relations—1953-1975. | BISAC:
    HISTORY / Europe / Russia & the Former Soviet Union. | BIOGRAPHY &
    AUTOBIOGRAPHY / Presidents & Heads of State. | HISTORY / Military / World
    War II. Classification: LCC DK268.S8 R83 2016 | DDC 947.084/2092—dc23
    LC record available at http://lccn.loc.gov/2015047378

A catalogue record for this book is available from the British Library.

10 9 8 7 6 5 4 3 2 1

CONTENTS

ACKNOWLEDGMENTS

A number of colleagues and friends helped me with this book. I am especially grateful to Heather McCallum, my editor at Yale University Press in London, who proposed the project to me. She proved to be a reliable friend and resource, firm, helpful, and clear-headed as I made my way through a thicket of historical events and challenges with the manuscript. My agents, Robin Straus and Andrew Nurnberg, were also particularly encouraging at moments when I wondered if I could sort out what needed to be said and how to get there.

Several colleagues at the Kathryn W. and Shelby Cullom Davis Center for Russian and Eurasian Studies at Harvard University, which has been my intellectual home for over three decades, provided much needed guidance and assistance. I relied on Mark Kramer for his remarkable knowledge of documents and historical writing on the period; he also proved to be a patient and insightful reader of the manuscript. Hugh Truslow, the librarian for the Davis Center Collection, was always ready to help me track down an obscure volume or find my way through online archival materials. He and other staff members at Harvard's Widener Library provided much needed bibliographic support.

Kimberly St. Julian worked as my research assistant when I first began this project, while Sydney Soderberg located material for me at the Dwight D. Eisenhower Presidential Library in Abilene, Kansas. I want to thank both of them for their help.

David Brandenberger at Richmond College was among the colleagues I first approached when I was considering how to fashion a book about the events surrounding Stalin's death; his feedback and encouragement were always welcome. Maxim Shrayer of Boston College was also a source of ideas and inspiration. My longtime friend, Boris Katz, was kind enough to read parts of the manuscript and, as always, was forthright and thorough in his criticism.

In addition, I would like to thank Sergei Nikitich Khrushchev who welcomed me to his home in Cranston, Rhode Island, near the outset of my research. I very much benefited from our conversation about his father and his own experiences during those fateful days in March 1953. And Tatiana Yankelevich shared a vivid story with me from the life of her mother, Elena Bonner, who came close to being a victim of the Doctors' Plot. Jonathan Brent also shared a good deal of material with me from his extensive collection of documents about the Doctors' Plot.

Finally, my wife, Jill Janows and our son, Ben, had to endure yet another deep dive into Soviet history which required me to be in libraries and behind a study door at all hours of the day and night. Their patient love continues to be a crucial source of emotional support.

INTRODUCTION

Joseph Stalin collapsed and died in an atmosphere of medieval recrimination. It was March 1953. The Kremlin seethed with fears of a broad, new purge against members of his Presidium. A public campaign against treasonous Jewish doctors threatened to engulf all of Soviet Jewry. Tensions with the West were more and more alarming: after three years of fighting, the war in Korea continued unabated while American and Soviet armies faced each other in a divided Germany. At the same time a new American administration led by President Dwight David Eisenhower and Secretary of State John Foster Dulles had come into office that January with the intention of "rolling back" communism only to find themselves confronting Stalin's heirs and a host of unexpected reforms.

At home and abroad Stalin's longtime "comrades-in-arms" faced a host of difficult dilemmas. They understood the need to release prisoners from the Gulag, disavow the Doctors' Plot, and provide higher living standards for the population. They also offered concessions to the West, a dramatic "peace offensive" that included renewed and serious negotiations to end the fighting in Korea and reduce tensions in Europe, including in the satellite countries in Eastern Europe where Stalin's extreme policies were leading to popular unrest against communist rule.

But their overriding concern was preserving their hold on power. Stalin had so dominated life in the country that his death provoked an enormous outpouring of disoriented grief. "Stalin was inside everyone, like the hammer alongside the sickle in every mind," as the writer Andrei Sinyavsky wrote.[1] The regime feared that his death would lead to panic and disorder, which in turn could undermine their legitimacy and the authority of one-party rule. They had to devise a way to distance themselves from Stalin's crimes while insisting that the Communist Party not be held responsible for the tyrant's brutality, that the party was more to be pitied for what it had endured than condemned for what it had applauded. This dilemma arose immediately after his collapse, then continued for decades, with occasional flashes of candor and truth followed by renewed, official respect for Stalin and his leadership. It affected his medical treatment, the conduct of his funeral, relations with the West, and everyday life in the country.

This book opens with Stalin's death, moves backward in time to the Nineteenth Party Congress in October 1952, when Stalin made his last public speech, then proceeds through the winter of 1952–53 when the Doctors' Plot and a broad campaign against the country's Jews unfolded. It explores how the Soviet and American press covered Stalin's death and how the new Eisenhower administration reacted to the dramatic changes in Moscow that followed. It concludes with the arrest of Stalin's longtime security chief, Lavrenti Beria, in June.

Stalin's death introduced an unprecedented opportunity. It gave his heirs the chance to reverse many of his policies and move the country forward in a hopeful, more relaxed direction. It presented the United States with an urgent need to review assumptions about how it could work with a brutal and menacing dictatorship that had suddenly lost its leader and seemed ready to negotiate a new beginning to its relations with the outside world. For complex reasons both Soviet and Western governments could not overcome the decades of mistrust that divided them. The arms race persisted. The division of Germany and Europe continued. The Cold War reached into far corners of the world where tensions between East and West spilled over into proxy conflicts of untold misery and destruction. And in the Soviet Union the promise of change that highlighted the initial months that followed Stalin's death collapsed into a pattern of exhilarating reform and disheartening repression that lasted until Mikhail Gorbachev pushed the limits of reform so far that the Soviet regime could no longer survive. Stalin's death gave the Kremlin and the West the chance to escape the grim reality of his nightmarish imagination, a challenge they failed to accomplish. That failure haunted the world for decades to follow.

CHAPTER ONE

THE DEATH OF STALIN

Early on Wednesday morning, March 4, 1953, well before dawn, the Soviet government issued a startling announcement over Radio Moscow, alerting its people and the world at large that Joseph Stalin had suffered a devastating stroke on Sunday night, March 1. According to official statements, Stalin had been stricken in his Kremlin apartment by a cerebral hemorrhage causing loss of speech and consciousness. He was paralyzed on his right side and both his heart and lungs were no longer functioning properly. The regime assured the Soviet people that Stalin was receiving suitable medical treatment "under the constant supervision of the Central Committee of the Communist Party of the Soviet Union and the Soviet Government." Nonetheless, everyone must "realize the full significance of the fact that the grave illness of Comrade Stalin will involve his more or less prolonged non-participation in leading activity." This would mean the "temporary withdrawal of Comrade Stalin" from affairs of state.

A medical bulletin provided more specific diagnostic detail, including measurements of his labored breathing, an elevated pulse and clinically worrisome high blood pressure together with arrhythmia of the heart. Despite Stalin's "grave state of health," the doctors were applying "a series of therapeutic measures ... toward restoration of the vitally important functions of the organism."[1] The bulletin was issued over the names of eleven prestigious doctors, including the minister of public health and the chief doctor of the Kremlin. The regime was making clear that it was providing the most effective care possible in response to a devastating medical event; that party leaders were monitoring the work of the minister of public health, while the minister was supervising ten other doctors; and that, as their names indicated, none of them were Jewish. This was crucially important because only seven weeks earlier, on January 13, the regime had announced the exposure of a sinister conspiracy involving a group of physicians, most of whom were Jews, who were said to be in league with imperialist and Zionist organizations to carry out the murder of leading Soviet officials by maliciously applying their medical skills. This was the notorious Doctors' Plot. Now Stalin had fallen ill. His successors and members of his inner circle—Georgy Malenkov, Lavrenti Beria, Nikolai Bulganin and Nikita Khrushchev—waited at least forty-eight hours to announce the news, wanting to be sure they agreed on how to divide party and government authority, both to calm the population and, not least, to protect themselves. They had been living in fear for their own lives, wondering if and when Stalin would target one, two, or all of them as he had dispatched so many other once-powerful men. Their shared interest in survival ensured their cooperation at this delicate moment. They also needed to be absolutely confident that Stalin was about to die. Suddenly, his ruthless, personal dictatorship was over. Their fear of him was evaporating.

Stalin's health had long been a question of deep speculation. Who did not dream about his dying? Or perhaps people were simply looking for hints of mortality knowing that except for death itself, nothing demonstrates a common humanity more vividly than aging and illness. But for some even that was too much of a prohibited instinct. Listening to the medical communiqués, the writer Konstantin Simonov thought it was "senseless to consider what the pulse, the blood pressure, the temperature and all the other details in the bulletins could mean, what they signified about the medical condition of a seventy-three-year-old man. I did not want to think about it and did not want to talk about it with others because it did not seem right to talk about Stalin simply as an old man who suddenly took sick."[2] As the writer Ilya Ehrenburg wrote in his memoirs, "We had long lost sight of the fact that Stalin was mortal. He had become an all-powerful and remote deity."[3] But Stalin did not share this illusion. There were countless rumors that he was supporting scientific research into extending human life, even that he spared the famous doctor Lina Shtern after her conviction for treason and espionage in 1952 because he thought her work could extend his own life span.[4]

Based on the reports of doctors who had treated Stalin and on other sources of information, it is possible to piece together at least a partial medical history. Stalin suffered from several disfiguring features. The toes of his left foot were webbed. His face was pock-marked from a bout of smallpox as a child. His left arm appeared to be withered, with an elbow that could not properly bend; there are different explanations for this injury, either that an accident as a young boy was not properly treated or that his left arm was injured during a difficult birth, leaving him with a condition called Erb's palsy. As he approached the age of fifty, he began to seek treatment for dull pains in the muscles and nerve endings of his arms and legs, a condition that doctors urged him to treat with cures at medicinal baths in southern Russia and the Caucasus. He also suffered from headaches and painful conditions in his throat. By 1936, his doctors noted problems with his ability to walk and stand, and they began treating him for the initial symptoms of arteriosclerosis.

Following the war, it is believed that Stalin suffered either a heart attack or small strokes in 1945 and again in 1947. Based on little hard information, there were a number of articles in the Western press which speculated about his faltering condition. In October 1945, the *Chicago Tribune*, the *Paris Press*, and *Newsweek* all claimed that Stalin had suffered two heart attacks at the Potsdam Conference the previous summer where he met President Truman for the first and only time. On November 11, the French journal *Bref* reported that Stalin had suffered a heart attack on September 13 and that he had retired to the Black Sea in order to write his political "testimony."[5] It remains difficult to clarify exactly what was going on. Stalin welcomed US Ambassador Averell Harriman to Sochi on October 24 and 25, and it was Harriman who reassured the press that "Generalissimus Stalin is in good health and rumors of his ill health have no foundation whatsoever."[6]

His medical condition, nonetheless, continued to deteriorate in the post-war years. A foreign diplomat who saw him in June 1947 was struck by how much he had aged since the conclusion of the war; Stalin was now "an old, very tired old man."[7] According to the Russian historian Dmitri Volkogonov, Stalin fainted at least three times in his office, twice in the presence of his secretary, Aleksandr Poskrebyshev, and once in front of members of the Politburo. Volkogonov described these attacks as sudden spasms in his blood vessels.[8] At Stalin's last appointment with his personal physician, the cardiologist Vladimir Vinogradov on January 19, 1952, his doctor urged him to consider retirement. Such advice angered Stalin and he dismissed it as a sign of disrespect. It was out of the question. (Vinogradov was later arrested in the fall of 1952 as part of the Doctors' Plot.)

But Stalin was not entirely oblivious to the need to take care of his health. Beginning in 1945 (following the war), he would leave Moscow for an increasing number of months—initially three months a year, then almost five months in 1950, and finally a full seven months from August 1951 to February 1952—finding it more restful to live and work at one of his southern dachas where the warm weather and familiar climate of the Caucasus revived him.[9] From there he could read reports and telegrams, all along never letting the country know that he was not working in the Kremlin. Rarely though did he take Vinogradov's advice. As a chain smoker who kept his pipe filled with tobacco, Stalin exacerbated his hypertension and did not stop smoking until early in 1952. By then, he had also stopped taking steam baths; sitting in a *banya* only increased his blood pressure. To treat his hypertension, he liked to drink boiled water with a few drops of iodine before dinner, a useless exercise in self-medication.

By 1950, interest in Stalin's health was widespread in the West, generating convoluted rumors of serious illness, even his death. In March, after Stalin failed to deliver an election speech, the US embassy in Moscow reported to Washington that he might be suffering from throat cancer. Two years later, in January 1952, the US embassy in Warsaw reported that Stalin was ill, leaving "Beria, Malenkov, and Molotov or Shvernik" to act in his place.[10] Three weeks later, the US embassy in Ankara reported that the Turkish prime minister, Adnan Menderes, had advised the American ambassador about an intercepted message out of the Polish embassy that Stalin was "seriously ill."[11] Two days after that, the US embassy in Moscow cited newspaper reports out of Amsterdam that Stalin's health was failing after a heart operation on December 19, 1951. There was also the claim that Soviet embassy officers in Amsterdam had been alerted by the foreign office in Moscow that Stalin was "no longer [a] young man" and that they should "not be alarmed to hear he had undergone [a] successful heart operation and might expect similar news in future in view his age."[12] Nonetheless, American diplomats added in the very same cable that Stalin had attended the annual Lenin anniversary ceremony at the Bolshoi Theater on January 21 where, the *New York Times* correspondent Harrison Salisbury later noted, Stalin appeared "in obvious good health and spirits."[13] The outgoing US ambassador to Moscow, Admiral Alan

Kirk, visited President Truman on February 4. When they discussed Stalin, the ambassador confirmed that he could not offer "concrete evidence of [Stalin's] failing health."[14] The Americans were grasping at straws.

Salisbury was following all of these rumors. On February 27, 1952, he sent a letter to his editors in New York—presumably the letter was taken out of the country in a secure manner to evade Soviet controls—about how he would alert them with a coded message should he learn of Stalin's death before an official statement came out. "Frankly," he added, "I think it is a thousand to one shot that anything will be known in advance of the official announcement, which almost certainly will be released for publication abroad as soon as it is made here." He also urged his colleagues to "query [him] before putting into print any rumors about [Stalin's health] such as the very silly item from Amsterdam which AP [Associated Press] carried."[15]

Western diplomats remained alert to any possible changes in Stalin's health. That June, US Ambassador George Kennan passed along rumors to Washington that Vyacheslav Molotov and Andrei Vyshinsky were about to replace Stalin, and that instructions were being quietly circulated to remove Stalin's ubiquitous pictures from public display. Such talk prompted Kennan to speculate that Stalin was withdrawing from at least some of his duties, that "his participation in public affairs is sporadic and relatively superficial as compared with [the] period before and during the war." Kennan, who was always among the most philosophical of American diplomats, could not help but comment on the unexpected longevity of Stalin's "comrades-in-arms." "Whims and vicissitudes of nature seem to me to have spared this body of men for abnormally long time. It is time nature began to play her usual tricks, and their effects may well be quite different from anything any of us have anticipated."[16] Nature did intervene, but not for another seven months.

That summer, American military attachés who attended a parade in Red Square reported to Kennan that the Stalin who stood atop the Mausoleum was probably a dummy; "the other members of the Politburo ... seemed to pay no attention to him and talked unceremoniously past his face."[17] Kennan knew enough to dismiss such a report, although it was widely assumed that Stalin sometimes employed a double. Kennan remained eager to hear from the new French ambassador, Louis Joxe, who had just seen Stalin in the Kremlin that August. Joxe and his colleagues found Stalin "showing his age very markedly. They said his hair was noticeably thin compared to his pictures, his face shrunken, his stature much smaller than they had expected. They had the impression that he moved his left arm only with considerable difficulty and that his bodily movements were in general labored and jerky." They left the meeting with the distinct feeling that they had been "confronted with an old man."[18]

Nonetheless, there are conflicting reports about Stalin's appearance and his level of energy in the final weeks of his life. Svetlana Alliluyeva visited her father for the final time on his birthday, December 21, 1952. She came away "worried over how badly he looked."[19] The last foreigners to visit with him were the newly appointed ambassador from Argentina, Louis Bravo, and the Indian ambassador K. P. S. Menon, who accompanied the Indian peace activist Dr. Saifuddin Kitchlew to the Kremlin. Bravo saw Stalin for nearly an hour on the evening of February 7, 1953, and reported him to be in "excellent physical and mental condition," belying his advanced age.[20] Stalin then welcomed Menon and Kitchlew on February 17, spending a half hour with Menon and then more than an hour with Kitchlew, who had just been awarded a Stalin Peace Prize.[21] Here again both men came away impressed by Stalin's "excellent health, mind, and spirits."[22] It is hard to know what to believe. Perhaps these men, progressives with a degree of sympathy toward the regime, were indulging in wishful thinking and were not going to reveal how Stalin's health was faltering. The reality would soon come to the attention of the world.[23]

On Saturday evening, February 28, 1953, Stalin entertained his inner circle at the Kremlin and then at the Nearby Dacha in the Moscow suburb of Kuntsevo. By the final years of his life, Stalin was spending virtually all of his free time there. The grounds of the Nearby Dacha included a rose garden, lemon and apple trees around a small pond, even a watermelon patch which Stalin liked to cultivate. Once inside, a vestibule welcomed visitors, with two cloakrooms on either side. To the left, a door led to Stalin's study equipped with a large desk that once accommodated military maps during the war; Stalin often liked to sleep on a sofa in the study. To the right, another door led to a long, rather narrow corridor with two bedrooms on the right-hand side. The same corridor led to a long, open veranda where Stalin would sometimes sit in the winter, enveloped in a fur hat and a sheepskin coat with traditional, Russian felt boots on his feet. The middle door off the front hall led to a large, rectangular banquet hall where a long, polished table dominated the space. It was here that Stalin held ceremonial banquets or welcomed the Politburo for meetings and late-night dinners. Modestly appointed, with standard chandeliers and rose-colored carpets, its only wall decorations were two large portraits—one of Lenin, the other of the writer Maxim Gorky. Stalin's bedroom stood on the other side of the dining room through a door that was almost invisibly placed in the wall; it contained a bed, two small dressers, and a sink. There was a large kitchen off to another side where a sizable oven for baking bread stood behind a wooden partition. When attacks of radiculitis (nerve inflammation) made Stalin particularly uncomfortable, he liked to undress and stretch out on a board above the oven, hoping the heat would relieve his symptoms.

The second floor, which could be reached by an elevator, was built to accommodate his daughter and her family, but she hardly stayed there and Stalin himself rarely went up there; the two rooms remained mostly empty and dark.

The dacha was designed as a place where Stalin could relax, distract himself with walks among the trees and rose bushes, or feed the birds. He could receive government officials and the occasional foreign guest, like Mao Zedong in the late 1940s, or Winston Churchill who stayed at the dacha during his first visit to Moscow during the war, in August 1942; he gave Stalin a radio which remained there. When Svetlana Alliluyeva last saw her father, the ordinary decorations on the walls "seemed strange" to her: "those awful portraits of writers . . ., the 'Reply of the Zaporozhe Cossacks' painting, those children's photographs taken from magazines." Stalin had the habit of cutting out pictures and illustrations from magazines, then hanging them on the walls of the dacha. "Another thing that seemed odd," his daughter wrote, "was the fact that a man who wanted something to put on the walls should never have considered hanging even one of the thousands of pictures he'd been given." She left unhappy after seeing her father; he looked unwell and the dacha depressed her.[24]

Stalin disliked being alone. As Khrushchev wrote of him, "The main thing was to occupy Stalin's time so that he wouldn't suffer from loneliness. He was depressed by loneliness and he feared it."[25] But he could always summon his inner circle for company. As often happened, Malenkov, Beria, Bulganin, and Khrushchev watched a movie with Stalin at the Kremlin on that fateful Saturday night. Two other longtime associates were not invited; neither Vyacheslav Molotov nor Anastas Mikoyan was there. They were living under a cloud.

Following the movie, the four "comrades-in-arms" drove out to Kuntsevo to join Stalin for dinner. They stayed until the early morning. This was not unusual because Stalin liked to keep them unbearably long hours and then sleep late into the next day. Again, according to Khrushchev, Stalin "was pretty drunk after dinner and in very high spirits." He walked them to the door, joking, friendly, jabbing Khrushchev "playfully in the stomach with his finger and calling [him] 'Mikita' with a Ukrainian accent. This was Stalin's habit when he was in a good mood. They all returned home happy"— Beria and Malenkov in one car and Khrushchev and Bulganin in another—"because nothing had gone wrong at dinner."[26] It was five or six o'clock in the morning.

But the next day, a Sunday, did not unfold as expected. According to Stalin's routine, the guards and household staff would expect to hear from him by 11 a.m. or perhaps 12 noon when he would ask for tea or some breakfast. As part of Stalin's security protocol, they were under strict orders not to enter his rooms without an invitation, a command they would break at their peril. But no call came and there seemed to be no stirring, no sound of footsteps or coughing. The guards waited. They noticed a light go on from inside his rooms that afternoon. In the early evening, as well, sentries outside the dacha saw a light through the window. But still there was no call, no request for tea or food. For security reasons, Stalin liked to sleep in different rooms, thinking it would confuse a would-be assassin. But this precaution also confused his guards who were never sure where he was sleeping.

According to Khrushchev, the guards did not call their superiors for instructions or think to sound an alarm that something might be amiss with Stalin. Khrushchev himself found it odd that he did not hear from Stalin all day. The silence from the Nearby Dacha seemed out of the ordinary, but there is no indication that Khrushchev called anyone to clarify what was happening. He reluctantly retired to bed himself.

By ten o'clock that night the guards grew so nervous that they decided to find a pretext for sending someone into Stalin's private rooms. An official packet of mail had arrived from the Kremlin, an everyday occurrence; Stalin needed to look over the material and it was the guards' responsibility to show it to him. So they decided to ask a longtime maid, Matryona Petrovna, to bring the packet in to him. She was an older woman who had worked for Stalin for many years. The reasoning was that if he were startled by her appearance in his rooms, she would be the least likely to arouse suspicion.

She found him lying on the floor in the library in his night clothes. He was unconscious, his clothes drenched with urine. He could barely move his limbs. When he tried to speak, he made only a strange buzzing sound. Matryona Petrovna quickly alerted the guards who lifted him onto a nearby sofa. In desperation, they called their boss, Minister of State Security Semyon Ignatiev. But he was too frightened to provide instructions and urged them to call Malenkov and Beria. They did reach Malenkov who mentioned how difficult it might be to find Beria. Malenkov knew Beria's habits and assumed he was with a mistress at an undisclosed dacha; the guards would not have either an address or a telephone number to reach him. It was Beria who called them, and, when he heard the news, insisted they tell no one about Stalin's condition. Malenkov also reached Bulganin and Khrushchev, urging them to come to the dacha.

Again, according to Khrushchev, Malenkov and Beria were the first to arrive, followed by Khrushchev himself. They approached Stalin quietly, either out of fear of disturbing him or not wanting to wake him if indeed he were asleep. Stalin was snoring. At this point, Beria assured the guards that Stalin was sleeping normally, that he was not to be disturbed. For an ordinary layman, it might be difficult to recognize the difference between someone who is asleep and someone who is unconscious and virtually paralyzed but is otherwise breathing. Most likely they understood that Stalin had suffered some kind of serious medical incident—the guards had found him on the floor and they could all see and smell how he had soiled himself— and that it would be best for all concerned, themselves in particular, to let him die. It also has to be considered that Stalin had not seen doctors for almost a year, except for an ear, nose, and throat specialist about a severe cold in April 1952. He had developed a pathological fear of medical professionals and had ordered the arrest of his own personal physicians. In the wake of the Doctors' Plot, Beria and Malenkov might well have decided that without definitive proof of some kind of medical emergency it would serve them better to hold off on summoning doctors. If in fact Stalin was sleeping normally they might well have decided to wait until morning when Stalin would awaken and they could sort out what, if anything, had occurred. In any event, no one immediately summoned medical assistance. Beria, Malenkov, and Khrushchev returned home. By that time Stalin had been ill for at least eight hours, perhaps as many as eighteen. We will never know for sure.

But the guards remained nervous. They again sent Matryona Petrovna in to observe him. He remained asleep but it seemed to be a strange kind of sleep. They called Malenkov to express their unease. And once again Malenkov called Beria, Bulganin, and Khrushchev. Only then did they decide to alert two other longtime party leaders, Kliment Voroshilov and Lazar Kaganovich, and to summon help.

Khrushchev's recollections of that night do not coincide with an account by Alexei Rybin, a security guard at the Bolshoi Theater who claimed to have spoken with several of Stalin's bodyguards. (Rybin himself was not present at the dacha.) According to Rybin, the bodyguards insisted that Stalin was not drunk, that he had imbibed only fruit juice before the guests departed around 4 a.m. Rybin, too, wrote how Stalin's failure to ask for breakfast or tea throughout the next day unnerved the guards on duty, but it was not Matryona Petrovna who was sent in. The deputy commissar for the dacha, Pyotr Lozgachev, took it on himself to bring Stalin the mail and check on his well-being. It was Lozgachev who found Stalin on a carpet, his body lying awkwardly on his elbow. Stalin was barely conscious, could hardly speak but raised a hand and responded with a nod when Lozgachev asked about lifting him onto a couch. Lozgachev quickly alerted the others on duty.

As the guards waited for medical help they decided to move Stalin to a nearby ottoman and cover him with a rug; his body was cold and they surmised he had fallen as long as seven or eight hours earlier. Lozgachev stayed with him, listening intently for the sound of a car bringing the doctors. But instead only Beria and Malenkov reached the dacha around 3 a.m. They approached Stalin with caution; Malenkov removed his shoes, carrying them in his hand. Just as in Khrushchev's account, Stalin was snoring, giving them reason to say that the guards had panicked. Even when Lozgachev tried to convince them that Stalin was gravely ill, Beria insisted he was sleeping normally and dismissed any concerns about his health, berating the guards for bothering them and even questioning their suitability to serve Stalin, at least according to Rybin. Without a nod from these party leaders, the guards did not have the courage to summon doctors on their own. They were not going to defy Beria.[27] As the writer Nadezhda Mandelstam noted, "Stalin inspired such terror that no one dared enter until it was too late."[28]

Although Stalin had deployed the full resources of his empire to protect himself, all these precautions served only to enhance his vulnerability. When he collapsed, his security arrangements made it harder for his staff to know what was going on, to assist him, to summon help. His chauffeur took different routes between the Kremlin and the dacha. His motorcade of five identical limousines, none with license plates, made its way over the twelve-mile route from the Kremlin to the dacha with the drivers passing one another to deter any would-be assassin. Hundreds of agents patrolled the dacha grounds with German shepherds. There were multiple locks on the gate and double rows of barbed wire around the compound, along with bodyguards among the household staff. None of these layers of security could prevent him from lying for hours in his own urine, paralyzed, and without the ability to scream.

As Stalin lay dying, his successors established a regimen to supervise his care: Lavrenti Beria and Georgy Malenkov during the day, Lazar Kaganovich and Mikhail Pervukhin, Kliment Voroshilov and Maxim Saburov, Nikita Khrushchev and Nikolai Bulganin throughout the night, a pair of them on hand at all hours. Beria took the most initiative at the dacha, summoning Malenkov to the second floor where they could talk discreetly. It was quiet there and away from the frantic activity below. For many hours they laid out plans for a revamped government that would soon take over. Khrushchev was well aware of Beria's energy and his thirst for power. According to his memoirs, Khrushchev warned Bulganin during their nighttime vigil that Beria was angling to take back control of the secret police "for the purpose of destroying us, and he will do it, too, if we let him."[29] But for now and for several months to follow they all agreed to work together and project an image of productive unity. Alert and wary, Khrushchev accepted the need for patience.

Although Stalin was unconscious, fear and anxiety continued to plague everyone around him. The doctors were afraid even to approach their patient. Khrushchev saw how Professor Pavel Lukomsky went up to Stalin "very cautiously . . . and touched [his] hand as though it were a hot iron."[30] Rybin, too, reported how the doctors' hands were shaking, that they could not remove Stalin's shirt and had to use scissors to cut it away. A young woman doctor took a cardiogram and quickly claimed that Stalin had suffered a heart attack. Although the other doctors suspected a cerebral hemorrhage, they were terrified of the possible repercussions if they failed to detect a heart attack. But then the woman doctor left the dacha and no further questions were raised. With the newspapers decrying a conspiracy to murder Kremlin leaders, no doctor could feel confident that he would not be held accountable for Stalin's demise.

But Stalin's condition was beyond the limits of what they could effectively treat. The stroke left him unconscious, his right arm and leg paralyzed. In a note that described their initial findings, the doctors included several details that were not shared with the public. Stalin's liver was severely enlarged, poking up several centimeters between his ribs. His right elbow was visibly bruised and swollen, an evident indication of how he had fallen. When they lifted his eyelids, his eyeballs moved left and right, showing no control of their focus. Faced with these symptoms, they recommended the following treatments: absolute quiet; the application of eight medical leeches to his ears; a cold compress on his head; an enema of milk of magnesia; and the removal of his false teeth. They also recommended that there be no attempt to feed him, but that fluids, like soup and sweet tea, could be carefully introduced through his mouth using a teaspoon as long as he was not gagging. He should have round-the-clock care with the attendance of a neurologist, a therapist, and nurses.[31]

But Stalin's lieutenants held off informing the population. On Tuesday morning, March 3, they asked the doctors for a definitive prognosis. "Death was inevitable," the doctors told them according to the account by Aleksandr Myasnikov. "Malenkov made it clear that he expected such a finding, but then stated that he hoped that medical measures could extend his life for a sufficient time, even if they could not save it. We understood that he was referring to the need to allow time to organize a new government and, at the same time, prepare public opinion."[32] The doctors cooperated as best they could.

We now know that other specialists were being consulted. One of the imprisoned Jewish doctors, Yakov Rapoport, who was a highly regarded pathologist, later reported how his interrogators abruptly turned solicitous. They began asking for medical advice about how best to treat a stroke victim, what was "Cheyne–Stokes respiration," and how could it be controlled. "It was a grave symptom, often attending the agonies of death," Rapoport told them, "and in the majority of cases death was inevitable." The interrogators also asked if he could recommend a specialist to treat an "important person." Here Rapoport was at a disadvantage; he "had no idea which major specialists were still free." When the interrogator insisted on hearing his recommendations, Rapoport listed nine doctors, all of whom turned out to be prisoners like himself. He later learned that at least two other doctors who had been arrested in connection with the Doctors' Plot had also been consulted. But the stroke was too damaging for their advice to matter.[33]

Stalin's children, Svetlana Alliluyeva and Vasily Stalin, were brought to him. Svetlana was called out of French class and told that Malenkov wanted her to come to the Nearby Dacha. "It was unprecedented for anyone but my father to ask me to come to the *dacha*. I went with a strange feeling of disquiet." It was not until she saw Khrushchev and Bulganin in front of the house that she grasped the severity of the situation. They were both in tears, inviting her inside where Malenkov would tell her the full details. Hearing them, she assumed her father was already dead.

The normally quiet dacha was bustling with activity, a swirl of anxious chaos around an inert Stalin. "There was a great crowd of people jammed into the big room where my father lay lying," Svetlana wrote. "Doctors I didn't know, who were seeing him for the first time ... were making a tremendous fuss, applying leeches to his neck and the back of his head, making cardiograms and taking X-rays of his lungs. A nurse kept giving him injections and a doctor jotted it all down in a notebook. Everything was being done as it should be."[34]

According to Khrushchev, only Beria behaved in an outrageous and offensive manner. "No sooner had Stalin taken ill than Beria started going around spewing hatred against him and mocking him," Khrushchev wrote. "But interestingly enough, as soon as Stalin showed ... signs of consciousness on his face and made us think he might recover, Beria threw himself on his knees, seized Stalin's hand, and started kissing it. When Stalin lost consciousness again and closed his eyes, Beria stood up and spat."[35] Khrushchev, of course, had many reasons to blacken Beria's reputation and it could well be the case that the behavior he described exaggerated the truth, if it was not fabricated altogether. Still, Svetlana also remembered that Beria's behavior was "very nearly obscene."[36]

In her memoir, Svetlana also recalled how unexpectedly tender and loving she was toward her father as he lay on his deathbed. She thought of his love for her and her brothers when they were young children and the heavy burdens of office he took on himself, how bereft she was as he lay dying, how she held his hand, kissed his forehead, and caressed his hair. Her behavior is similar to what every adult child would be expected to do in the face of a parent's imminent death. But she was no ordinary daughter and he was not an ordinary father.

Her brother Vasily sat nearby. "But he was drunk, as he often was by then, and he soon left," Svetlana recalled. "He went on drinking and raising Cain in the servants' quarters. He gave the doctors hell and shouted they had killed or were killing our father. Finally he went home."[37] Soviet newspapers liked to claim that Vasily Stalin had served with distinction as a jet fighter pilot during World War II, flying two dozen sorties against the Germans and shooting down enemy planes. Whether or not the tales of his heroics were true, and it is doubtful that they were, he rose nimbly through the ranks after the war, benefiting from his paternal connection. Vasily became commander of the Air Force in the Moscow Military District in 1948, and prominent enough to be featured on the cover of *Time* on August 20, 1951, recognized as a lieutenant general and his father's "little watchman"; perhaps the editors were speculating that Vasily would succeed his father. It is unclear whether Stalin ever had such plans for his son. Stalin would also scold him mercilessly, especially on one occasion when he learned that Vasily's method of fishing, on a trip to Poland, was to throw hand grenades into the water. Vasily held this post until the summer of 1952 when he was dismissed because of an accident during the May Day parade. Against the orders of his superiors, he had insisted that the Air Force proceed with the fly-by even though the weather was too windy and overcast. The pilots could not stay in formation and their planes "nearly brushed the spires of the Historical Museum" in Red Square. Stalin himself signed the order removing him from his august position.[38]

* * *

In March 1953, it was not easy for word of Stalin's medical condition to spread. Although Western reporters in Moscow, including the lonely group of six American correspondents, had received a Tass communiqué about Stalin, they still faced severe controls. Telephone calls to their home offices could only be made through the Central Telegraph Office in the heart of the capital. There were no telex facilities, no telephone lines that could be used independently of an operator, no independent means to alert the world. Eddy Gilmore of the Associated Press remembered the confusion of those days and nights in downtown Moscow. Writing in his memoir, *Me and My Russian Wife*, he recalled that

> The place we had to work in was a room about twenty-five feet long by twelve feet wide. It contained three telephone booths for making long-distance calls, a few cheap wooden desks, and a pay telephone for local calls screwed to the north wall. ... Every Western correspondent was there, in the same room, beating out the story of Stalin's illness. We had an official Tass communiqué to go by and the censor was taking his time about passing our

copy, which we sent in to him a paragraph at a time. The line was open to London, and as quickly as we got a paragraph through the censor, we telephoned it. . . . Not that we didn't work fast enough, for we were sitting there with our telegrams written and already handed in to the censor. The trouble was, he, too, was sitting—sitting on our telegrams. When Moscow Radio gave the first news, then our copy began to pass.[39]

Taking advantage of the difference in time zones, the *New York Times* was able to alert its readers to Stalin's illness later that same day. A headline across most of the front page announced "Stalin Gravely Ill After A Stroke: Partly Paralyzed and Unconscious: Moscow Discloses Concern For Him."[40] Harrison Salisbury added more details about what he was seeing on the streets of the capital:

No one knows when the next medical bulletin will come out. Radios are turned on constantly. There were long lines at the kiosks—some a hundred or more—to buy papers. Many believers have gone to the churches to pray for Stalin. The patriarch issued a general proclamation asking for prayers for Stalin and is to conduct a solemn service himself in the Yelokhovsky cathedral. At seven o'clock this evening the chief rabbi will hold special services in the Choral synagogue.

A few hours later, Salisbury added still more details in his diary:

The chief rabbi called for a day of fasting and prayer in the Jewish community tomorrow that Stalin's life might be spared.

At the big cathedral the patriarch called on God to spare Stalin's life. The congregation chanted "Amen." Acolytes held aloft the Bible in its golden case, and the patriarch with his gold rod and gown of gold and purple passed through the multitude of praying believers. Around the altars hundreds of tiny candles burned like golden stars of hope. All over Russia this scene was repeated in one form or another.[41]

It was the middle of the night when the news about Stalin's collapse reached Washington, DC. Neither President Dwight Eisenhower nor Secretary of State John Foster Dulles was alerted to Stalin's collapse with any sense of urgency. CIA director Allen Dulles (the younger brother of Foster Dulles) called James Hagerty, Eisenhower's press secretary, to alert the White House. But rather than rouse the president, who had instructed his staff to awaken him only with news that required "immediate action,"[42] Dulles and Hagerty argued for a half hour about whether or not to awaken the president before agreeing that since no quick decision about Stalin's illness was required there was no need to call him. Only an hour later, at 6 a.m., when Eisenhower normally got up, was he informed. A call to the home of Foster Dulles yielded a similar result. When State Department officials telephoned, a butler answered and informed the caller that the secretary of state was still asleep. Rather than awaken him early, they agreed that the butler would inform Foster Dulles when he got up later in the morning.

Eisenhower, who had just assumed office in January, struggled with his closest advisers over how to react to Stalin's illness. He summoned Allen Dulles to the White House for a meeting at 7.30 a.m. They were joined by Hagerty, C. D. Jackson, who was a special presidential assistant on psychological warfare strategy, and General Robert Cutler, who served as head of the planning board of the National Security Council. Eisenhower understood that Stalin's likely death could present a major opportunity for the United States and wanted to act quickly, to issue a statement and initiate some kind of action. "Well, what do you think we can do about this?" he challenged them.[43] But his advisers had nothing concrete to offer. Unable to agree on a way forward, the group called for a full meeting of the National Security Council, which gathered at the White House later that morning.

As Stalin lay dying in Moscow on the morning of March 4, Eisenhower presided over a meeting of senior officials and sought their advice over what kind of statement to issue. Their discussion revealed a fundamental assumption that was to plague the administration in the months to follow. Foster Dulles, Vice President Richard Nixon, and Eisenhower himself all assumed "that the situation might very well be worse after Stalin's death." This would be, in fact, a common reaction to Stalin's death, including inside the Soviet Union, and led the president's advisers to caution him against speaking publicly at that moment. Eisenhower, nonetheless, remained convinced about the need for some kind of public comment. Foster Dulles recalled that Calvin Coolidge had not commented on Lenin's death in January 1924. Perhaps it would be best not to "make any statement at all," Foster Dulles advised, that it would be an unnecessary "gamble" and "might be read as an appeal to the Soviet people in mourning to rise against their rulers." In spite of his reputation as a hardliner, the secretary of state believed the administration should adopt a cautious approach and not appear to be capitalizing on a moment of deep and uncertain tension. But Eisenhower was adamant, leaving it to others to draft a statement over his name; it would be issued later that afternoon.[44]

Former president Harry Truman and British prime minister Winston Churchill, remembering the wartime alliance with the Kremlin, quickly expressed their personal regrets over Stalin's illness. Churchill even dispatched his private secretary to the Soviet embassy in London to convey his concern. Speaking from his home in Kansas City, Missouri, Truman called Stalin "a decent fellow." "Of course I'm sorry to hear of his trouble," Truman told the press. "I'm never happy over anybody's physical breakdown. . . . I got very well acquainted with Joe Stalin, and I liked old Joe. . . . But Joe is a prisoner of the

Politburo. He can't do what he wants." Or so Truman believed, a misconception that Eisenhower seemed to share.[45]

But at least publicly Eisenhower and Foster Dulles resisted any niceties in what they had to say. Eisenhower, who had met Stalin in Moscow in 1945, did not offer a word of sympathy over his ill health. As Eisenhower recalled in his memoirs, he knew Stalin to be "an absolute dictator . . . and his baneful influence was felt universally."[46] His official statement, directed to the Soviet people, struck a religious note and did not mention Stalin by name.

At this moment in history when multitudes of Russians are anxiously concerned because of the illness of the Soviet ruler the thoughts of America go out to all the people of the USSR—the men and women, the boys and girls—in the villages, cities, farms and factories of their homeland.

They are the children of the same God who is the Father of all peoples everywhere. And like all peoples, Russia's millions share our longing for a friendly and peaceful world.

Regardless of the identity of government personalities the prayer of us Americans continues to be that the Almighty will watch over the people of that vast country and bring them, in His wisdom, opportunity to live their lives in a world where all men and women and children dwell in peace and comradeship.[47]

The Indian ambassador in Moscow, K. P. S. Menon, read the statement out of Washington. As he observed in his diary, "History does not record a more sanctimonious attempt to drive a wedge between a people and their leader at the moment of his death." Menon was sensitive to how Cold War tensions compromised diplomatic protocol. But the effect of Stalin's passing on Soviet society was still immediate and refreshing, "as if a fortochka had been suddenly opened into a stuffy and rather suffocating room." It was the tone of the message out of Washington that startled him.[48]

The British foreign secretary, Anthony Eden, had already arrived in Washington earlier in the week. (At Churchill's urging, Eden was intending to encourage Eisenhower to meet with Stalin.) He was scheduled to see the president on Friday, but that Wednesday Eden met with Eisenhower and Foster Dulles for nearly an hour in the evening, and then, after Foster Dulles left, Eisenhower and Eden continued meeting for another half hour. All this unusual activity reflected the combination of apprehension and promise that Stalin's likely death posed for the United States and its allies. Eisenhower and Eden agreed, according to *Newsweek*, "that for the next three to six months the West need not expect any startling surprises from Moscow," an assumption that quickly proved to be wrong.[49]

US embassies began reporting to the State Department on the response to Stalin's collapse. In Venezuela, a rumor circulated that Stalin had already died and the embassy, confused about what to do—the government of Venezuela did not have diplomatic relations with the Soviet Union—wondered if it should fly the American flag at half-mast, a question that would vex US officials over the next five days. From Brussels, the embassy shared a mocking lyric written by an American employee, hoping to brighten the day of Charles Bohlen, the new ambassador-designate to Moscow, who was in the midst of his confirmation hearings in Washington:

Uncle Joe is sick in bed—
Rush in blood up in his head—
If he can't walk and he can't talk—
By whom now are the Communists led?[50]

From Bonn, US diplomats cited the advice of a West German "expert on [the] Soviet Union," Klaus Mehnert, who urged caution in how the Western powers should respond. "Prime aim for West is to do nothing which will relieve strain of internal contradictions and struggle within Kremlin. Western statements which can be interpreted by Kremlin as threats or gloating probably will serve to unite Soviet people," the telegram observed. "Stalin's death should be no (rpt no) occasion for Western rejoicing or for relief that international situation has been eased. [Mehnert] feels Stalin has exercised a restraining influence and until it is clear what policy will be adopted by Moscow, he is urging his own people to be most circumspect in any expression of official opinion from Bonn. In short," the telegram concluded, "well-informed but not (rpt not) necessarily widespread German opinion can best be summarized by the remark 'better a devil you know than one you don't.'" Mehnert, like so many others, believed that without Stalin the situation inside the Soviet Union and its relations with other states could grow more strained and dangerous.[51]

John Foster Dulles felt the need to clarify how US diplomats should conduct themselves. Addressed to the embassy in Moscow, his telegram instructed US diplomats to "be guided by minimum protocol procedures. You should not (repeat not) send any individual message to Foreign Office until you have received further instructions."[52]

From Munich, a telegram reached the State Department advising against "diatribes on [Stalin's] 'evevlrole' [sic] or speculating on struggle for power. By the same token, nothing could contribute more to Kremlin's uncertainty, disunity and suspicion than an ominous silence from official sources. Such action would not preclude other sources from stressing the impossibility of finding anyone big enough to fill his shoes. In short, do not induce a reaction of unity but let the yeast work."[53] Given the assumption that Soviet officials and the society at large would face "confusion and uncertainty . . . in an empire that rested so heavily on a one-man dictator," there was also talk in Washington of dropping leaflets on Soviet cities with the text of Eisenhower's message of sympathy for the Soviet people and his "prayer for their freedom." Washington officials were also considering ways to encourage Mao Zedong "to break away from the Kremlin."[54] It is understandable that American policymakers would dream of rankling Soviet officials at this moment of transition, but the ideas they were toying with—sending a religious-sounding message of condolence, refusing to gloat as Stalin lay dying out of a strategic belief that silence would have a greater impact on their nerves, thinking they could cause a rift between Mao Zedong and the Kremlin—seem hopelessly naïve.

America's diplomatic corps was also in transition. Jacob Beam was America's chargé d'affaires in Moscow. An experienced and capable diplomat, he had served in Nazi Germany in the 1930s and then in London during the war, followed by postings to Indonesia and Yugoslavia before going to the Soviet Union. After October 1952, George Kennan was no longer in the Soviet capital; the Kremlin had declared him *persona non grata* over public remarks he had made about life under Stalin, comparing conditions in Stalin's Moscow to his experiences in Hitler's Berlin. His successor, Charles Bohlen, remained in Washington awaiting the conclusion of his confirmation hearings, which Senator Joseph McCarthy had been holding up because of dubious concerns over Bohlen's previous work at the State Department, in particular his assignment as a translator during the Yalta conference in 1945.[55]

Beam, who did not speak Russian, reported directly to Foster Dulles in Washington, DC, and awaited instructions as each day passed with its unforeseen developments.[56] At midday on March 5, Beam let Foster Dulles know that "British and French Ambassadors personally expressed sympathy at Foreign Ministry re Stalin's illness as did Scandinavian, Argentine and Belgian mission chiefs." He went on to advise Foster Dulles that the dean of the Diplomatic Corps was planning to send a message of condolence in the event of Stalin's death "on behalf of the diplomatic corps and send a wreath in their name." It would also be customary to "fly flags half-mast day of death and day of funeral but if interim official period of mourning set, he proposes fly flags half-mast also during that time. I hope we may concert our practice with British and French." Foster Dulles responded quickly, confirming for Beam that he should coordinate US reaction with them.[57]

Foster Dulles remained eager for news, "urgently interested" about the "popular reaction in USSR and satellites" to Stalin's illness.[58] In Germany, American diplomats began to see stirrings among officials and the population. Rumors sprouted that East Germany's deputy prime minister, Walter Ulbricht, had left for Moscow, while the United Press reported that communist leaders throughout Eastern Europe were being summoned to the Soviet capital. From Berlin, US officials noted how numerous "East Berliners and East Germans [were coming] to West Berlin specifically to obtain true news about Stalin in order to know whether time had come to bring out wine bottles they have been saving for this special occasion."[59]

The government of Yugoslavia, which had broken with the Kremlin in 1948 and withstood threats against its existence, could hardly restrain its delight. The communist regime of Marshal Joseph Broz Tito understood that Stalin's heirs would only be announcing his illness because his imminent death was assured. Radio Belgrade issued a commentary at 5 p.m. on March 4 under the title "Death rattle in the throat of world's greatest dictator." For Tito, "nature [was] the ally of justice."[60]

At midnight, as Thursday, March 5, began, Salisbury sent a coded message to his editors, this time to confirm that censorship was being imposed on the subject of Stalin's health and so it would likely be difficult to report anything beyond the contents of official communiqués. Two hours later, a second medical bulletin came out. It confirmed what everyone understood was about to take place. The doctors reported that Stalin's health was growing increasingly fragile. They observed that Cheyne–Stokes breathing, an abnormal condition often seen in comatose patients, was more frequent. "The condition of the blood circulation deteriorated and the degree of the lack of oxygen increased."[61] As they did before, the doctors provided information about his heart rate, a slightly elevated temperature, and dangerously high blood pressure. Their medical measures included: clapping on an oxygen mask when his breathing became labored, feeding him a glucose solution through a vein since he was comatose and could not eat, applying leeches to help reduce his blood pressure, injecting penicillin to guard against pneumonia, caffeine to stimulate his nervous system, and camphor compounds to strengthen his heart. These were all standard procedures at the time, although by 1953 the use of camphor for the treatment of heart disease was mostly out of fashion among Western doctors, as was the application of blood-sucking leeches to reduce the volume of blood in the body and therefore the pressure. In the West, doctors might have punctured a vein, an easier and perhaps more effective means to draw blood slowly. Stalin's doctors may also have been thinking that the use of leeches "would convince even the most old-fashioned Russian that nothing was being left undone that might save [him]," as *Time* magazine observed.[62] But all their efforts were hopelessly ineffective. Nonetheless, this did not deter Harrison Salisbury from commenting, with some degree of hyperbole, that "every device and treatment known to modern medicine was employed."[63] With the eyes of the world on Moscow, the death watch continued. Reading the news coverage in multiple papers and seeing how little there was to say, the great *New Yorker* journalist A. J. Liebling could not restrain his sense of irony. "The annoying hiatus that the old Bolshevik permitted to intervene between his syncope and his demise put a strain on even the most rugged professional seers, who had to start explaining the significance of his death and then keep on inventing exegeses until he was in his tomb." For Liebling, Stalin had "the bad taste to die in installments," making editors meet deadlines about a big story with little hard information to offer.[64]

At a press conference in Washington that Thursday, President Eisenhower acknowledged that he and his closest advisers had been discussing the possible effect of Stalin's absence from the Moscow political scene but after much back-and-forth "ended up largely where they started." In response to questions, Eisenhower found himself expressing more substantial concerns than he had perhaps intended to. One journalist asked about the Kremlin's recent and vicious press campaign directed against the Jews. Eisenhower was forthright in his answer. "Turning very grave then, Mr. Eisenhower said that of course he deplored the rise of anti-Semitism. It was heartbreaking, he continued, particularly for one such as himself who knew something of the [Nazi] horror camps of World War II and had seen the remnants of Jews who had been ground down by Hitler. To think that this sort of thing was going on again, the President continued, was distressing, and a person in the position of President of the United States really didn't know whether to say anything about it publicly lest his words be used as an excuse to make things even harder for the Jews."[65] But, yes, he had offered to meet with Stalin if such a meeting would advance the cause of world peace and the same offer remained on the table for any Soviet leaders who would succeed him. Still, the *New York Times* added that "Directives [had been] sent to the Voice of America to play up the news of Stalin's fatal illness" while at the same time avoiding any speculation about a possible successor.[66]

As public officials and the world's press pondered the news, prisoners in the Gulag were also learning about Stalin's collapse. The writer Lev Razgon was in the midst of serving an eighteen-year term in the camps. "So I finally made it to that day in March," he later recalled, when all the sudden we heard this heavenly music on the loud-speakers. Bach, Handel, Beethoven, and then we heard the health announcement. I remember how we all ran to the camp infirmary and the doctors discuss this among themselves and tell us what we could hope for. So the chief doctor, his assistant and the male nurse all of whom were convicts of course, went into the banya to hold their meeting. Meanwhile we're all huddled in the changing room, our teeth chattering with anticipation. They met for about 20 minutes, then the chief doctor walked out. He was a professor, a very well educated man. He was beaming, and he said, you guys, the bastard is finished. No hope for him. And we began kissing one another.[67]

Back in Moscow, the Western press corps was doing its best to gather even wisps of information in between the official updates. Eddy Gilmore of the Associated Press had difficult memories of that week. "I shall not labor here with the details of those long sleepless nights we all spent at the Central Telegraph. No food for hours. No real sleep for days. To the eternal credit of every Moscow correspondent, he stayed on the job. Tempers became frayed and we cursed and screamed at one another. Several times there were near fights. The trouble was that telephone. There were only two lines to the West and there were six correspondents. Someone had to be last and everyone was trying to be first."

During those two days when the world understood that Stalin lay dying, Gilmore "made it [his] business to go through Red Square . . . at least ten or fifteen times a day or night." He kept seeing automobiles with men and women "in white going in and out of the Kremlin." Although he could not be certain, he assumed they must be doctors and nurses. And there was also an "open-bodied truck hauling what appeared to be oxygen tanks." Given that the regime had announced that Stalin had fallen ill in the Kremlin, it was only natural for

29

Gilmore to be impressed with the frantic arrival of medical personnel and equipment.[68]

If, in fact, what Gilmore saw were true, then it was all part of an elaborate charade. Stalin had collapsed at his dacha in Kuntsevo in the city suburbs. But so many myths surrounded his exercise of power—including the idea that he was always working on behalf of the Soviet people, so that a light in the window of his Kremlin office looking onto Red Square was kept on throughout the night—it must have seemed too awkward to announce that he was actually at the dacha when he collapsed. When years later Svetlana Alliluyeva, and in a separate account Nikita Khrushchev, described the death watch at Kuntsevo, it did not occur to either of them to mention the falsehood in the Kremlin's announcement. A harmless lie like this was not worth explaining.

* * *

That Thursday morning, Stalin's condition grew worse. He began to vomit blood, causing his blood pressure and pulse to grow weaker. This was an unexpected turn and puzzled the doctors. They gathered around him, and injected him with medications to address the drop in his blood pressure. Bulganin was in charge that morning, monitoring their every move. Aleksandr Myasnikov was among the doctors. He noticed how Bulganin was looking at them "suspiciously and perhaps even with hostility." He asked the reason for Stalin's vomiting of blood. Myasnikov could only offer the opinion that it might have to do with small hemorrhages in the lining of the stomach connected to his blood pressure and the stroke. Bulganin responded sarcastically. "Is it possible?" he said to them, mimicking the tone in Myasnikov's voice. "Perhaps Stalin has stomach cancer?" His voice carried an unmistakable threat, but he allowed them to proceed with their treatments. Bulganin was probably as scared as the doctors were.[69]

They proceeded as best they could. Concerned about bedsores, the doctors rubbed camphor onto his back. He had hiccups, while his lips and skin showed increasing signs of cyanosis. Wanting to nourish their patient, they applied enemas, one set with glucose twice a day plus another set, what they called "nutritional enemas," with 100 grams of cream and an egg yolk, twice a day. There was little more they could do.[70]

The Kremlin issued a third bulletin about Stalin's condition late that afternoon. The news was sobering. An electrocardiogram indicated newly developed lesions to the back wall of the heart and "disturbances in blood circulation in the coronary arteries." At one point, his blood pressure had dropped precipitously.[71]

With their country and the world alerted to Stalin's condition, Beria and Malenkov called for an extraordinary meeting of party and government officials for that evening. Konstantin Simonov was among the 300 members of the Central Committee, the Council of Ministers, and the Supreme Soviet who gathered in the Kremlin's Sverdlov Hall. "A few hundred people," he wrote,

> . . . they knew each other from work, they recognized each other's faces, they knew one another from many meetings—a few hundred people . . . sat completely in silence, waiting for the meeting to begin. They sat next to each other, shoulder to shoulder, looked at each other, but no one said anything to anyone. No one asked anyone a question. It seemed to me that not one of those who were present even felt the need to speak. From the very beginning there was such a silence in the hall that I, if I had not sat for forty minutes in that silence, would never believe that three hundred people who were sitting so closely to one another could be so quiet.

They all thought, of course, that Stalin was under medical care down a corridor or two. His presumed presence nearby reinforced the gravity of the moment. When the dozen or so leaders sat down at the front of the hall, among them sat two little-known figures in national economic planning, Maxim Saburov and Mikhail Pervukhin, because Stalin had included them in the newly created Bureau of the Presidium only months earlier, while Molotov and Mikoyan, who had been excluded by Stalin, sat to the side. Since Stalin was still breathing, the new leadership gave the appearance of continuing to abide by his plans.

Malenkov began the evening, explaining that Stalin was battling for his life and that even if he were to cheat death, he would not be able to work for long stretches of time. At such a time, the international situation required that the country have stable leadership. Malenkov then called on Beria. Beria walked to the lectern and took a moment to propose that Malenkov be recognized as chairman of the Council of Ministers, a decision that was quickly endorsed by acclamation. As Beria then moved back to his seat, he and Malenkov both needed to fit through a narrow space among the chairs, face to face, their ample girths creating an awkward pause as they moved in opposite directions. At the time, Simonov did not recognize the comic angle to this unexpected choreography. As he wrote in his memoir, "Back then, I did not think to grin." Malenkov then explained the changes that were being instituted, rightfully expecting there would be no need for questions or deliberation. Stalin was being removed as leader of the government and of the party. The meeting closed with no further word about his condition. But a momentous decision was now behind them. As Simonov recalled, "There was a sense that right there, in the Presidium, people were being freed from something that had been weighing them down."[72]

Stalin's daughter remained by his side at the Nearby Dacha, watching as her father's life drained away. "For the last twelve hours the lack of oxygen was acute," she wrote.

His face altered and became dark. His lips turned black and the features grew unrecognizable. The last hours were nothing but slow strangulation. The death agony was horrible. He literally choked to death as we watched. At what seemed like the very last moment he suddenly opened his eyes and cast a glance over everyone in the room. It was a terrible glance, insane or perhaps angry and full of the fear of death and the unfamiliar faces of the doctors bent over him. The glance swept over everyone in a second. Then something incomprehensible and awesome happened that to this day I can't forget and don't understand. He suddenly lifted his left hand as though he were pointing to something above and bringing down a curse on us all. The gesture was incomprehensible and full of menace, and no one could say to whom or at what it might be directed. The next moment, after a final effort, the spirit wrenched itself free of the flesh.[73]

Death came at 9.50 p.m.

Khrushchev and the others were there as well. Just as Stalin died, "a huge man came from somewhere and started giving him artificial respiration," Khrushchev wrote, "massaging him to get him breathing again." Khrushchev was appalled and felt sorry for Stalin. He could tell it was useless and voiced his discomfort. But the doctors had to demonstrate that they were trying every method imaginable to keep Stalin alive. Khrushchev's words made it easier for them to stop.[74]

"As soon as we determined that the pulse and breathing had stopped, and the heart was still," Aleksandr Myasnikov later wrote, "it grew quiet in the spacious room among the party and government leaders, his daughter Svetlana, his son Vasily, and the guards. Everyone stood motionless in solemn silence for thirty minutes or even longer. . . . A great dictator, who had only recently been all-powerful, had turned into a pitiable, poor corpse, who tomorrow pathologists would hack into pieces."[75]

Beria alone immediately mobilized into action, rushing to the door and ordering assistance. "The silence of the room where everyone was gathered around the deathbed was shattered by the sound of his loud voice, the ring of triumph unconcealed," Svetlana recalled.[76] As he shouted for his driver, his words, "Khrustalev, my car," have entered the lore of Russian history and culture. "Beria was radiant," Khrushchev later claimed. "He was regenerated and rejuvenated. To put it crudely, he had a housewarming over Stalin's corpse before it was even put in the coffin. Beria was sure that the moment he had long been waiting for had finally arrived. There was no power on earth that could hold him back now. . . . You could see these triumphant thoughts in his face as he called for his car and drove off to the city." Beria was "a butcher and an assassin," but Khrushchev would have to wait patiently before moving against him.[77]

Svetlana remained in the room. She watched as the bodyguards and household staff came in to pay their respects. "Many were sobbing." The housekeeper, Valentina Istomina, who had worked for Stalin for eighteen years, "dropped heavily to her knees, put her head on my father's chest and wailed at the top of her voice. . . . She went on for a long time and nobody tried to stop her." It was not until much later, near dawn on Friday, March 6, that the body was taken away for the autopsy. Bulganin walked with Svetlana as she followed the gurney outside. They were both crying. The regime waited six hours and ten minutes to lower the Kremlin flag and announce Stalin's demise to the world. While Svetlana and the household staff sat quietly in the dacha kitchen, they heard the somber news on the radio. It was now official. Stalin was dead.[78]

CHAPTER TWO

A NEW PURGE

In the final months of his life Stalin intended to engineer a dramatic change within the party leadership. Surprising both the country and foreign diplomats, the Kremlin issued a startling announcement in August 1952 that the Nineteenth Party Congress would be held in Moscow at the beginning of October, the first congress to be held after a lapse of thirteen years. (Party rules called for them to take place every three years.) As the initial notice made clear, Stalin was announcing a major reform of the leading party structure: the abolition of the nine-man Politburo and its replacement by an expanded Presidium of twenty-five. The congress would also feature a report from the Central Committee by Georgy Malenkov. Since Stalin had delivered the chief report at every party congress since 1925, this signal of a possible succession portended an historic meeting.

Stalin further compounded expectations for the congress with a statement on economic policy. Three days before the congress was to open, the party's principal theoretical journal, *Bolshevik*, carried his long essay, approximately 25,000 words in length, under the title "The Economic Problems of Socialism in the USSR." Although Stalin was said to have completed the piece months before, he was deliberately publishing it now in order to overshadow the congress's agenda. Consistent with his megalomania, the Kremlin used every means to elevate the significance of the essay. *Bolshevik* printed an additional 300,000 copies above its usual circulation of 500,000. Then *Pravda* appeared in greatly expanded editions over the next two days with the full text of Stalin's article. A special pamphlet edition of 1.5 million copies was also distributed at that time; by January 1, 1953, 20 million copies of the pamphlet were published. In Moscow alone 200,000 trained agitators read and discussed it in factories, schools, and offices throughout October.[1]

This was to be Stalin's last authoritative statement on a matter of important public policy. On the surface, he was responding to a long-standing discussion, one that had reportedly gone on for fifteen years, about a new textbook on the country's political economy. He had particular reasons of his own to settle matters. Even though his article was replete with "sublime theoretical verities" which hardly rose "above the level of the commonplace," in the words of the historian Adam Ulam, there was a serious purpose behind Stalin's initiative and it did not bode well for Soviet society.

Stalin was using this statement to set a tone for the congress and to set the stage for a new purge. He recommended, for example, a further tightening of controls over the country's collective farms. For Stalin, as Ulam remarked, the collective farm system "was insufficiently socialist."[2] He was now proposing that the last vestiges of personal cultivation on the farms be elevated to the level of "public or national property," that the peasants' household lots, which they cultivated on their own to ensure a minimum amount of food for their families, be turned over to the state.[3] There had also been calls to reduce the priority investment in heavy industry and broaden the production of consumer goods. Here again, Stalin would have none of such talk. The country continued to face "capitalist encirclement" and required disproportionate investments in heavy industry to sustain the production of armaments; Soviet consumers would have to wait. He did include an impractical call for a shorter work day, urging the creation of a six-hour day and then a five-hour day when conditions warranted as part of the transition from socialism to communism. He called for better housing conditions, for the doubling of real wages—proposals that led nowhere.

While Stalin devoted a great many pages to a discussion of the economy, one early portion of his statement grabbed the attention of his readers inside and outside of the country. The imperialist powers were in crisis, Stalin asserted, competing with each other over access to natural resources and new markets, and chafing under American domination. For Stalin, the economic recovery of Germany and Japan foreshadowed a renewal of their competition with the United States. The Americans had promoted the Marshall Plan to extend their control over post-war Europe, even hoping to seduce the new "people's democracies" to join the Marshall Plan and thereby extend the reach of American imperialism. But the socialist bloc had resisted the temptation—Stalin, in fact, had coerced Poland and Czechoslovakia to reject the Marshall Plan—and successfully created a competing market of its own. This decision protected the natural resources of these countries from the greedy designs of American capitalism. The socialist bloc countries, Stalin was claiming, operated in complete harmony with each other. It was the capitalist countries which would experience a crisis. There would now be more fierce competition among them over a market that was appreciably smaller and over access to a shallower reservoir of natural resources than they had anticipated. As Stalin made clear, "Some comrades affirm that, in consequence of the development of international conditions after the second world war, wars among capitalist countries have ceased to be inevitable. They consider that the contradictions between the camp of socialism and the camp of capitalism are greater than the contradictions among capitalist countries." For Stalin, though, "the inevitability of wars among the capitalist countries remains."

This warning overshadowed his extensive pronouncements about the economy and affected the mood and discourse of the party congress. He remained in charge. No one would be allowed to thwart his ideological hard line for the country's economy or international relations. As Harry Schwartz of the *New York Times* observed, Stalin was giving "notice to the world that he regards his rule as far from finished and that, in his opinion, any speculation about the succession to him is still premature." It was Stalin who remained "the primary source for the party line to which all others must defer."[4]

As the party congress was about to convene, the delegates eagerly waited for Soviet leaders to make their way onto the stage. One of the French delegates, Auguste Lecœur, expected to see Stalin lead in the group, just as Maurice Thorez, the French communist chief, would always take his place first. Lecœur sat in the hall anxiously waiting, as if he were a religious acolyte about to see his deity. But instead, when Soviet leaders entered through a small door off the platform they were in alphabetical order, leaving Stalin to make his way near the end. Stalin then interceded with a handful of guests to demonstrate the graces of a host. Noticing that Maurice Thorez, Klement Gottwald of Czechoslovakia, and Dolores Ibárruri of Spain—the famous La Pasionaria—were sitting in a specially designated loge rather than at the Presidium dais, Stalin stood up and summoned them to the dais, even holding a chair for each one, a staged piece of theater designed to draw attention to himself and cause a buzz throughout the hall. The gesture had its desired effect. For Lecœur and no doubt for others, Stalin's behavior "seemed to me the very essence of modesty and only increased my admiration."[5] Stalin then sat down in a chair off to the side behind the rostrum, leaving two empty chairs between himself and Lazar Kaganovich and the rest of the Presidium.

Dmitrii Shepilov was the editor of *Pravda* at that time. He was among the guests at the congress and years later recalled several of its most vivid moments. For Shepilov, it was particularly important to watch Stalin as Malenkov delivered the report of the Central Committee. This had always been Stalin's moment, the occasion for his triumphant pronouncements when he rode roughshod over opponents like Trotsky and Bukharin. Now,

> throughout Malenkov's speech, which took up five hours, ... [Stalin] remained almost motionless, gazing stonily ahead. Malenkov went unbelievably fast ..., giving Stalin an occasional sidelong glance, as a well-trained horse might glance at its rider. As Stalin's longtime favorite who was accustomed to his master's ways, Malenkov was trembling inside: What if Stalin made one of his familiar, impatient gestures or took out his gold Longines watch? That would signal displeasure, and Malenkov would have to cut short his speech and end it no matter where he was. After all, to arouse Stalin's displeasure, to say nothing of his anger, would be much worse than to make a fool of himself before an audience of a thousand. But all was well. Stalin listened to the speech to the end.[6]

He was far from retiring.

To the casual observer, the speeches during the congress all seemed to echo the standard wooden language of Stalinist rhetoric: declarations of loyalty, pledges to meet the goals of the Five-Year Plan, promises to rededicate attention to the proper examination of Marxism–Leninism—the basis for all reliable economic and political work. But a worrisome theme of ideological vigilance suffused many of the speeches, particularly the report from the Central Committee— the cornerstone statement of the congress. Given the stark developments that unfolded in the months to follow, these remarks, however buried within triumphant-sounding rhetoric, were warning party activists to be on their guard.

In a chilling reminder to the audience, Malenkov harked back to the purges of the 1930s when the party waged "an implacable struggle ... against ... the capitulators and traitors who tried to deflect the Party from the right path and to split its ranks. It has been proved that these infamous traitors and renegades were waiting for an armed attack upon the Soviet Union, counting on stabbing the Soviet state in the back in its hour of trial." But the elimination of enemies like Trotsky and Bukharin, along with their followers, ensured the consolidation of the country's unity, making it impossible for "a fifth column" to undermine morale during the war. "If this had not been done in time," Malenkov claimed, "we should, during the war, have found ourselves under fire both from the front and the rear, and might have lost the war." Malenkov was undoubtedly sincere when he proclaimed that the purges had eliminated "a fifth column" which otherwise would have endangered the country during the ensuing war. The call for vigilance was a major theme of the congress, a clear and menacing signal that the country needed to internalize the tensions of the Cold War.[7]

Malenkov was invoking a painful and ominous lesson, one he did not want his audience and the country at large to misunderstand. Yes, after the triumph of the communist revolution in China and the establishment of socialist democracies in Central and Eastern Europe, the Soviet Union was "no longer a solitary island surrounded by capitalist countries," a claim that contradicted the warning of "capitalist encirclement." But changes in the international field must not allow the Soviet people to take the country's security for granted. Stalin always said that as the country moved toward communism, class antagonisms would only grow sharper. "Nor are we guaranteed against the infiltration of alien views, ideas and sentiments from outside," Malenkov declared, "from the capitalist countries, or from inside, from the relics of groups hostile to the Soviet state which have not been completely demolished by the Party." If an earlier struggle against "enemies of the people" had prepared the Soviet state for its mortal struggle against Nazi Germany, then, Malenkov claimed, a renewed campaign against hostile, ideological elements may well prove necessary to ensure the country's safety. It was this paranoid perspective that Stalin was about to impose on the country once again.[8]

Aleksandr Poskrebyshev, who headed Stalin's office in the Kremlin, invoked a similar theme and provided some of the most extreme language during the congress. He asserted that "Comrade Stalin teaches that the safeguarding of socialist property is one of the basic functions of our state, . . . that a thief who pilfers public property and undermines the interests of the national economy is the same as a spy and a traitor, if not worse."[9] The significance of his remarks would become clear soon after the congress.

Stalin's own speech came on the final day of the meeting. Until then, except for sitting through Malenkov's report, he had kept his distance, appearing at odd moments for fifteen or twenty minutes. This elusive quality had always been part of his allure. As Shepilov recalled,

> Stalin rarely spoke in public. . . . Sometimes he spoke only once over a period of years. To be present at one of his appearances, to see and hear Stalin in the flesh, was deemed a rare and great opportunity. Anyone lucky enough to be there did not want to miss a single word. Moreover, for thirty years the entire press, radio, and cinema and all of the oral propaganda and arts had been inculcating the view that Stalin's every word was a lofty revelation, absolute Marxist truth, a gem of wisdom that contained knowledge of the present and a prediction for the future. That was why the hall listened to Stalin as though under a hypnotic spell.[10]

This was to be Stalin's last public speech. When Voroshilov introduced him, announcing that "Comrade Stalin has the floor," the entire audience rose to its feet "as though galvanized," a wave of unrelenting ovations surging through the hall." But Stalin appeared indifferent to their adulation. "The expression on his face revealed nothing of his feelings at the moment," Shepilov wrote. "Now and then he shifted from one foot to the other, smoothed his mustache with his index finger, or stroked his chin. Twice he raised his hand as though requesting the audience let him begin, only to cause the ovation to redouble."[11]

Stalin remained in command, but his voice and his aging appearance must have caught everyone's attention. He slurred his words—an evident sign of previous small strokes—while his sallow complexion and thinning white hair underscored his mortality. His remarks were brief, hardly more than ten minutes long, and were confined to one theme. He thanked the fraternal communist parties whose ranks were represented in the hall, singling out leaders of the French and Italian parties for their presence—Comrades Thorez and Togliatti—because they had pledged that "their people will not fight the peoples of the Soviet Union." There was no mention of Mao Zedong, although the Chinese leader was the most prominent communist after Stalin himself. Stalin left it to other speakers to single out the Chinese delegation and their country's triumphant revolution. He called on his fellow communists to persist in their efforts to struggle for peace, to make it impossible for capitalist governments to wage war, an overriding priority of Soviet foreign policy since the Americans had dropped atomic bombs on Japan.

Stalin then added a task for them to pursue. The bourgeoisie was becoming "more reactionary," was losing "its ties with the people." It used to be able to "play the liberal, to uphold the bourgeois-democratic liberties, and thus gain popularity with the people." Stalin insisted that "the rights of the individual are now extended only to those who possess capital, while all other citizens are regarded as human raw material, fit only to be exploited. ... The banner of bourgeois-democratic liberties has been thrown overboard." It would be up to communist parties to "raise this banner and carry it forward, if you want to gather around you the majority of the people. There is nobody else to raise it." The audience, all stalwart believers, sat spell-bound. When he finished—Stalin closed with the words "Down with the warmongers!"—the audience knew how to respond. As *Pravda* noted, they rose from their seats. There was "Stormy, unabating applause, turning into an ovation. Cries of 'Hail Comrade Stalin!' 'Hurrah for Comrade Stalin!' 'Hail Comrade Stalin, the greater leader of the working people of the world!'"[12] The ritual continued for many minutes, no doubt satisfying Stalin's vanity. No one else commanded such contrived adoration. Years later, Khrushchev claimed that Stalin's brief speech made clear to him and his colleagues that Stalin was faltering. "We all concluded from this that he must be very weak physically if it turned out to have been an incredible accomplishment to make a speech of seven minutes."[13] But Khrushchev and the others, if they really had thought that way at the time, would never have shared such an impression out loud.

The delegates returned home reassured. No serious changes seemed to be on the horizon. All the major party figures had made an appearance: Molotov had opened the meeting, Voroshilov had closed it. Beria, Kaganovich, and Khrushchev had all addressed the delegates, while Malenkov had delivered the report of the Central Committee in place of Stalin. The congress had also adopted two minor resolutions: to change the official name of the party, which had long used the awkward title of All-Union Communist Party (of the Bolsheviks) to the easier-sounding Communist Party of the Soviet Union, and to rename the Politburo the Presidium and expand its numbers to an unwieldy twenty-five.

It was here that Stalin was carrying out his underlying intentions for the congress. Decades had passed since the country had undergone a transition of leadership. Stalin was determined to hold on to power and to remind his lieutenants how unprepared they all were to succeed him. As Khrushchev wrote in his memoirs, "He loved to repeat the statement to us: You are blind like little kittens. Without me the imperialists would strangle you."[14] Stalin was putting his veteran lieutenants on notice. The expanded Presidium would have several little-known and hardly seasoned men whose presence among the broader group would signal the vulnerability of Stalin's "comrades-in-arms." As Shepilov recognized, the prestige of the new Presidium was diluted by "mediocrities who were unknown to the party and the people."[15]

Stalin liked to sully the names of potential heirs and reveal how each could not measure up to the job. According to Khrushchev, Stalin enjoyed taunting them.

> Who will we appoint chairman of the Council of Ministers after me? Beria? No, he is not Russian, but Georgian. Khrushchev? No, he is a worker, we need someone more educated. Malenkov? No, he can only follow someone else's lead. Kaganovich? No, he won't do, for he is not Russian but a Jew. Molotov? No, he has already aged, he won't cope. Voroshilov? No, he is really not up to it. Saburov? Pervukhin? These people are only fit for secondary roles. There is only one person left and that is Bulganin.[16]

Within two days after the party congress, Stalin went even further in his attacks.

On October 16, a Central Committee plenum convened in the Kremlin's Sverdlov Hall. A closed-door meeting of around 200 delegates, it lasted two and a half hours. It would be the plenum's formal responsibility to elect the members of the newly expanded Presidium. Stalin spoke for almost half the time and his remarks took the meeting in an unexpected direction. Dmitrii Shepilov had just been elected to the Central Committee. He came to his first meeting thrilled to be included among the leaders of the party.

He quickly saw, though, how things worked differently away from the public. When Stalin entered the room, a group of younger new members sprang to their feet, ready to applaud and raise their voices in praise just like at the party congress. But Stalin showed his displeasure, "muttering something like 'never do that here.'" Evidently, there was a sense that behind closed doors it was unseemly to engage in such ritual displays of adoration.[17]

But it was Stalin's speech that disturbed Shepilov, the writer Konstantin Simonov, and others. Stalin had limited himself to brief remarks at the party congress, but now at the plenum he spoke for over an hour without notes. His tone was as chilling as his words. "He spoke in a severe manner from beginning to end, without humor," Simonov noted. "There were no pages or notes lying on the lectern in front of him." He spoke about getting old, even offered to resign as general secretary and only remain as head of the government. Stunned by his proposal, the audience insisted he continue leading the party, a response that Stalin, not surprisingly, accepted. (Years later, Malenkov expressed the opinion that Stalin had not been serious about resigning; he had only wanted to flush out his hidden enemies.) Nonetheless, "it was nearing the time when others would have to continue to do what he had been doing, that the international situation was complicated, while a difficult struggle with the capitalist camp loomed ahead of them, and that the most dangerous thing in this struggle would be to flinch, to be afraid, to retreat, to capitulate." Stalin wondered if his heirs would be up to the task.[18]

But then, to the surprise of everyone in the hall, he directed his attack against three longtime associates: Vyacheslav Molotov, Anastas Mikoyan, and Kliment Voroshilov. He spoke "contemptuously" of Molotov, "saying that he had been intimidated by American imperialism and had sent panicky telegrams back from the United States, that a leader like him was untrustworthy and had no place in the party leadership."[19] He went on to denounce Mikoyan and Voroshilov with similar words, questioning their political reliability. The scholars Yoram Gorlizki and Oleg Khlevniuk believe that Stalin was particularly angry with Molotov and Mikoyan because of their support for increasing the state's investments in agriculture. The country was experiencing a severe shortfall in food production, but Stalin, who mistrusted the peasantry and insisted on a "long-term policy of accelerated growth in the military and heavy-industry sectors," opposed any concession to collective farmers.[20] He was always happy to squeeze more out of them. This may well have been the immediate reason for his rage. But his malicious remarks fit within the pattern of "deceiving charm, unprovoked sadism, suspicion, and contempt" that marked his relations with all of his closest associates.[21] His fear of being overshadowed, his resentment of anyone whose competence could cast doubt on his own omniscience, his reluctance to plan ahead for a succession—all moved Stalin to denounce each of them at one time or another.

Listening to Stalin, Shepilov was both fascinated and repelled. He felt "as though a slab of ice had been placed on my heart." Like everyone else in the hall, "my gaze shifted from Stalin to Molotov to Mikoyan and back to Stalin. Molotov sat immobile at the Presidium table. He was silent. Not a muscle twitched on his face as he stared straight at the assembly through his pince-nez, occasionally moving three fingers of his right hand over the baize tabletop as though kneading a ball of bread."[22] As Khrushchev's son, Sergei, later wrote, "Stalin was putting Molotov on his list of American spies, Voroshilov was a British spy, and as for Mikoyan, well, Stalin had yet to determine."[23] Nikita Khrushchev, as well, recalled how Stalin had grown increasingly hostile to Molotov and Mikoyan, snapping at them when he saw them. For Khrushchev, it seemed obvious that "their lives were in danger."[24] Mikoyan was well aware of Stalin's plans. In the weeks before Stalin died, Mikoyan heard from an unnamed comrade that Stalin was intending to convene a Central Committee plenum where he could "settle scores" with himself and Molotov, then expel them from the Presidium and the Central Committee. It was all heading not just to their political disgrace but "to physical annihilation."[25] Khrushchev believed this as well. In his Secret Speech in 1956 he stated that "Stalin evidently had plans to finish off the old members of the Political Bureau."[26]

Molotov was widely regarded as Stalin's closest associate. He had worked with Lenin and enjoyed many years of service near the top of the Soviet hierarchy, including his role as chairman of the Council of People's Commissars in the 1930s and then foreign minister during World War II. He was easily the most recognized Soviet diplomat of his day, famous for his rimless glasses and his unyielding posture as a negotiator. Stalin, though, had a long history of humiliating Molotov, a pattern of behavior he could deploy against any and all members of the Politburo to ensure their personal loyalty. During the Great Terror in 1937 and 1938, Molotov's assistants were arrested and a case was even prepared against Molotov himself. In 1939, the secret police fabricated a case against his wife, Polina Zhemchuzhina (who was Jewish); a veteran Bolshevik with experience in the country's perfume, food, and fishing industry, Zhemchuzhina was accused of harboring a nest of "vandals," "saboteurs," even German spies, within her office.[27] She lost her position as people's commissar of the fishing industry, a demotion that could have led to more drastic measures. But then Stalin decided to back off for reasons of his own. She was not arrested and continued to serve in Soviet commerce, assigned to a position in the haberdashery division of the People's Commissariat of Light Industry. Rumors abound over why Stalin disliked her. It is said that she was particularly close to his second wife, Nadezhda Alliluyeva, and that she may have been the last person to see her alive before Alliluyeva committed suicide in November 1932.

Molotov continued to be vulnerable. In May 1941, just a month before the German invasion, he was removed from his position as chairman of the Council of People's Commissars. Months after the war, in December 1945, Stalin wrote a tough-minded letter to Beria, Malenkov, and Mikoyan in which he expressed his lack of confidence in Molotov. "I have become convinced," Stalin wrote to them, "that Molotov does not hold the interests of our state and the prestige of our government in very high regard—all he cares about is popularity in certain foreign circles. I can no longer consider such a comrade to be my first deputy." Stalin then compromised him further, instructing the three of them to summon Molotov and read the telegram to him. As Stalin explained, he did not want to send Molotov the note because he did not have "faith in the trustworthiness of certain of his close associates," so he preferred to recruit other members of the leadership to participate in this humiliating ritual. Molotov responded in a typically servile fashion. "I will try to earn your trust through my deeds. For any honorable Bolshevik, your trust represents the trust of the Party, which is dearer to me than life itself."[28]

Stalin returned his attention to Zhemchuzhina in 1949. She was arrested, accused of nationalistic activity in collaboration with other important Soviet Jewish figures, including Solomon Mikhoels, the Yiddish actor and theater director who had been murdered on Stalin's personal orders in January 1948, his death camouflaged as a traffic accident. (It was "nationalistic" to be too concerned with Jewish suffering or support the establishment of a Jewish state in the Middle East.) Following her arrest, Zhemchuzhina was sent into internal exile in Kazakhstan for five years. Molotov was further humiliated; he was pressured by Stalin to divorce his wife and then dismissed from his post as foreign minister. Andrei Vyshinsky replaced him in March 1949. "A black cat had run between me and Stalin," was all Molotov could say.[29] But as first deputy chairman of the Council of Ministers, he remained a member of the Politburo.

Stalin was still not done with Molotov. At the party plenum in October 1952, Stalin announced the appointment of a nine-man

Bureau for the Presidium which was supposed to assume the executive responsibilities of the previous Politburo, a kind of inner cabinet whose existence and membership were not announced to the public. Stalin, of course, would lead it. While Molotov, Mikoyan, and Voroshilov remained on the Presidium, their names were being excluded from this new Bureau. Stalin was demoting Molotov, in particular, making clear that no one could cast a shadow over his preeminence. Feeling targeted and threatened, Mikoyan came away with a more cynical reason for the creation of a larger Presidium. As he put it in his memoirs, "With this broad makeup of the Presidium, it would not be so noticeable for Stalin to make any Presidium members disappear if he did not like them. If, let's say, out of twenty-five people, five or six would vanish in between congresses, it would be viewed as an insignificant change. If the same five or six would disappear from a group of nine Politburo members, then that would be far more noticeable."[30] Nonetheless, Stalin's verbal assault had only inconsistent repercussions. Molotov continued to receive government documents about foreign affairs even when he was being excluded from the ruling group.

At least two participants in the meeting came away with the feeling that Stalin was psychologically impaired. Shepilov wondered to himself if "all this [could] be a product of Stalin's schizophrenic paranoia?"[31] Admiral Nikolai Kuznetsov thought that Stalin "gave the impression of being a sick man."[32] Their comments, of course, came out years later. They could well have been sincere, but they could also reflect the condemnation of Stalin that Khrushchev initiated in 1956 at the Twentieth Party Congress and then expanded upon in 1961 at the Twenty-Second Party Congress. Until party leaders like Khrushchev gave a signal with their own remarks, it would have been impossible for Shepilov or Kuznetsov to question Stalin's mental health.

At first glance it is not easy to understand why Stalin was choosing to target Molotov, Mikoyan, and Voroshilov in the fall of 1952. Why not Kaganovich or Khrushchev? Kaganovich had played an especially prominent role in the party; when Stalin would leave Moscow in the 1930s, Kaganovich would take on his responsibilities. By the 1950s, he remained the sole surviving Jew in the Politburo and it would not have been difficult to implicate him in any one of several "plots" or "conspiracies" that Stalin was brewing. During the Great Terror of 1937, several threads of repression had come close to compromising him. There were numerous arrests among his closest associates and deputies in the Transport Commissariat which he headed. Kaganovich had been friendly with General Iona Yakir, one of the principal victims of the purge of the military, who was also Jewish, a fact that Stalin questioned Kaganovich about as the purge unfolded. Stalin explained to him that some of the arrested officers had pointed to Kaganovich's involvement in their "counter-revolutionary organizations," a charge that secret police interrogators would have had to concoct. And Kaganovich's brother Mikhail had once served as commissar of the aviation industry before being removed over accusations of "counter-revolutionary activities"; Mikhail Kaganovich committed suicide soon afterwards.

Khrushchev, as well, coming out of Ukraine, could have been equally vulnerable. It is well known that one after another Ukrainian figure within the party leadership had been singled out over the years for alleged misdeeds and acts of disloyalty. Khrushchev, moreover, had been publicly rebuked in the press for some failings in agricultural policy as recently as 1951, a charge that could easily lend itself to the usual inflation of criminal behavior—"wrecking" or "sabotage," for example; during his speech to the party congress Malenkov had even referred to this incident. But Khrushchev, like Kaganovich, was not singled out in the way that Molotov and Mikoyan were obviously targeted. As Oleg V. Khlevniuk, one of the most well-informed and insightful of contemporary scholars of the Stalin era, has observed, "historians will never be able to penetrate the gloomy depths of Stalin's psyche to fully understand the calculations and inclinations that wound up determining the fates of those with whom he had shared the leadership."[33] Khlevniuk was writing about the 1930s and the Great Terror, but similar mechanisms of opaque calculation apply to the final years of Stalin's life. Still, it would be plausible to believe that Molotov, Mikoyan, and Voroshilov were being targeted because they were the last remaining "Old Bolsheviks" in the upper reaches of the party. Their prominent roles went back to the revolution and the civil war, making their vulnerability less arbitrary than it might have seemed.

Stalin's "comrades-in-arms" never forgot the fate of Lenin's initial Politburo. Lev Kamenev and Grigory Zinoviev were executed in August 1936 following the first purge trial. Grigory Sokolnikov was a defendant in the second purge trial, held in 1937; convicted and sentenced to ten years in the camps, he was reportedly killed by other prisoners on the orders of the secret police in May 1939. Andrei Bubnov was arrested in 1937 and executed sometime during the following year or two under unknown circumstances; he was never brought to trial. Leon Trotsky was assassinated in Mexico City in August 1940 on Stalin's personal orders. Only Lenin and Stalin would enjoy a natural death. As Khrushchev once admitted, after a meeting with Stalin no one ever knew if he would return home alive. To the public, they were his "comrades-in-arms." In reality, they were potential victims as long as he remained in charge.

* * *

As a candidate for the presidency, Dwight Eisenhower was well aware of Stalin's essay on the Soviet economy and his speech to the party congress. He was in New York a few days after the congress closed to deliver a talk at the Alfred A. Smith Memorial Foundation dinner at the Waldorf Astoria Hotel. Introduced by Cardinal Francis Spellman, who called Eisenhower one of the "All-Time Great Men of American History," Eisenhower included a brief response to Stalin's pronouncements in his speech. He said that Kremlin leaders had outlined "a diplomacy that envisioned the nations of the free world eventually falling into factions and preying on themselves." He suggested that "the Soviet Union might be ready to embark on a new international program of 'cold peace,' possibly as a mask for future aggression." Eisenhower challenged Stalin. "There is this most curious of all contradictions," he continued. "The fact that Soviet policy constantly becomes frightened by demons of its own invention. Thus its self-induced hysteria over fear of Western attack led it into a truculence which solidified the free world against it as nothing else could have done."[34] With the election only weeks away, Eisenhower was hardly in a mood to be conciliatory. The Kremlin was engaging in heated rhetoric about a likely war among Western powers, while the conflict in Korea pitted American forces against North Korean and Chinese communist troops.

In spite of Stalin's rhetoric, it was the communist world that was enduring political turmoil of its own. On September 17, *L'Humanité* denounced the "factional work" of two historic figures in the French Communist Party (PCF), André Marty and Charles Tillon.[35] Active communists for decades, they had first gained renown for their involvement in the Black Sea Mutiny when the crews of two French warships went on strike in 1919 in part out of sympathy with the Bolsheviks during the Russian Civil War. Both men were sentenced to prison but were pardoned within a few years. The experience radicalized them and they joined the PCF upon their release. Tillon went on to lead French communist guerrillas in World War II, when his units carried out bombings and sabotage against the occupying Germans. After the liberation, Tillon became one of a handful of PCF leaders to join the cabinet, serving successively as minister of aviation, armaments, and industrial reconstruction under Charles de Gaulle and other prime ministers between 1944 and 1947. Marty in particular was famous for his role as a political commissar with the International Brigades in Spain, where his fierce enforcement of party ideology led to the arbitrary execution of countless volunteers. Ernest Hemingway painted a disturbing portrait of Marty in *For Whom the Bell Tolls*: "To question him was one of the most devastating things that any man could do."[36] Ilya Ehrenburg had also known Marty in Spain. He disliked Marty and did his best to avoid speaking with him. In his memoirs, published in Moscow in the 1960s, Ehrenburg was allowed to describe Marty "as imperious, short-tempered, and always suspecting everyone of treason. . . . He spoke and sometimes acted like a man suffering from paranoia."[37]

But Marty's fanatical devotion to Stalin was not enough to keep him in the good graces of the PCF. Writing in the *New York Times* on October 5, just as the Nineteenth Party Congress was opening in Moscow, C. L. Sulzberger noted how the impending reorganization of the Bolshevik hierarchy was likely to lead to other parties' "streamlining [their] machinery." He then cited an article in the French communist press which affirmed that "in every country the combative ability of the party must be strengthened and unified. This idea, which sounds somewhat menacing," Sulzberger observed with a good deal of prescience, "probably bodes more ill for the Communists than other world citizens."[38] A purge soon overtook the PCF, one that only vaguely resembled the more violent proceedings in Eastern Europe. As happened elsewhere, former members of the Resistance and veterans of the Spanish Civil War were targeted, their fealty to the party line coming into question perhaps because in the antifascist struggle they had demonstrated courage and initiative, qualities that made them suspect in Stalin's eyes. Subjected to a closed "kangaroo court" by the party's Central Committee, Tillon was removed from leadership positions within the party but not expelled altogether, unlike Marty, who was thrown out in December. This being France, the party had no authority to impose any further sanction; they could not be arrested, tortured into making false confessions, or executed for their failure to support the party line. But the Marty–Tillon Affair dragged on for months, highlighted by news articles and opinion columns in *L'Humanité* and other French newspapers. Other communists faced more dreadful consequences.

In Prague, the former general secretary of the Czechoslovak Communist Party, Rudolf Slansky, a Jew and a man with a long record of obeisance to Stalin, awaited his fate in a jail cell. He had been arrested in November 1951 amid a chorus of allegations that he and other leading Czechoslovak officials were "Titoists" and had been engaging in espionage on behalf of Western powers to undermine socialism in Czechoslovakia. Faced with Tito's defiance in Yugoslavia, Stalin felt compelled to make absolutely sure that no other communist leader would follow his example and be allowed to contaminate another regime.

The Slansky case, emerging after a series of show trials in other satellite states, would be the concluding and most terrifying of them all. Subjected to torture, the defendants—eleven of the fourteen were Jews—would confirm that they were not only Titoists, but Zionists, and had engaged in a broad conspiracy with the Americans and the Israelis to undermine socialist rule. The trial would cast a shadow on Moscow itself. Malenkov had warned at the party congress that Soviet society still contained "vestiges of bourgeois ideology" and remained vulnerable to the "infiltration of alien views, ideas and sentiments from outside." What applied within the Soviet Union applied with equal gravity to other communist parties, particularly where party officials exercised political control of their countries. Stalin was laying the groundwork for something sinister, perhaps a renewed round of purges at the top or a broader assault on Soviet society itself in order to expose and destroy a newly identified "fifth column." These were hardly new themes, but in the atmosphere of

Cold War tension Slansky's impending trial, with all of its explicit anti-Zionist rhetoric, suggested something more alarming and immediate: a campaign against Jews throughout the socialist bloc and a continuing purge of leading officials, including inside the Soviet Union, during the final months of Stalin's life.

CHAPTER THREE

STALIN'S PARANOIA AND THE JEWS

With the opening of the Slansky trial in Prague on November 20, 1952, Soviet policies took a more openly antisemitic turn. Stalin himself had orchestrated the case, dispatching interrogators from Moscow as far back as 1949 to oversee the investigation and ensure the defendants' compliance. One of the Soviet interrogators, Vladimir Komarov, had particular experience tormenting Jewish prisoners. At the height of his career Komarov served as deputy chief of the investigative unit for especially important cases in the Soviet Ministry of State Security (MGB). He himself was arrested in early 1951 during a purge of the security services. Fearing for his life as he sat incarcerated in the internal prison of Lefortovo, Komarov sent an ugly letter to Stalin in February 1953 in which he bragged about his cruelty and his particular hatred for Jewish nationalists. What better way, he must have hoped, to wheedle his way back into Stalin's favor:

Defendants literally trembled before me. They feared me like the plague. ... I especially hated and was pitiless toward Jewish nationalists, whom I saw as the most dangerous and evil enemies. Because of my hatred of them I was considered an anti-Semite not only by defendants but by former employees of the MGB who were of Jewish nationality.[1]

Based on Komarov's own words, it is easy to see why Stalin thought he would be useful in Prague.

Accused of high treason, espionage, and economic sabotage, Rudolf Slansky and his thirteen co-defendants confessed to their crimes and pleaded with the court to impose the most severe punishment. After a week of testimony, during which the defendants confirmed the fantastic conspiracy that they had attempted to carry out as "Trotskyite–Titoist Zionists, bourgeois–nationalist traitors and enemies of the Czechoslovak people," the court announced its verdict and sentenced eleven of the defendants to death. That three of the defendants were spared was the only surprise. The judges noted that they had played minor roles and had been following Slansky's orders, thereby diminishing their criminal liability. But there could well have been an underlying reason for this gesture; the three were all Jewish. The Czechoslovak leader Klement Gottwald, who had the final say, may well have decided to soften the impression that the trial had reeked of antisemitism. As for the condemned men, they were hanged early in the morning of December 3. Their bodies were cremated, the ashes strewn by the side of an icy road to help the driver, who was a secret policeman, gain traction for his tires.

This was the largest post-war trial in Eastern Europe and the final, public face of Stalin's machinery of repression.[2] *Pravda* reported on the trial every day, emphasizing the defendants' guilt and highlighting their connections to Zionist and "bourgeois Jewish nationalist" conspiracies. As Radio Bucharest proclaimed in a typical statement, "We also have criminals among us, Zionist agents and agents of international Jewish capital. We shall expose them, and it is our duty to exterminate them."[3] By mid-December, the governments of Czechoslovakia and Poland insisted that Israel recall its ambassador, Arieh Kubovy, who represented the Jewish state in both countries; he was accused of abusing his diplomatic privileges. No step of this sort, which escalated tensions with Israel and the West in general, could have been initiated without Stalin's approval.

The question of why Rudolf Slansky became the chief defendant defies an easy answer. He did not resemble the other major purge victims in Eastern Europe. He was not a veteran of the Spanish Civil War nor was he a hero of the anti-Nazi resistance. He had spent the war in Moscow and was a reliable follower of the party line, far from the kind of "national communist" that so unnerved the Kremlin after Tito's defiance. When it came to leading Jewish and non-Jewish communists, Stalin was happy to exploit their blinkered loyalty, their naïve idealism, their cynical desire to exercise power, or whatever it was that bound them to the cause. And when it was time to use them in another way—as prisoners in the dock—Stalin was more than ready to finger whoever seemed most suitable for the roles he had in mind. Accused of economic sabotage, branded as traitors, Slansky and his co-defendants stood in the dock as flesh-and-blood incarnations of Western and Jewish perfidy. But the "Prague trial was only a curtain-raiser for a drama soon to be announced," as *The Times* observed in London.[4] As 1952 drew to a close, it was only natural to fear what would come next.

* * *

The Nineteenth Party Congress in Moscow and the Slansky trial in Prague prepared the ground for Stalin's next series of actions. By using the congress to reform the Politburo and the Slansky case to rekindle antisemitic repression in Eastern Europe, Stalin was getting ready to carry out a broader purge within the party leadership at home. The Jews could serve as both a scapegoat and a screen. He could arouse public emotions against the Jews while pursuing a step-by-step strategy that would combine accusations of disloyalty against the Jews with a reshaping of the security services and the country's broader leadership. At some point soon, he would have to make his intentions more public. A series of alleged crimes in Ukraine signaled the new direction to his madness.

During the final week of November 1952, *Izvestia* reported that severe sentences were being imposed on people convicted of commercial crimes, including the production of substandard goods, embezzlement, corruption, and the theft of state property. On December 1, a special military court in Kiev condemned three people to death for "counter-revolutionary wrecking"; their names were K. A. Kahn, Yaroshetsky, and Gerson, all three recognizably Jewish. Accused of criminal conspiracy in the field of trade, they were held responsible for the loss of "hundreds of thousands of rubles."[5] This was the first time that a military court was impaneled to cover a business-related crime. Just weeks earlier at the party congress, Poskrebyshev had warned that "a thief who pilfers public property and undermines the interests of the national economy is the same as a spy and a traitor, if not worse." Now his threat was bearing fruit. Stalin's target was clear to anyone who could read.

But it was not only individual Jews who were being singled out. On December 22, the biweekly party journal *Bloknot agitatorov* (Agitators' Notebook) carried a prominent article against Zionism. In unusually blunt language, it defined Zionism as a "reactionary trend of the Jewish bourgeoisie" which serves as a loyal agent of American imperialism.[6] While the Communist Party had always been opposed to Zionism, now Jews as Zionists were being accused of "[carrying] out espionage and subversion for the benefit of the United States," as the *New York Times* reported.[7] Nearly five years earlier, the Kremlin had been the first to recognize the new Jewish state after its founding in May 1948 and had even authorized the sale of weapons to Israel by the Czechoslovak communist regime.

Stalin had reasons of his own to support Israel's founding, not least the opportunity to see British withdrawal from the Middle East. But just as Stalin was increasing the antisemitic atmosphere within the country, Soviet foreign policy was growing more antagonistic toward Israel. It was now "[identifying] Zionism with American imperialism and alleged American subversion," as Salisbury alerted his editor in New York.[8] *Agitators' Notebook* was no ordinary journal. It was produced for party workers—45,000 in the Moscow region alone—in order to explain the party line on important issues. Reading the article, Salisbury assured his editors that it was inspired by the Slansky trial in Prague.

Stalin, in fact, had begun to go sour on his support for Israel five years earlier. In September, 1948, after the arrival of Golda Meyerson to Moscow as Israel's first diplomatic representative—she would soon change her name to the Hebrew surname Meir—the Soviet press covered the presentation of her credentials, providing false hope to Soviet Jews over the meaning of the Kremlin's support. In September and October, Meyerson visited the impressive Choral Synagogue on the Sabbath and on the Jewish holidays of Rosh Hashanah and Yom Kippur. Moscow's Jews could not restrain their enthusiasm. As she walked through the streets of the capital thousands of Jews welcomed her, while enormous crowds gathered in front of the synagogue.

Stalin had no patience for such passionate support for the new Jewish state. He blamed the Jewish Anti-Fascist Committee—a group that the Kremlin had created during the war to encourage support in the West for Stalin's alliance with Western democracies—for the demonstrations. By November the regime disbanded the committee, claiming that it was "a center of anti-Soviet propaganda and regularly submits anti-Soviet information to organs of foreign intelligence."[9] Within months, Yiddish-language periodicals and publishing houses were closed, and professional Yiddish theaters shut down, while hundreds of Yiddish cultural figures, including fifteen people associated with the Jewish Anti-Fascist Committee, were arrested. Yiddish was the principal vehicle for Jewish self-expression in the country and now its public institutions were being eliminated.

For Stalin, the whole episode raised questions about the loyalty of his Jewish subjects. After three decades of Soviet rule, with all the attendant pressures to assimilate, to reject religious ritual and adopt Russian culture as the primary expression of their moral and cultural identity, here were thousands of Jews in the streets showing without restraint that they remained Jews with longings and dreams that extended beyond the physical and spiritual borders of the Soviet state. It was time to remind them of where they were living: the Kremlin's support for Israel did not mean that Soviet Jews would be able to emigrate or volunteer to help defend the new Jewish state.

But the attack on the committee and Yiddish-language organizations left prominent Jews in the country's Russian-language cultural institutions untouched; their turn came in 1949 when the regime's anti-Western and "anti-cosmopolitan" campaign began to target Jewish figures by name. (To accuse someone of being a "cosmopolitan" was a crude way of questioning their loyalty to Soviet culture.) On January 28, *Pravda* highlighted "an anti-patriotic group of theater critics."[10] They were clearly Jewish, with names like Yuzovsky, Gurvich, and Kron. The article kicked off a broad press campaign targeting Jews for their questionable loyalties as if their primary attachment was to America, Europe, and the West. All this propaganda created an atmosphere of intimidation, isolating Jews in their places of work and putting their jobs in jeopardy. The consequences ranged from warnings and dismissals to expulsions from artistic unions. Some were also expelled from the Communist Party and even faced arrest.

Olga Freidenberg was a professor of classical philology in Leningrad. For many years she carried out a detailed and heartfelt correspondence with her cousin, the poet Boris Pasternak. In 1949 she shared a note with him from her diary. "Moral and intellectual pogroms have spread like a plague through the cities of Russia. . . ."

> Intellectuals with Jewish names are subjected to moral lynching. One should see the pogrom as carried out in our department. Groups of students rummage through the works of Jewish professors, eavesdrop on private conversations, whisper in corners. They make no effort to conceal their purposeful vigilance.
>
> Jews no longer receive an education, are no longer accepted at universities or for graduate study. The university has been devastated. The finest professors have been dismissed. The murder of the remaining intelligentsia goes on without cease. . . . They strike at scholars with whatever means they have at their disposal. Throw them out of work, force them to retire, condemn them to nonexistence by banishment. Professors who survived last year's pogroms are dying one after another from strokes and heart attacks.[11]

This was the atmosphere in myriad Soviet institutions as a result of the "anti-cosmopolitan" campaign.

Unbeknownst to the public, the Kremlin was also continuing to investigate the Jewish Anti-Fascist Committee, interrogating and torturing its arrested members. After three or more years of confinement they were brought to a secret trial in May 1952. Held within the confines of the Lubyanka, the secret police headquarters in central Moscow, the trial lasted for two months. The fifteen defendants were accused of "Jewish bourgeois nationalism," espionage, and treason based on their work with the committee. Their efforts during the war, even how they had gathered information about the Nazi massacres and tried to commemorate the victims, were held against them. Thirteen were executed on August 12. One defendant collapsed during the trial and subsequently died in a prison hospital. Only the distinguished scientist Lina Shtern survived the ordeal. Although she was sentenced to five years of internal exile, she was allowed to return to Moscow a year after Stalin's death. It took the Kremlin forty years to release the transcript of the trial and reveal the antisemitic nature of the entire case. With the execution of the defendants, five of whom were famous Yiddish poets and writers—David Bergelson, Peretz Markish, Leyb Kvitko, David Hofshteyn, and Itsik Fefer—Stalin was reaching the zenith of his assault on Yiddish-language culture. Held in secret, however, the trial could not serve the broader purpose of intimidation. Something more dramatic would have to be devised.[12]

By the fall of 1952 Stalin had been pulling together elements of an alleged conspiracy by high-ranking Jewish physicians who were accused of plotting against Kremlin leaders. A number were arrested that November, among them Stalin's personal doctor, Vladimir Vinogradov, and the chief doctor of the Red Army (who was also a cousin of the actor-director Solomon Mikhoels), Miron Vovsi. They were subjected to brutal interrogations; according to Khrushchev, Stalin ordered Vinogradov "to be put in chains." The regime wanted confessions about their links to foreign intelligence services and their plans to murder Soviet officials. "If you do not obtain confessions from the doctors," Stalin warned his security apparatus, "we will shorten you by a head."[13] The beatings grew so severe that a special room was outfitted in Lefortovo prison to accommodate the torture. Such pressure led to quick results. Vovsi briefly resisted before denouncing other doctors, accusing them of espionage on behalf of the Americans and the British; by December he was ready to claim that Mikhoels had been a "Jewish bourgeois nationalist." Vinogradov broke down, as well, "admitting" to his role as a spy and a terrorist along with his criminal ties to living doctors, including Miron Vovsi.[14]

Only Stalin could have been behind such cases. By then he was openly expressing his paranoid anxiety about Jews and Americans. On December 1, he declared during a Presidium meeting that "every Jew is a nationalist and an agent of American intelligence. Jewish nationalists believe that the USA saved their people. There you can become rich, bourgeois, and so forth. They believe they are indebted to the Americans."[15] Statements like this set a tone within the regime, providing guidance to security officials over how to pursue investigations and handle the accused.

* * *

In the wake of the Slansky trial, the Israeli government found itself in a perplexing position. It wanted to maintain workable, if not friendly, relations with the Kremlin and avoid siding with the Americans in the burgeoning Cold War. But David Ben-Gurion's government was under pressure to respond to the antisemitic and anti-Zionist demagoguery of the Prague trial. According to Israel's renowned UN Ambassador Abba Eban, the Americans wanted the Israelis to add their "loud and resounding voice to those who disparage the Soviet Union along with the entire propagandist and political spectrum the world over."[16]

The Israeli press and public, at least, could not be expected to restrain themselves. A mock trial was held in Tel Aviv directed against the Kremlin and the Israeli Communist Party, while newspapers carried articles and editorials decrying the trial's outright antisemitic dimensions. More ominously, someone carried out acts of vandalism against the Czechoslovak legation. On November 23, while the trial was still unfolding, a stone was thrown through an office window, and on December 4 a bomb was thrown in the underground garage of the legation building, damaging a wall and a car. A few days later, someone attempted to set fire to the Soviet legation's car. In reporting on such incidents, Soviet diplomats echoed the accusations out of Prague: "The attitude of Israeli ruling circles and Zionist parties to the Prague trial, in addition to the content of the trial itself, confirms that Zionism and its representatives and participants are direct agents of American imperialism."[17]

But the Israeli government maintained its restraint, not wanting to worsen relations with the Kremlin. In early January, Eban reported to Tel Aviv that Jewish leaders in New York were "confused and divided among themselves" over the meaning of the Slansky trial. "The question is whether to accuse the Soviet Union of a clearly anti-Semitic attitude which would put it among Israel's enemies and thus abolish the last moral distinction between it and the Nazi regime." Eban advised Ben-Gurion to "denounce the Prague trial as a separate anti-Semitic episode which raises fears about the attitude of the Soviet authorities, without, however, pronouncing judgment on the Soviet Union as if anti-Semitism had become a permanent element of its policy."[18] Ben-Gurion agreed, even though he was confident that the Slansky trial had been "planned down to the last detail in the Kremlin and one must be prepared for a serious change of course in Soviet policy in an anti-Jewish or at least anti-Israeli direction." For now he adopted a wait-and-see attitude and refrained, however reluctantly, from regarding "this prognosis as a fact."[19] The Kremlin soon confirmed his worst fears.

Stalin, as always, insisted on keeping up the appearance of normality. On the night of January 12, he attended the Bolshoi Theater for a concert by visiting Polish musicians and was accompanied by five members of the Presidium. The public face of the regime and its ideological façade remained opaque and defiant. But the announcement of the Doctors' Plot the next day sent shock waves through Soviet society; reading the announcement, Harrison Salisbury wrote how "it chilled my blood."[20] In spite of how the regime prepared the groundwork—the outright anti-Jewish demagoguery of the Slansky trial and the execution of alleged Jewish thieves in Kiev—there was no precedent in more than three decades of Soviet rule for the overt antisemitism of the Doctors' Plot. As the dissident historian Roy Medvedev observed, Stalin was "[casting] aside almost all ideological screens and made anti-Semitism an open, obvious part of state policy."[21]

"Some time ago," Tass announced to the world on January 13, 1953, "the agencies of state security uncovered a terrorist group of doctors who had made it their aim to cut short the lives of active public figures of the Soviet Union by means of sabotaged medical treatment." These doctors had now confessed to their crimes. It then revealed that two prominent Soviet leaders, Aleksandr Shcherbakov and Andrei Zhdanov, who had died in 1945 and 1948 respectively, had not succumbed to natural causes, as had long been believed; the accused doctors had maliciously sabotaged their medical treatment. The doctors had also been targeting leading military officers, among them three Soviet marshals, an army general, and an admiral, "but arrest disrupted their evil plans and the criminals did not succeed in attaining their aim." They were nothing less than "monsters in human form."

The article listed nine doctors, all of whom occupied senior positons in the Soviet medical elite. Six were Jewish: M. S. Vovsi, M. B. Kogan, B. B. Kogan, A. A. Feldman, Y. G. Etinger, and A. M. Grinshteyn. And to reinforce the point, the article went on to claim that they were in league "with the international Jewish bourgeois nationalist organization, 'Joint' [the American Jewish Joint Distribution Committee], established by American intelligence for the alleged purpose of providing material aid to Jews in other countries"; it also accused Vovsi of seeking to "wipe out the leading cadres of the USSR" with the assistance of "the Moscow doctor, Shimeliovich, and the well-known Jewish bourgeois nationalist Mikhoels."

Here again, the communiqué was sharing startling claims that could only have confused and frightened its readers. Boris Shimeliovich was no ordinary doctor. He had been chief medical director of Moscow's prestigious Botkin Hospital where he supervised the treatment of party and government leaders as well as foreign dignitaries. But unbeknownst to the world, Shimeliovich had been arrested on January 13, 1949, as part of the regime's assault on the Jewish Anti-Fascist Committee. He then disappeared into the confines of Lefortovo prison where he endured systematic beatings in an attempt to compel him to confess to "bourgeois Jewish nationalism," treason, and espionage. But Shimeliovich resisted and refused to confess to any crime; this did not save him from execution in August 1952. Now the regime was alleging that Shimeliovich had been involved in a conspiracy to kill Soviet leaders. It did not say whether or not he was under arrest, or reveal that he was already dead. Nor did it refer to his trial where such an accusation had not been presented. But by invoking his name, the regime may well have been preparing to connect the case against the Jewish Anti-Fascist Committee—which remained a highly secret process—with the Doctors' Plot, which was only now being exposed. The communiqué also impugned the reputation of Solomon Mikhoels, who had been killed five years earlier to the day. These were the first words against Mikhoels to appear in the Soviet press, although Soviet interrogators in Prague had referred to him as "a treacherous Zionist" during the investigation of the Slansky case.[22] The Tass communiqué ended with an ominous claim: "The investigation will soon be concluded." For Soviet readers, the implication was clear: the accused would face imminent justice for their crimes.

Along with the Tass announcement, *Pravda* carried a separate editorial on its front page with the medieval-sounding title "Foul Spies and Murderers in the Mask of Doctors and Professors." The editorial raised questions that were designed to incite fear and hatred among Soviet citizens:

Whom did these monsters serve? Who directed the criminal terrorist and wrecking activity of these vile traitors to the motherland? What purpose did they want to achieve through murders of active public figures of the Soviet state? . . .

The bosses of the USA and their British "junior partners" know that it is impossible to secure mastery over other nations by peaceful means. Feverishly preparing for a new world war, they are sending more and more of their spies into the USSR and the people's democracies, trying to succeed where the Hitlerites failed—trying to create a subversive "fifth column" in the USSR.

So the accused doctors were doing more than seeking to murder Soviet officials. The regime was now linking them to the Nazis, alleging they wanted to provoke a new world war. The Jews had suffered during the previous war—which *Pravda* did not bother to mention—but now, it seemed, they were turning the tables on the very regime that had saved them. In addition, the image of a "fifth column" bent on subverting Soviet society echoed the language of the 1930s when Stalin justified the purges as a way to cleanse the country of elements that would undermine unity in the face of a war.

But the editorial was not only concerned with the criminal activity of the doctors. It also expressed concern over how "Soviet agencies and their officials [had] lost their vigilance and were infected with gullibility. The agencies of state security did not discover the doctors' wrecking, terrorist organization in time."[23] This was a direct threat against other Soviet leaders, for it had long been a practice to convert lack of vigilance into active complicity. Stalin was using the Doctors' Plot to accuse them of failing to monitor the work of people who were prone to commit espionage, even murder. Lavrenti Beria had long been associated with the security services and even though in January 1953 he was no longer minister of state security he remained involved in matters of internal security as a deputy minister. Moreover, the previous November, in a subtle downgrading of his status, his portrait had been dropped two notches in the order in which over-size portraits of Stalin's "comrades-in-arms" were carried in the parade to mark the anniversary of the revolution. He was now preceded by Molotov, Malenkov, Voroshilov, and Bulganin. Harrison Salisbury noticed that "this sequence was repeated hundreds and hundreds of times" as civilian marchers passed the viewing stand, an unmistakable indication that Stalin was up to something.[24]

Soviet leaders were always sensitive to their place in the hierarchy. Soon after Stalin's death, the former Moscow radio reporter Mikhail Soloviev explained to the *New Yorker* just how carefully such matters were monitored.

I was describing the 1939 May Day parade in Red Square. At one point, I mentioned the government officials who were reviewing the parade with Stalin—Andreyev, Voroshilov, Molotov, Kaganovich. . . . That same night, I was called before Malenkov. . . . He asked me to explain why the names of the officials at the parade had not been announced in the proper order. I told him, "Tovarich Malenkov, I put Andreyev first simply because 'A' comes first in the alphabet." Malenkov said, "The Soviet alphabet always begins with 'S,' then comes 'M,' then 'V,' then 'K,' and then 'A.' He meant, of course, Stalin, Molotov, Voroshilov, Kaganovich, and Andreyev. Since we knew each other, I took the liberty of asking, "This alphabet is permanent?" "No," he said. "It may be changed tomorrow, but remember that the alphabet is decided here in the Central Committee, and not in a radio station."[25]

Over the winter of 1952–53, Beria knew he was a marked man.

* * *

On January 13, the denunciations in the Soviet press did not mention Israel by name, giving the Israelis pause. Even as the Foreign Ministry instructed Israeli embassies on how to word objections to the accusations—that it was "madness" to accuse the Joint Distribution Committee of such crimes and that the "pejorative use of 'Jew' and 'Zionist' demonstrates that the Russian leaders are in need of scapegoats"—it insisted that "Israel is not interested in being drawn into an open conflict with Soviet Russia because it is of vital importance to maintain our position as fully as possible in Moscow and in the capitals of the satellites."[26] Abba Eban objected to this approach; he wanted to see a stronger response coming from Israel. But other Israeli leaders, including Ben-Gurion and its leading diplomat on Eastern Europe, Shmuel Eliashev, favored restraint. They continued to fear a break in relations over the Doctors' Plot, which would undermine any hope of dialogue with the Kremlin and jeopardize Israel's contacts with Jews in Eastern Europe and the Soviet Union. Israel was not ready to take sides in the Cold War.

But Ben-Gurion faced other unexpected domestic tensions. The Israeli Communist Party (known by its acronym, Maki) held a handful of seats in the Israeli parliament—the Knesset. Its leaders and its newspaper, *Kol Ha'am* (Voice of the People), did not hesitate to mouth the propaganda out of Moscow, endorsing the accusations against the Jewish doctors and against Zionism as if they were made in good faith and based on actual facts. Even as government ministers and other Knesset members denounced the false allegations out of Moscow, Ben-Gurion found it necessary to denounce Maki, calling its behavior "pathological and criminal" and challenging the parliament to take action against the party and its newspaper. "Is it conceivable that [Israel] should tolerate accomplices of and collaborators with the enemies of Israel in foreign countries?" he wrote to members of the Knesset.[27] While Ben-Gurion muted his response, knowing full well that diplomatic relations with the Kremlin were hanging by a thread, he could not be patient in the face of ideological support for Stalin within Israel itself.

But reaction to the Doctors' Plot in the West was forthright and immediate. Writing in Paris, the sociologist and political commentator Raymond Aron summarized the troubling nature of the accusations with questions of his own. "Let's suppose," he wrote in *Le Figaro*, "that the accused are telling the truth: what must be thought about a country where the greatest doctors assassinate leading state officials? And if the confessions had been extorted by violence, what must be thought of a country where men of science are made to publicly display their humiliation and where the population will be prepared to accept the truth of their confessions which are as disgraceful for the judge as they are for the accused."[28] In London, *The Times* decried the accusations; not since the 1930s had it seen "so lurid and fantastic a story" out of Moscow.[29] An editorial in the *New York Times* entitled "Soviet Anti-Semitism" opened with a startling comparison. "Taking one more leaf out of Hitler's book the Stalin regime has now openly and unmistakably adopted anti-Semitism as a weapon in its own internal dissensions and as an instrument of both Communist tyranny and Soviet imperialism. . . . Now, undeterred by world-wide revulsion against a revival of the Nazi madness, the Soviet rulers have put their stamp of approval on it, and neither their disclaimers of prejudice nor their differentiation between Jews and Zionists can disguise their adoption of the Hitler technique."[30]

But even as the *New York Times* decried the accusations, it engaged in confused speculation as to why the Kremlin was initiating such a campaign. On January 18, for example, a news article suggested that "There may actually have been some kind of conspiracy and the Kremlin may have got wind of it." And how would the leading American newspaper explain the possibility that there really could have been a plot by Jewish doctors to do away with Soviet leaders? By claiming that something similar had happened "a number of times in the past. For example, the bloody purge of the Red Army in 1937 stemmed from the Kremlin's charge that certain officers were plotting with Germany against the Soviet Union." Yes, the *Times* reminded its readers, "many Westerners regarded this charge as a frame-up, but it may have had some basis in fact." The article then referred to the memoirs of Winston Churchill where he expressed the belief that there were "pro-German elements" in the Red Army in the 1930s, leading him to regard the 1937 purge—where over 30,000 officers were killed!—as "merciless but perhaps not needless." But Churchill was wrong. Stalin had his own paranoid reasons for this wholesale slaughter, but with the likelihood of war with Germany it was the height of reckless leadership for him to engineer a broad-scale purge of the officer corps. The *Times* was misleading its readers by suggesting that this repugnant idea could even be remotely true.[31]

* * *

The announcement on January 13 was only the opening salvo in a tsunami of antisemitic propaganda. Virtually every day for the following six weeks the Soviet press questioned the loyalty of the country's Jewish citizens. National and republic-level newspapers reprised the same incendiary language, echoing the anti-Jewish invective of the initial Tass communiqué. *Trud* denounced the doctors as a "despicable band of wreckers who posed as learned doctors [while seeking] to cut short the lives of public figures in the Soviet Union."[32] Medical journals highlighted dubious accusations against doctors almost all of whom bore Jewish names: Asya Borisovna Epshtein, Celia Markovna Nesnevich, Regina Grigoryevna Blokh, and Dora Moiseyevna Paperno, among others, were malingerers. And if Paperno's family name seemed too ethnically neutral-sounding, her patronymic "Moiseyevna," or "daughter of Moses," made her origins unmistakably clear. Another doctor, M. Z. Izraelit, was said to have fraudulently passed for an expert on venereal diseases without the proper medical diploma. A long list of Jewish physicians associated with the Central Clinic of Legal Psychiatry was accused of refusing to apply the methods of "patriotic Russian psychiatry" and of propagating the "false and harmful theories" of Freud and Bergson.[33]

As the Soviet press campaign continued, the magazine *Krokodil* stretched the limits of the Kremlin's ugly rhetoric. *Krokodil* was known for its satire as it took aim at permitted targets within Soviet society, like bureaucrats who avoided hard work or heavy drinkers who compromised their family and professional lives. Its caricatures could also be counted on to lampoon "enemies of the state," foreign and domestic opponents of the regime who were ripe for attack. The Doctors' Plot provided a suitable target for its brand of humor. Taking its cue from the language of *Pravda* and Tass earlier in the month, *Krokodil* could tickle its readers' thirst for laughter:

> Vovsi, B. Kogan and M. Kogan, Feldman, Grinshteyn, Etinger, Vinogradov, and Yegorov knew how to change the expression in their eyes to give their wolves' souls a human aspect. . . . For this purpose they attended a well-known school directed by the hypocrite Mikhoels, to whom nothing was sacred and who, for thirty pieces of silver, sold his soul to the "land of the yellow devil" which he chose to be his homeland. . . . In the people's memory they [the arrested doctors] are the personification of baseness and abomination, the same kind as that Judas Iscariot. . . . The black hatred of our great country has united in one camp American and British bankers, colonialists, kings of arms, Hitler's defeated generals dreaming of vengeance, representatives of the Vatican, loyal adherents of the Zionist *kahal* [a Hebrew word for "community"].[34]

Krokodil topped off its nasty article with a cartoon that recalled the outright antisemitic caricatures of the Nazi periodical *Der Stürmer*.

The cartoon took up the entire back page of the magazine and featured a physician being restrained by the hand of justice as it grabbed his white medical gown from behind. Only this was not a distinguished-looking professional doctor, but a modern-day Shylock, a figure with a hooked nose and thick lips lusting for dollars and blood, whose true face—underneath a mask that was now being swept aside—bore the unmistakable, extreme image of a Jewish predator.

As this hateful press campaign continued without let-up, *Pravda* reported how a Russian doctor, Lidia Timashuk, had alerted officials to the deliberate misdiagnosis of Andrei Zhdanov's condition in 1948. As an experienced physician with a specialty in reading electrocardiographs, it was alleged that she had challenged older, more senior physicians when she noticed how they were misinterpreting electrocardiographs of Zhdanov's heart. She had written to the Kremlin to express her unease back in 1948 (or so it was claimed) and it was this appeal that helped Soviet officials uncover the truth. For her courage, she was being awarded the Order of Lenin. As part of its campaign, the Kremlin celebrated her bravery for several weeks. It orchestrated a letter-writing campaign to newspapers and to Timashuk herself, lauding her outspoken courage and thanking her for standing up to more senior doctors who had abused the trust of their patients.

As anti-Jewish incitement spread, panic engulfed Soviet society. Yakov Rapoport would soon be among the imprisoned doctors. Decades later he recalled how a young mother "announced that she would not give any more medicine to her baby, . . . [declaring] with frenzied determination that she would prefer her baby die of pneumonia rather than poison."[35] Her attitude was not unusual. "It was like hell in the hospitals," Ilya Ehrenburg wrote in his memoirs. "Many patients regarded the doctors as insidious scoundrels and refused to take any medicines." One friend told Ehrenburg about a doctor who "had to swallow pills, powders, a dozen medicines for a dozen diseases"; her patients "were afraid she was a conspirator."[36] Ehrenburg was in a better position than most people to gauge the effect of the Doctors' Plot on his fellow Jews. As perhaps the most prominent Jewish public figure in the country—aside from Kaganovich—he had written eloquently and repeatedly about Jewish suffering during the war. Individual Soviet Jews often wrote to him to express their worries and concerns, about harassment they were suffering at school or work. Most called on him to denounce the arrested doctors as traitors; they were desperate and looking for ways to protect themselves.[37]

In spite of growing alarm in the West, the Kremlin could still rely on the support of its compliant followers. A submissive French Communist Party enlisted support for Stalin's unmasking of the alleged conspiracy. On January 27, *L'Humanité* published a statement by a group of French physicians, among them four Jews, who declared their support for Soviet officials in their "war" against the criminal acts of the accused medical personnel.[38] Three weeks later, 12,000 French communists, along with the film actress Simone Signoret, packed the Vélodrome d'Hiver to protest the death sentence that had been imposed by an American court on Julius and Ethel Rosenberg for their atomic espionage on behalf of the Soviet Union. According to a Reuters' dispatch, "Jacques Duclos, acting leader of the French Communist party, used the fact that the Rosenbergs were Jews to 'prove' that Communists were not waging an anti-Semitic campaign."[39] Stalinists like Duclos were more than happy to invoke the controversy over the Rosenberg case to help camouflage the nature of the Doctors' Plot.

* * *

The final month of Stalin's life remains the most enigmatic and frightening of his reign. Rumors swirled about his health, about the vulnerability of his "comrades-in-arms," about his intentions toward the Jews. With Mikhoels being publicly denounced, the regime was now after his family. Near the end of January, the secret police searched their apartment "for almost an entire day and night, after which not the smallest scrap of paper was left in the flat." As his daughter, Natalya Vovsi-Mikhoels, recounted the scene, the officers grew suspicious of anything with the word "Jew" in it.[40]

About a week later, in the early morning hours of February 7, the secret police returned for his son-in-law, the distinguished composer Mieczysław Weinberg, who was a devoted friend of Dmitri Shostakovich; they often played piano for four hands together and dedicated new compositions to each other. Weinberg's arrest marked a typical turn of fortune. Stalin liked to play with his victims, often honoring them with awards or offering tributes in newspapers just as warrants for their arrest were being arranged. Only hours before Weinberg's arrest, the violinist David Oistrakh had performed the premiere of his *Moldavian Rhapsody* in Tchaikovsky Hall, the capital's most prestigious concert hall. Now, well past midnight, Weinberg was led away without his tie and belt. Accused of Jewish bourgeois nationalism—his *Sinfonietta No. 1* was held against him—he was held in solitary confinement. In such an atmosphere of uncertainty and terror, Shostakovich took two extraordinary steps on his behalf. He and his wife arranged for power of attorney so that if Natalya Vovsi-Mikhoels were to be arrested as well the Shostakoviches would become the guardian for their seven-year-old daughter; she would not be sent to an orphanage where children of "enemies of the people" were consigned. In addition, and at no small risk to himself, Shostakovich sent an appeal to Beria, describing Weinberg "as a very talented and promising new composer, who wasn't concerned with anything except music, and saying that he, Shostakovich, was willing to vouch for his honesty."[41] But Weinberg remained in custody.

An incident in Israel further complicated matters. Late on the night of February 9, a small group of right-wing Israeli extremists, who were incensed over the antisemitic campaign in Moscow, placed an incendiary device inside the compound of the Soviet legation in Tel Aviv. The bomb blew out windows and damaged other property, injuring the wife of the ambassador as well as the housekeeper and the chauffeur. Ben-Gurion was furious, knowing where such an act would lead. He immediately denounced the crime, assuring the Kremlin that Israel would find the perpetrators and hold them accountable. But Stalin was not appeased. For the Kremlin, the bombing provided the perfect pretext to break diplomatic relations with the Jewish state. It did not merely announce the severing of relations; it used the incident to broaden its propaganda against Zionism, only now it could denounce Israel as an outright enemy that had deliberately carried out an attack. As *Pravda* commented in the days that followed, "The pack of mad dogs from Tel Aviv is loathsome and vile in its thirst for blood."[42]

The bombing provoked harsh, public feelings among the Soviet population. Local party officials were quick to organize meetings in factories and other institutions both to reinforce an anti-Zionist message and to gauge public opinion in the wake of the ongoing propaganda campaign. As their reports make clear, the incident in Tel Aviv reinforced the coarsening effects of the Doctors' Plot and often resulted in a "harmful interpretation" of these events by ordinary citizens. Based on a handful of once top-secret reports, it is possible to glimpse inside the popular reaction to the party's campaign against Zionism and the Jewish doctors.

On February 13, four days after the bombing, a Communist Party instructor at a Moscow bread factory described the workers' indignation over this "outrageous provocation" and their unanimous endorsement of the breaking of relations with Israel, an expected echo of the party line. But her report went on to cite "displays of anti-semitism" that she found troubling. Several workers complained that there "are hardly any honest people among the Jews, that they try to arrange 'easy jobs' at work where there are good salaries; and that during the Great Patriotic War hardly any Jews were front-line soldiers." A worker at a Moscow textile plant called for the Jews "to be removed from managerial positions in institutes and ministries, in consumer goods stores and trade organizations." Still another claimed that "the Jews had grabbed all the good apartments so they should be expelled from Moscow, and their apartments given to workers who are fulfilling the five-year plan and building communism."

The population had been schooled in how and what to think for decades, so it was hardly surprising that people parroted the party line. But now they were going beyond the prescribed reaction and engaging in explicit, antisemitic baiting. A welder declared: "I would pack all of these monsters without exception to Palestine." Someone wrote graffiti on the walls of a train station: "Beat the Kikes, save the USSR"; party officials saw this as a provocation, a direct rephrasing of a notorious, tsarist-era slogan. School children were threatening a fellow Jewish student, calling him a "traitor, saboteur, and 'kike'"; such an incident prompted officials to write that "something like this had not happened before." From the language in the reports, it is clear that party officials were both inciting animosity against the Jews and wanting "to curtail provocative actions and rumors." The press campaign had been so ugly and unrelenting that at least some officials realized that it was tapping into a deep well of anti-Jewish prejudice, provoking denunciations and physical threats that went beyond what the regime was intending to accomplish.[43]

Individuals were feeling free to voice their antisemitic resentments. A teacher of logic in a Leningrad high school took it on himself to ape the accusations in the press. He wrote an odious syllogism on the blackboard:

A (the doctor-assassins) = B (the Jews)
A (the doctor-assassins) = C (spies)
Then it follows that:
B (the Jews) = C (spies).

He then asked each student to stand and declare his or her agreement with his clever formula. They all remained silent and received a failing grade.[44]

A group of anonymous students complained to the Central Committee on February 28 that "critics–cosmopolitans" were controlling access to Moscow's prestigious literary journals, closing off opportunities for native Russian critics to advance their careers. These "subversive editors" were insinuating their views and making it possible for the journals to be taken over by "Zionist sentiments, nepotism, and clannishness." It was "intolerable for our Russian critical literature to be in the hands of Jewish rogues." The letter came to the attention of Malenkov, who noted that this was "an important matter," then passed it along to other party functionaries.[45] It is a reflection of the depth of anti-Jewish feeling at the time that the highest party officials felt compelled to follow up on such allegations and expect their subordinates to investigate. The ongoing public denunciations of Israel, Zionism, and individual Jews were agitating the population, leading to incidents that went beyond the officially sanctioned acts of discrimination.

* * *

The Slansky trial had ended in November, but Stalin remained determined to extend the purge elsewhere in Eastern Europe. In Hungary, the regime was arresting prominent Jews, including Lajos Stoeckler, president of the country's Jewish community, while a purge targeted leading Jewish officials inside the party and the government. Similar reports emerged out of East Germany where a group of ten Jewish communal leaders fled to West Berlin in mid-January after the regime accused various East German communists of "conspiring with the fourteen Czech 'traitors.'"[46]

In Romania, the foreign minister Ana Pauker—a longtime and once-powerful communist official—was arrested on February 18, 1953. Like Slansky and other East European communist leaders, she was Jewish and had a reputation as a convinced and unrelenting Stalinist. The daughter of orthodox Jewish parents, Pauker matched the profile of a vulnerable communist official. Her position in government made her the highest-profile woman in Eastern Europe, a status that singled her out in a heavily male-dominated world. Her fame and importance in the country were widely acknowledged, particularly since 1947 when she had been appointed foreign minister, the first woman in any modern country to reach this pinnacle of authority. *Time* featured her on its cover on September 20, 1948, declaring her "the most powerful woman alive."

Following her arrest, interrogations of Pauker, of her brother, Zalman, who was arrested on the same day, and of other party officials, focused on Pauker's alleged conspiracy with Israeli diplomats and Zionists, and her espionage support for the Americans. The investigation also roped in Rabbi Moses Rosen, the most prominent rabbi in Bucharest, intending to include him among the defendants in what was meant to be a Romanian version of the Slansky trial. Romanian and Soviet investigators intended to open such a trial within weeks after Pauker's arrest, adding another intimidating spectacle to Stalin's anti-Jewish campaign.

* * *

It was in this poisonous atmosphere that rumors began to spread that Stalin intended to deport Soviet Jews to far-off places of exile: to

Kazakhstan, to Siberia, perhaps to Birobidjan, the "autonomous Jewish region" near the border with China. Ever since Stalin's death, the truth behind these rumors has remained among the most difficult to explore or confirm. The arguments that such a plan never really existed are compelling, and are often and most persuasively based on the fact that not a single document has been located that can confirm that such a plan was ever considered. When Mikhail Gorbachev opened hitherto closed, sensitive, official archives in the late 1980s and allowed both Soviet and foreign scholars to unearth once inaccessible material about myriad crimes—a process that Boris Yeltsin and even to some extent Vladimir Putin have continued—documents relating to Stalin's alleged plan to deport the Jews were among the most highly sought. But nothing has been found. That there should be no explicit directive from Stalin's office is not surprising. But neither are there records from within the Gulag bureaucracy calling for the construction of extensive new camps or settlements; nor orders within the railway administration to assign rolling stock; nor written plans to deploy soldiers, security officers, or ordinary police to round up Jews.

In their book, *Stalin's Last Crime*, Jonathan Brent and Vladimir Naumov point to orders for the construction of new special camps for German, Austrian, and other foreign criminals, but these documents refer to a few thousand prisoners and do not mention the Jews.[47] They also cite protocols of interrogations and face-to-face confrontations involving two senior officials of the secret police, Mikhail Ryumin and Isidor Maklyarsky, as evidence that such a plan was being considered. Maklyarsky had been arrested in November 1951. Under questioning by Ryumin several months later, he was pressured to denounce other people for engaging in Jewish nationalism. He was also told by Ryumin that he had "intended to put the question to the government about the expulsion of the Jews from Moscow."[48] Brent and Naumov, who like all students of this period were frustrated by the lack of explicit documentation about such a plan, concluded that "the testimony of Maklyarsky concerning Ryumin's threats gives ample reason to believe that, as in so many other cases, a policy was being developed without explicit written directives, that it had emanated from the Central Committee and had penetrated the investigative units of the security services."[49] This interpretation implies that officials like Ryumin were responding to some kind of signal "from above," that the drumbeat of propaganda against "Zionists" and now Jewish doctors created a situation reminiscent of how Nazi officers sought to "work toward the Führer."[50] They engaged in atrocities of their own without an explicit order, based on their understanding of what Hitler expected from them when it came to Jews, subversives, or the disabled. Officials like Ryumin, who were always anxious to demonstrate their ideological reliability, could well have been "working toward Stalin" and initiating rumors or even preliminary plans for a general assault against the Jews before Stalin or the Presidium actually reviewed or sanctioned such a plan.

Around 2.5 million Jews were living in the Soviet Union at that time. They were overwhelmingly urban, with a significant presence in Moscow, Leningrad, Kharkov, Kiev, Minsk, Odessa, Vilnius, and Riga. As a whole, they were highly educated and often enjoyed visible roles in scientific and cultural institutions. To round them up and dispatch them to camps would have been far more complicated than had been the deportation of several small ethnic minorities in 1944—the Crimean Tatars, the Ingush, the Balkars, the Karachevtsy, and the Kalmyks—whose members numbered in the hundreds of thousands and who had been living for the most part in well-defined areas of the country.

Although these mass deportations were state secrets, enough people knew about them and understood what the regime was capable of.[51] In the wake of the Doctors' Plot and the unrelenting propaganda against Zionism and alleged Jewish criminals, a mood of terror and dread spread so broadly that it created an atmosphere in which such a fantastic act of repression could seem like an inevitable conclusion to the case against the doctors. Such fears were not confined to the Soviet Union. In London, *The Times*, for one, cited a column from the Israeli newspaper *Haaretz* (The Land) when it voiced its distress over the announcement of the Doctors' Plot: "We cannot suppress fears that Moscow's purge of Jewish doctors may serve as the introduction to, and perhaps justification for, the mass expulsion of Jews from European Russia to Asiatic Russia. Who knows whether the fate of the lost 10 tribes is not in store for Russian Jewry." And it was this British newspaper that speculated in mid-January that it was "even possible that those [Jews] in western Russia will be removed, as some of the Caucasian tribes and the Crimean Tatars were removed, into the interior of the Union as a precautionary measure."[52]

According to the rumors, the condemned doctors would publicly confess to their heinous crimes in a show trial, then face public hanging in Red Square rather than be secretly dispatched in a prison basement. Following the executions, prestigious Jewish scientific and cultural figures would appeal to Stalin to save the Jews from "the wrath of the people"—who had been incited against the Jews by the nefarious crimes of the doctors—by dispatching them into exile; the Jews would then be rounded up *en masse* and sent away. It was even rumored that security troops would fire on the trains transporting the Jews as they passed through the countryside.

Over the years, several Soviet dissident figures, many of them respected and independent-minded students of history, among them Roy Medvedev, Anton Antonov-Ovseenko, Mikhail Heller, Aleksandr Nekrich, and Aleksandr Solzhenitsyn, all expressed the belief that such a deportation plan for the Jews existed. Medvedev wrote matter-of-factly about such a plan in his path-breaking book

Let History Judge: "Everything indicated that [Stalin] was beginning preparations for a mass deportation of Jews to remote districts."[53] Heller and Nekrich in *Utopia in Power* expressed their belief that the bureaucracy was ready to carry it out, even that a member of the Presidium, D. Chesnokov, had prepared a book explaining the reasons for the deportation of the Jews.[54] Antonov-Ovseenko went even further, claiming in his book *The Time of Stalin* that the Central Committee would allow some Jews to remain in Moscow, but they "would have yellow stars sewn on their sleeves,"[55] a rumored scenario that completely contradicted Stalin's way of camouflaging his actions. And Solzhenitsyn, couching his claims with a measure of caution, wrote that "It would appear that Stalin intended to arrange a great massacre of the Jews," and then in a footnote described the rumors of a planned mass deportation to the Far East and Siberia.[56] None of them offer any documentary evidence for their claims. The book by Chesnokov, for example, has never been found, although it is referred to by several writers.[57] Other allegations—that a great many barracks were under construction in Siberia or Central Asia, that lists of Jews by their addresses were being compiled—have also been advanced but without any documentary evidence.[58] All this leads to a cautionary conclusion: that the rumors about an impending deportation were so widespread, frightening, and believed that they seeped their way into the intellectual and cultural legacy of Stalin's critics, including those who had made it to the West. No less a figure than Aleksandr Yakovlev, who became a principal adviser to Mikhail Gorbachev and chair of Russia's Presidential Commission for the Rehabilitation of Victims of Political Repression, believed that "preparations for mass deportations of Jews from Moscow and other major industrial centers to the northern and eastern regions" were underway in February 1953.[59] Under Yakovlev's direction, numerous, hitherto-secret documents about Stalin's regime were published, so one would have thought that his opinion was based on what he found in the archives. But Yakovlev, too, was unable to point to a single document to confirm what he thought to be true.

Without some measure of documentary evidence, it is impossible to reach a definitive conclusion about Stalin's ultimate plans. What can be said is that the antisemitic campaign was gathering such momentum in the press and in the mood of the population that it could well have been intended to reach some kind of monstrous denouement. Only Stalin knew the answer to this question, and with his death the answer could well be lost to history.

Stalin's heirs also contributed to the popular belief in such a scenario. Following Khrushchev's denunciation of Stalin in February 1956, the Western press began carrying wildly implausible claims about how Presidium members had stood up to Stalin when he detailed his plans to deport the Jews. Appearing in *Le Monde*, *France-Soir*, or *The Times* of London, these reports were based on self-serving accounts by Stalin's heirs designed to enhance their own stature while further blackening his image as a tyrant. Rather than confirming that such a plan was afoot, they do more to undermine the credibility of the claim.

Running these stories, the Western press was not always careful to couch them with some degree of skepticism. On April 16, 1956, barely two months after Khrushchev's "Secret Speech," *The Times*, for example, reported that Khrushchev had told a small party gathering in Moscow that after Stalin had described his plan to the Presidium to banish the country's Jews to a remote region of the country, "His hearers were aghast. Mikoyan and Molotov both protested. ... Marshal Voroshilov declared that the proposal was criminal, the kind of outrage that had roused the world against Hitlerism. Stalin worked himself into a fury and the next that was known was that he had had his stroke." *The Times*, at least, had the sense to equivocate, concluding its brief article with the caution that "whatever the truth of the story ... it is being passed around

Communists in Eastern Europe."[60] But on June 8, 1957, the *New York Times*, citing *France-Soir* as its source, elaborated on this story in an article under the melodramatic title "Stalin's Death Ascribed to Rage at Voroshilov for Opposing Him," with the subtitle "Dictator Stricken After Angry Dispute Over His Plan To Deport Soviet Jews To Far East, Paris Paper Reports." According to the *New York Times*, the original source for the article out of Paris was based on an account by Panteleimon K. Ponomarenko, the Soviet ambassador to Poland, who was said to have been speaking with communist journalists in Warsaw. He claimed that Stalin summoned the Presidium members to the Kremlin in late February 1953 where

> he announced his plan to send all Russian Jews to Birobidjan. . . . Stalin explained that he was taking the action because of the "Zionist and imperialist" plot against the Soviet Union and himself. . . . He was described as speaking in "delirious" terms. . . .
>
> When Stalin finished outlining his deportation plan ... a heavy silence fell until Lazar M. Kaganovich, the "only Jewish member," hesitantly asked if the measure included every single Jew in the country. Stalin replied that a "certain selection" would be made, after which Mr. Kaganovich said no more. . . .[61]
>
> Vyacheslav M. Molotov, then foreign minister, was next said to have suggested in a "trembling" voice that the measure would have a "deplorable" effect on world opinion.[62] Mr. Molotov's wife is Jewish. France-Soir said that, as Stalin was about to reprimand Mr. Molotov, Marshal [Kliment] Voroshilov rose, threw his Communist party card on the table and cried: "If such a step is taken, I would be ashamed to remain a member of our party, which will be completely dishonored!" An enraged Stalin was then said to have shouted into Marshal Voroshilov's face: "Comrade Kliment! It is I who will decide when you no longer have the right to keep your membership card!"[63]

Then, with the meeting in an uproar, Stalin fell to the floor. Since the doctors who had attended Stalin were in prison, a quarter of an hour passed before other medical assistance could be found.[64]

And again in September 1959, in London *The Times* followed up on its earlier story with a report of a meeting two years earlier between Khrushchev and an "American Christian Sociologist," Dr. Jerome Davis. Khrushchev had told Davis that he and other party leaders had "forced Stalin to stay his hand" in response to the planned deportation, that they had "saved" the Jews from Stalin's paranoid hatred.[65]

This scenario, which continued to appear with variations on where it was held (in the Kremlin or the dacha), in the timing of the alleged meeting (either in February or in March), and who had the courage to challenge Stalin (was it Kaganovich or Voroshilov?), had no basis in fact and was circulated for the sole purpose of distancing Stalin's heirs from crimes in which they themselves had colluded.[66] In Khrushchev's memoirs, which he dictated after his removal from power in 1964—and which were meant to serve as the most definitive defense of his legacy—he never mentioned such an episode, not in connection to Stalin's antisemitism or to the manner of his death. This same group of men, whose hands had been awash with the blood of countless victims—during collectivization, the Ukrainian famine, the purge of the military, the purges of the party itself—were now floating the idea that they had finally found the limit to their compliance and the moral strength to prevent yet another roundup, this time against the Jews. But there was no such confrontation and until the day Stalin collapsed not a single member of the Presidium challenged him. He remained in control, exerting his fear over them to the very end.[67]

* * *

The alleged plan to deport the Jews has long been connected to the complicated story of a collective letter to be published in *Pravda* over the signatures of scores of prominent Jewish figures. Although this episode, as well, is shrouded in mystery, there are documents and personal memoirs that shed at least some light on what happened.[68]

At the end of January, the regime began circulating a letter addressed to Stalin which prominent Jewish figures in cultural, scientific, and military institutions were expected to sign. Even Lazar Kaganovich was included.[69] A handful were approached individually; many were summoned to *Pravda* and expected to provide their signatures on the spot. The text of this letter—at least the draft that was initially shown to people—has never been located and those who wrote about it have provided only their general impressions of what they read. But we know that it frightened them. The poet Margarita Aliger was sitting next to Vasily Grossman at *Pravda* when they both signed the letter. Grossman was particularly upset and muttered that he had to see Ehrenburg as soon as he left the meeting. Aliger also recalled in an interview that two older cultural bureaucrats whom she did not know stood up and loudly objected to the letter, refusing to sign their names.[70]

Ilya Ehrenburg was handled differently. In his memoirs he could only hint at what he had experienced, in a brief and enigmatic account of what had occurred that February:

> Events were supposed to unfold further. I will omit the story of how I tried to prevent the appearance in print of a certain collective letter. Happily, the project which was absolutely insane, did not come about. I thought at the time that I dissuaded Stalin with my letter; now it seems to me the whole business was delayed and Stalin did not succeed in doing what he wanted to do. This is history, of course, a chapter of my biography, but I believe the time has not yet come for me to say more.[71]

To his friend, the Moscow artist Boris Birger, Ehrenburg revealed a good many details about this episode.[72] The Kremlin had delegated two well-known Moscow figures, both Jews, to collect signatures— the historian and academician Isaac Mints and the Tass editor Yakov Khavinson, who was known by his pseudonym M. Marinin. They visited Ehrenburg at his dacha outside of Moscow within two weeks after the announcement of the Doctors' Plot and urged him to sign a collective letter to Stalin that was to appear in *Pravda*. But Ehrenburg refused to sign it and sent them away. At the time, it seemed to Ehrenburg that they had approached him on their own initiative.

Another writer, Veniamin Kaverin, was summoned to *Pravda*. When Khavinson showed him the letter, Kaverin asked whether Ehrenburg had signed it and was told that Ehrenburg agreed with the letter and would be endorsing it. Kaverin did not believe Khavinson. He made clear that he needed more time, then left *Pravda* directly for Ehrenburg's apartment. Ehrenburg confirmed that he had not signed, that his discussion with Mints and Khavinson had only been "preliminary." As for signing it, "each of us has to decide for himself." In the end, Kaverin was among a handful who refused to sign the letter.[73]

But Mints and Khavinson were not done with Ehrenburg. Near the end of the month they came to him at his apartment on Gorky Street in central Moscow. Ehrenburg again refused to sign, telling them that it "could do harm to the country." He then offered several editorial suggestions which were meant to soften the language and make it seem that whatever action was being considered it would not descend on all the Jews. Mints and Khavinson took Ehrenburg's editorial comments to Malenkov, who shared the suggestions with Stalin. The dictator approved of the changes, leading to a new version of the letter. But that still left open the question of Ehrenburg signing the letter himself. Malenkov ordered Mints and Khavinson to obtain his signature.

They returned to his Moscow apartment on February 3, this time more determined to fulfill their assignment. When Ehrenburg refused to sign even this revised version, they made clear that Stalin expected Ehrenburg's compliance. Today, more than six decades after this episode, researchers have found the version which incorporated Ehrenburg's earlier suggestions and which Mints and Khavinson showed him on the evening of February 3.

It remains an ugly and disturbing piece of antisemitic demagoguery. It acknowledged the guilt of the arrested doctors and called for "the most severe punishment" for their crimes, meaning their execution. In its most extreme paragraph, the letter declared: "To increase vigilance, to utterly rout and uproot bourgeois nationalism—these are the obligations of working Jews, Soviet patriots, and defenders of freedom for all people."

In this draft, there are no references to a broad plot involving the country's Jews, no accusation of "fifth column" subversion, just as there is no call for collective responsibility for the crimes of the accused doctors or a call for deportations or mass repressions of any kind. At the end of the letter, the final paragraphs acknowledge that "the vast majority of the Jewish population is a friend of the Russian people. No tricks by our enemies will succeed in undermining the trust of Soviet Jews in the Russian people or cause a falling out between them."

While the idea that "this collective Jewish letter" was part of a broader plan to deport the country's Jews cannot be dismissed altogether, it is far more likely that Mints and Khavinson were told to mobilize prestigious Jewish figures to denounce the doctors and other alleged Jewish nationalists, and that this was the "insane" idea that so unsettled Ehrenburg and others. It meant the creation of an internecine struggle—an internal witch hunt—that would pit one group of Jews against another, compelling people to either target "Jewish bourgeois nationalists" or stand vulnerable to a similar charge against themselves. It was an exercise in moral blackmail, designed to wreak emotional and moral havoc among Soviet Jews. Ehrenburg wanted none of it.

To the chagrin of Mints and Khavinson, Ehrenburg insisted that he would write to Stalin himself. While he worked in his study, drafting and correcting a personal letter to Stalin, Mints and Khavinson remained with Ehrenburg's wife, Lyubov Kozintsev. They tried to intimidate her, vividly describing what would happen to her and her husband if Ehrenburg refused to sign. As she recounted years later, that hour was "not only among the most terrifying of her life but also among the most loathsome"; it was all she could do to avoid fainting in front of them. When Ehrenburg finished and rejoined them in the front hall, Mints and Khavinson still tried to prevail on him, but he refused to speak with them further and ushered them to the door, insisting that they deliver to Stalin his own letter, which he handed to them in a cleanly typed copy.

Ehrenburg understood that it was impossible to make a moral appeal to Stalin. Adopting a tone of deference and respect, he urged Stalin to consider how a public statement "signed by scientists, writers, and composers, who speak of a so-called Soviet Jewish community, could fan repellent anti-Soviet propaganda." It would undermine "the broadening and strengthening of the world movement for peace," which was a major Soviet propaganda initiative and a fundamental mission for Western communist parties. "The text of the letter speaks of a 'Jewish people,'" Ehrenburg wrote. And he then reminded Stalin that such a formulation "could encourage nationalists and others who have not yet understood that there is no such thing as a Jewish nation," a position Stalin himself had long advocated but which, Ehrenburg was pointing out, the collective letter was contradicting.[74]

Mints and Khavinson brought Ehrenburg's letter to Dmitrii Shepilov, the editor of *Pravda*. He read it, then summoned Ehrenburg to his office. He warned Ehrenburg that for him to pass along the letter was "the equivalent of a prison sentence" for Ehrenburg himself. He also confirmed that the collective letter had been written at Stalin's initiative. But Ehrenburg stood firm, insisting that he would only reconsider signing it after receiving Stalin's response. "Shepilov," according to Boris Birger, "told him that he had lost his mind. Their conversation lasted around two hours. Shepilov finished by telling Ehrenburg that he would do all he could for him, and since he insisted he would pass along the letter to Stalin, and after that Ehrenburg would have only himself to blame. Ehrenburg left Shepilov with the full confidence that he would soon be arrested."

Ehrenburg's letter was shown to Stalin by the middle of February. The dictator responded with instructions that he considered it necessary for Ehrenburg to sign the collective letter to *Pravda*. He also ordered that Shepilov draft a new "softer" version that eliminated many demagogic elements of the earlier collective statement. Summoned once more to *Pravda*, Ehrenburg dutifully affixed his signature. He returned home, expecting to see the collective Jewish letter, which was dated February 20, 1953, in *Pravda* within days. But it failed to appear.

The text of this final version of the collective letter exists. If in fact Stalin had been planning to round up the country's Jews and to use a "collective letter to *Pravda*" as part of his plan, this final version bears no hint of such an intention. It is almost entirely about enemies outside the country, especially imperialism as represented by the United States and Zionism as represented by Israel. Israel had now become "an American domain," "a beachhead" to assist American imperialism. The collective letter also blamed the Israeli government for the explosion at the Soviet legation in Tel Aviv. As for the unfortunate doctors, the collective letter echoed the initial charges from January 13. It referred to their betrayal on behalf of American intelligence, their attempt to murder Soviet leaders and compromise the country's defense. As the letter emphasized, "Only people without

honor or conscience, who have sold their soul and body to the imperialists, could resort to such monstrous crimes." But there was no call
for their execution, no accusation of "fifth column" subversion, no
admission of collective responsibility for the crimes of the accused
doctors. The final version of the collective letter even denounced
antisemitism as a "frightful holdover from the past" and went on to
repeat the assurance from an earlier draft that "No tricks by our
enemies will succeed in undermining the trust of Soviet Jews in the
Russian people or cause a falling out between them and the great
Russian people." Finally, the only recommended action in the letter
was the establishment of Jewish newspapers so that "the true situation
of Jewish workers in various countries will be known" among Jews
throughout the Soviet Union and abroad. Given that the original
letter horrified Ehrenburg and others, this softer "collective letter to
Pravda" leaves the distinct impression that Stalin had reconsidered his
original plan, whatever it was. Ehrenburg, in fact, had tried to convince
Stalin that proposals in the original collective letter to *Pravda* might
destroy Western communist parties, and it was this pragmatic warning
to Stalin that may have swayed the dictator's judgment.

As the wave of propaganda continued into February, the
momentum of the Doctors' Plot appeared to be heading to some
kind of terrifying conclusion, a final act designed to demonstrate the
full treachery of the doctors and the full determination of the regime
to punish its enemies, real or imagined. What is curious and has yet
to be explained is that the final piece in either *Pravda* or *Izvestia* to
have accusations against the doctors appeared on February 20; this
was an article about supportive mail addressed to Lidia Timashuk.
While Stalin was alive only he could have ordered an end to the
public campaign. And the doctors were never brought to trial in spite
of the promise in the original Tass communiqué that the investigation would soon be concluded. Either the investigation of the
Doctors' Plot was never completed or Stalin had second thoughts on

whether to proceed. Most importantly, no such collective Jewish statement ever appeared in *Pravda*. Something either changed his mind or, as Solzhenitsyn once wrote, "God told him ... to depart from his rib cage," which put an end to the scheme.[75] With Stalin's collapse, power quickly passed into other hands. And the machinery of destruction with regard to the Jews—wherever it was headed—was turned off altogether. A tyrant's dreams do not always come true.

* * *

Stalin's death did not put an end to many ugly episodes. As February led into March, the anti-Jewish campaign sustained a momentum of its own. On March 6, the day after Stalin died, a secret decree withdrew the Order of Lenin that Solomon Mikhoels had once received, as if a bureaucrat in a tidy office suddenly and belatedly recalled an honor that had best be rescinded before his superiors recalled the oversight. Murdered in 1948, denounced in 1953, Mikhoels could not be allowed to rest in peace.[76]

In the Writers' Union, reports had begun to circulate right after the announcement of the Doctors' Plot claiming that too many members had not been actively publishing for an unduly long time, that they constituted "ballast," that they sought material support for stays in comfortable rest homes. The members cited in almost every case were Jews who had joined the Writers' Union at the time of its founding in 1934 when a Yiddish writers' section formed part of the broader union. Under pressure from the Central Committee, leaders of the Writers' Union did a careful survey of the membership and pledged to the party and to Khrushchev personally as late as March 23 that it would exclude "critics-cosmopolitans" and other undesirable elements.[77]

The very next day, Konstantin Simonov, who was editor of the Writers' Union weekly newspaper *Literaturnaia gazeta* (Literary Gazette), followed up on the pledge. Writing to the Central

Committee on behalf of the union leadership, he passed along a list of Jewish writers who should be purged from its ranks; he called them "dead weight."[78] Such an act was particularly shameful coming from Simonov; in July 1944, he had traveled to Lublin, Poland, within days after the liberation of Majdanek, the first functioning concentration camp to be liberated by the Allies. His three-part article in *Krasnaia zvezda* (Red Star) in August had been the very first to report the reality of the Nazis' industrial-style killing: Simonov made clear that tens of thousands of Jews from all corners of Europe had been taken there to be murdered in gas chambers. And in January 1953, in the midst of Stalin's anti-Jewish hysteria, a whispering campaign had targeted Simonov himself, accusing him of being a Jew who was camouflaging his origins for subversive purposes.[79] Simonov dismissed the rumors, but he was not above confirming his loyalty to Stalin and the regime by engaging in antisemitic baiting of his own.

Even on the first day after Stalin's death, with his body now lying in state, an anonymous complaint reached Khrushchev that 95 per cent of the musicians performing in the Hall of Columns were Jews and that they "sounded insincere." The writer went on to comment that just hearing the word "Jew" elicited "a feeling of disgust and loathing." Obviously prompted by the propaganda that had dominated Soviet media for months, such a crude letter was still taken seriously. Five days later—during the dramatic days following Stalin's death, when the eyes of the world were on Moscow—Khrushchev was sent the reassuring news that only 35.7 per cent of the orchestra was made up of Jews, that more Russian musicians than Jews had been added in the previous season, that ten additional musicians would soon be retiring—among them two Russians and eight Jews—and that more "indigenous nationalities would be added via a competition in the fall."[80] Stalin was dead, but the antisemitism he had instilled in the Kremlin outlived him.

CHAPTER FOUR

THE KREMLIN MOVES ON

Stalin had died, but his regime did not collapse. Mobs did not topple statues or storm the walls of the Kremlin. They did not break into prisons and labor camps. After decades of abject terror and relentless propaganda, a state of fear paralyzed the population. They were not going to revolt. At the same time, grim faces of familiar gray men still looked from the pages of *Pravda* and from placards displayed in the streets. They had survived and were prepared to lead the country forward. Establishing their claim to legitimate authority, they were also engaged in the delicate task of putting Stalin to rest.

A close examination of *Pravda*'s pages reveals how they improvised. When the first announcement of his illness appeared, the official bulletins dominated the front page; there was no photograph of Stalin. But on March 6, with the headlines about his death, broad black borders surrounded the front page with a living, heroic image of Stalin. Dressed in his marshal's uniform, his right hand between the chest buttons of his jacket, Napoleon-like, he looked as commanding as the public was used to seeing him. It was a familiar picture, his hair thicker than it was in real life—dark with only a hint of gray—with no wrinkles on his face, the signs of aging obscured by a deft airbrush. Reports about his illness and death, and plans for the funeral the following Monday, filled out the rest of the page. (Curiously, the remainder of the issue resembled the *Pravda* of any other day, with routine dispatches about domestic and foreign concerns.) It was on March 7 that *Pravda* shared the autopsy results. As expected, they specified the full extent of the damage to Stalin's brain and heart due to high blood pressure and severe arteriosclerosis. "Accordingly," the report concluded, "the energetic measures of treatment which were undertaken could not have led to a favorable result or averted a fatal end." An impressive list of medical specialists, including the minister of public health and the president of the Academy of Medical Sciences, signed their names to the post-mortem examination. The country needed confirmation that Stalin had died a natural death.[1]

But Aleksandr Myasnikov, who had treated Stalin at the dacha and then observed the autopsy, drew additional conclusions which could not be shared with the public. In a memoir which was seized by the KGB when he died in 1965, Myasnikov wrote that Stalin's progressive hardening of the arteries in his brain clouded his judgment during the final years of his life. He lost the ability "to discern good from bad, useful from harmful, the permitted from the prohibited, a friend from an enemy. At the same time, the condition aggravated his personal qualities: an angry person becomes vicious, a somewhat suspicious person becomes morbidly suspicious.... I contend that Stalin's cruelty and paranoia, his fear of enemies, his losing the ability to soberly assess people and events, as well as his extreme stubbornness were all in large part the result of arteriosclerosis of the arteries in his brain. ... In essence a sick man ruled the state," Myasnikov wrote.[2] (It is not clear when Myasnikov wrote these words but it is unlikely he would have committed his impressions to paper until well past Stalin's death and perhaps only after the Twenty-Second Party Congress in 1961.) While this diagnosis might explain Stalin's increasingly paranoid behavior after the war, he had been equally cruel and murderous throughout the 1930s when he had been a much younger man with healthy arteries. Arteriosclerosis cannot adequately explain Stalin's thirst for power, his megalomania, his willingness to personally order the execution of untold thousands and arbitrarily consign other millions to death. His demise marked the passing of a nightmare.

It was also on March 7 that *Pravda* showed Stalin's corpse. The photograph took up the top right-hand quarter of the second page. Stalin is lying in repose on a raised bier, while his heirs stand to one side of the casket. They look relatively small and insignificant because the picture of the flower-bedecked corpse was enlarged to appear several times its actual size. They stand in two rows with Malenkov nearest to Stalin's head. To his side stand Beria, Voroshilov, Bulganin, Kaganovich, and Molotov in the front row, while Mikoyan and Khrushchev are visible between the shoulders of others. Of those in the second row, Khrushchev stands the farthest from Malenkov, his head barely visible between Kaganovich and Molotov, a possible indication of which leaders are being elevated above others.

The following day, the open coffin is shown in the center while the same eight men stand at attention. On the left of the image, from Stalin's head toward the viewer, Malenkov is shown followed by Beria and then Khrushchev. That Khrushchev now stands alongside them may have reflected a reconsideration of his place in the emerging hierarchy. On March 9, the day of the funeral, the casket is still in the center of the photograph, but now farther in the background and viewed from its side, with a uniformed soldier standing at each end. Stalin can be seen above a bank of flowers, his body lying on a pedestal above the heads of the same eight men who stand nearby in two columns facing each other. Malenkov and Beria remain in the prime position near Stalin's head. These solemn-looking figures appear to be sizing each other up, while Stalin's body with its unmistakable profile dominates the center of the photograph. There was something about the image of a deceased Stalin, his body held above his heirs, that underscored their subordination; their claim to legitimacy could only be secured in the shadow of the man they were about to inter.

For a time, all the signs pointed to Malenkov as the future leader. Standing by Stalin's casket, his position among the others was a vivid signal of his preeminence. And only Malenkov was independently featured on other pages of *Pravda*. On March 8, he was shown on page two giving the keynote report to the Nineteenth Party Congress the previous October. Stalin is visible sitting behind and above him, listening intently, his white hair contrasting with a dark-haired and much younger-looking Malenkov as if Stalin were anointing him as his chosen disciple. And on March 10, when *Pravda* reported on the funeral, Malenkov appeared on the front page standing atop the Mausoleum among Kremlin leaders and foreign communists. But only he was shown speaking behind microphones—all five of them— with the name "STALIN" in capital letters arrayed beneath "LENIN" on the Mausoleum's façade. Malenkov's speech was featured below the photograph, claiming almost half a page. (The speeches of Beria and Molotov appeared side-by-side on page two.)

To further underscore Malenkov's ascendancy, he was shown again on the third page in a photograph with no less than Mao and Stalin. They are in the background, while Malenkov, in the foreground, stands with his right arm across his jacket, the same Napoleon-like pose that Stalin favored. The photograph had been doctored, of course. The original dated from February 15, 1950, when it first appeared on the front page of *Pravda* to mark the signing of the Sino-Soviet Treaty of Friendship, Alliance, and Mutual Aid. It shows eighteen men. All are standing, with the exception of Andrei Vyshinsky, who is seated and about to sign the document in his role as foreign minister. Molotov, Stalin, and Mao stand behind him facing the camera, while Malenkov is shown in profile on the far right of the scene, gazing in the direction of Stalin. From the view-point of the reader, Gromyko, Bulganin, Mikoyan, Khrushchev, Voroshilov, and the Chinese premier Zhou En-lai all stand to the left of Molotov, while on the other side of the room, both Beria and Kaganovich stand behind Malenkov, along with several Soviet and Chinese aides. Three years later, only Stalin, Mao, and Malenkov survived the editor's airbrush. But Malenkov overplayed his hand. The photomontage had been awkwardly assembled. Unlike Stalin's manipulation of photographs which had once included famous revolutionaries whom he subsequently murdered, Malenkov was erasing his living "comrades-in-arms" who remained among the leaders of the country, as if he were consigning them to an Orwellian memory hole while they still commanded authority within the party and the government. With this clumsy and transparent maneuver, Malenkov was revealing a lack of self-assurance in the days following the funeral.[3]

* * *

As the images in *Pravda* indicated, the new leadership was reorganizing the government, appearing to establish collective rule in place of Stalin's dictatorship. First announced over the radio late on Friday night, March 6, their plan was meant to demonstrate that the government would function with suitable vigilance and that the old guard, Stalin's longtime "comrades-in-arms," were reasserting their place in the hierarchy. But the ensuing messages out of the Kremlin expressed the new leaders' own anxiety. Any unexpected transition can be chaotic, even in a constitutional democracy with a defined succession, but in a dictatorship like the Soviet Union where one man had dominated the life of the country for a quarter of a century, his heirs feared the effect of a vacuum at the center of political power. Prompted by feelings of insecurity they called for avoiding "any kind of disarray and panic," as if they were afraid that the patina of enforced unity could break down at any moment and collapse into turmoil.[4] If terror of Stalin was all that held the country together, then how could his heirs hold onto power and still relinquish the cudgel?

For the population, it was utterly irrelevant whether the leadership group would be called the Politburo or the Presidium, or whether it contained twenty-five members or nine. Initially, the appointment of Georgy Malenkov as chairman of the Council of Ministers reaffirmed the widely held assumption that he had been Stalin's choice to succeed him. Malenkov was the consummate bureaucrat; he had never been responsible for directing a local party or government organization, let alone a regional or republic-wide apparatus. He was a servant of Stalin, an indefatigable producer of government documents and reports. He was also a survivor of several brushes with oblivion when mistakes on his part—for example in 1946 when he was held responsible for failures associated with airplane production, leading to a temporary demotion and the loss of Stalin's favor—could have led to the end of his career, if not his life. Malenkov was also noticeably corpulent, which in some eyes undermined his ability to project the image of leadership.[5]

But the announcement that the Ministry of State Security and the Ministry of Internal Affairs would now be consolidated into one ministry and be headed by Lavrenti Beria, Stalin's longtime security chief, was the most significant change in both the reorganization of the government and the direction it might be headed. Beria was now grabbing the most powerful levers of domestic coercion. He was the most notorious man in Stalin's entourage: his years as security chief and his reputation for brutality toward prisoners made his appointment the most worrisome of all. But Beria had also played a major role in supervising the Soviet atomic bomb project; his intelligence and capacities as an administrator made him a formidable presence within the leadership.

Other appointments did not seem as momentous. Vyacheslav Molotov was now back in favor; he was restored to his position as foreign minister, while Andrei Vyshinsky, the notorious prosecutor from the purge trials who had replaced Molotov as foreign minister, was demoted to first deputy foreign minister and ambassador to the United Nations. Nikolai Bulganin became minister of defense. With his barbered goatee, Bulganin was an impressive-looking man; he was often seen in the bemedaled uniform of a marshal. But Bulganin, in fact, had never commanded troops. He owed his military rank to Stalin, who had picked him out in the 1930s to help lead the party in Moscow and then used him to monitor and control army commanders during the war. Lazar Kaganovich and Anastas Mikoyan joined the Presidium among the four deputy chairmen. Mikoyan was a veteran Bolshevik of Armenian background who was respected for his work in the field of foreign trade. Kliment Voroshilov had once been close to Stalin, especially during the civil war when they commanded Red Army units together. He later played a major role in the purge of the armed forces in 1936 and 1937, further cementing his relationship with Stalin. But Voroshilov lost all real power during the Winter War with Finland in 1939 when the Red Army suffered major setbacks, exposing his incompetence as a military planner; he was dismissed as People's Commissar for Defense. He retained a formal place among the leadership, however, and became chairman of the Presidium of the Supreme Soviet, or head of state, upon Stalin's death. Mikhail Pervukhin and Maxim Saburov were hardly known within the broader population and their appointments to positions within the economic apparatus had no bearing on the unfolding division of power. Other plans appeared to shunt aside Nikita Khrushchev; he was relieved of his duties as party head in Moscow and assigned to unspecified responsibilities at the Central Committee. His star seemed to be on the wane. Stalin's veteran "comrades-in-arms" were reclaiming their pride of place.

Still, Khrushchev was selected to lead the funeral commission. He had risen from a lowly miner's family to become a leading party official as first secretary in Moscow, then head of the party in Ukraine during World War II before returning to Moscow in 1949 where he became one of Stalin's most trusted lieutenants. Ruthless when he needed to be—he helped Stalin carry out purges in Ukraine—Khrushchev also had a reputation for being friendly and approachable, open to contacts with lower-ranking party members and ordinary people, more human and down-to-earth than his colleagues, characteristics that the world came to recognize when he later ascended to power. During World War II, unlike most of his colleagues, he made a point of touring the countryside during and after Hitler's invasion. He saw the heroism of the soldiers, the devastation, the stupidity of the party commissars who interfered with the competent generals and officers who had survived the purges. He "got his boots muddy," as the Russians say; indeed, he never liked being summoned to Moscow, away from the miners and farmers whom he genuinely liked. In addition, and this is not a trivial point, Khrushchev had a warm, intelligent wife who, by all reports, moderated his temper and encouraged whatever humane and generous instincts he managed to retain. These qualities distinguished Khrushchev from Stalin's other lieutenants.

The funeral commission also included Lazar Kaganovich, a longtime member of the Soviet leadership, the only Jew remaining at this level of power, and, at least according to the *New York Times*, a man who was also Stalin's brother-in-law, an unfounded claim the newspaper repeated throughout the year.[6] Tall and broad-shouldered, with a signature mustache, Kaganovich was known for his brutal behavior during the purges of the 1930s, when he carried out waves of targeted arrests and executions in Ukraine and elsewhere. These survivors—Malenkov, Beria, Molotov, Mikoyan, Bulganin, Khrushchev, Voroshilov, and Kaganovich—had worked closely with a number of now-executed security chiefs, men like Henryk Yagoda and Nikolai Yezhov. It is doubtful that a murderous gang ever exercised greater power in the course of modern history than Stalin and the men he had personally assembled.

* * *

As expected, the regime announced that Stalin's body would lie in state in the Hall of Columns in the House of Unions, one of Moscow's most impressive buildings. Initially constructed in the late eighteenth century within a few hundred yards of Red Square, and later renovated and enlarged into a club for noblemen, the building was famous for its central hall where twenty-eight marble Corinthian columns reached three stories to the ceiling and where enormous crystal chandeliers illuminated the space. Its history resonated through decades of Russian culture: in *Eugene Onegin*, Aleksandr Pushkin described how Russian aristocrats celebrated a magnificent ball in the Hall of Columns, while Leo Tolstoy chose the same hall for a scene in his *War and Peace*. Lenin had lain in state in the Hall of Columns for four days[7] and the last of the three famous show trials of the 1930s—the trial of Nikolai Bukharin and twenty others— unfolded there in March 1938. (The American U-2 pilot Francis Gary Powers was brought to trial in the same building in August 1960, a spectacle the Kremlin was happy to open to the world's press.)

By the time the sun rose in Moscow on March 6, "heavy black-bordered red Soviet flags" decorated the House of Unions, while a "great forty-foot portrait of Mr. Stalin in his gray generalissimo's uniform was erected on the front of the building. It was framed in heavy gilt."[8] The red flag which always adorned the Supreme Soviet building behind Lenin's tomb remained at half-mast. Stalin's body would lie in state for three days, beginning at 3 p.m. that Friday. On

Saturday and Sunday, the hours would be extended from 6 a.m. to 2 a.m. the following day. And then on Monday morning, March 9, the funeral would take place in Red Square. Following the funeral, his sarcophagus would be placed alongside Lenin's in the Mausoleum. On those four days, film shows, concerts, and all forms of entertainment were cancelled. With Stalin dead, the country needed time to come to grips with his passing. It seemed blasphemous to permit anything to diminish the image of universal grief that had descended on the empire he was leaving behind.

The regime added even more elaborate plans, announcing that a "monumental edifice—a Pantheon" would be constructed in Moscow to where the sarcophagi of both Lenin and Stalin would later be transferred and "also the remains of the eminent figures of the Communist Party and Soviet State buried by the Kremlin wall."[9] The Bolsheviks knew their history well. If the Pantheon in Paris could be a fitting tribute to France's heroes, then Moscow deserved nothing less. Caught up in the emotional moment following Stalin's death and eager to demonstrate their undying fealty, Stalin's heirs gave the appearance of honoring him in a way that would evoke the tributes to Lenin in January 1924 and so link the legacies of both Lenin and Stalin to the legitimacy of the regime whose leadership they were now inheriting. But this Moscow Pantheon was never built.

* * *

Crowds began gathering spontaneously that Friday morning. By the afternoon, hundreds of thousands of people spread from the House of Unions and Red Square to many blocks away and the first garden boulevard. Eddy Gilmore estimated that they eventually reached eight miles into the Moscow suburbs; he "counted them out on the speedometer" as he passed them in his car.[10] (Other reports confirmed the lines stretched to ten miles.) From his room in the Metropol Hotel, Salisbury watched workers add "bunting and fresh-cut evergreens," along with powerful floodlights, to the House of Unions. Mounted cavalry from the Ministry of Internal Affairs, "sabers gleaming and harness sparkling," patrolled the immediate area, while other ministry detachments began to direct traffic and pedestrians away from the city center. Public transportation was shut down for a considerable distance away from the Kremlin. The Moscow radio continued to play "solemn and melancholy music—Tchaikovsky, Scriabin, Rachmaninoff, Dvořák, Mussourgsky, and Chopin." It was not until 3 p.m. that Salisbury observed "a blue vanlike vehicle of the Moscow City Sanitary Department" bearing Stalin's coffin, surrounded by large official vehicles, leave the Kremlin by the Spassky Gate, circle several city blocks, then approach the House of Unions.[11] This cortege was also in keeping with the myth that Stalin had been lying ill in the Kremlin until the moment of his death. According to Vyacheslav Molotov, who continued to burnish Stalin's image to the end of his own life, Stalin was so frugal that he needed to be buried "in his old military suit which had been cleaned and repaired."[12] Stalin, in fact, was dressed in his generalissimo uniform.

After government and Communist Party officials paid their respects, the doors were opened to the endless line of mourners who began to stream past the bier. "The people are fed into the hall eight abreast," Salisbury recorded in his diary.

Each of the beautiful crystal chandeliers is darkened by gossamer wisps of mourning crepe. In the corridors are countless wreaths. As we ascend the broad staircase, a solid file of guards stands at attention.

The deeper one penetrates, the deeper becomes the ceremonial atmosphere of mourning. Enormous floodlights illuminate the columns. There are cameramen, both movie and still. In the great hall Stalin lies against a bank of thousands of flowers—real, paper, and wax. A symphony orchestra plays funeral music. The line moves swiftly, and it is difficult to see in the dazzling lights who is standing honor guard. Stalin lies, his face pallid and quiet, wearing his generalissimo's uniform and the ribbons of his orders and medals. On small pillows of deep maroon velvet at his feet are the decorations themselves. There is an air of repose about his figure. Almost before I realize it I am out in the open air.[13]

The diplomatic corps lined up the following day near the Kremlin to pay its respects. The Chinese delegation was placed ahead of the corps dean—traditionally, the longest serving ambassador in residence at any given time, in this case the Swedish ambassador—who protested, compelling the Soviets to recognize his tenure. For three days, an array of party leaders, republic-level officials, trade union chiefs, artists, and writers stood by the bier, constituting a quiet, rotating honor guard. The ceremonial grandeur of the funeral contrasted with the chaos and emotion in the streets outside. Ilya Ehrenburg lived on Gorky Street, an otherwise easy walk to Red Square and the House of Unions. But in order to walk outside his building he had to have "a policeman's permission to cross the street, a process that entailed long explanations and the inspection of documents. Very large trucks stood blocking the way and, when the officer gave me leave, I climbed on to a truck and jumped off it on the other side, only to find that, fifty paces further on, I was again stopped and had to go through the same performance." He saw many people in tears in the street and "some shouting as the crowd pressed toward the Hall of Columns."[14]

The regime prepared extraordinary measures to control the crowds, transforming "the heart of Moscow into a kind of citadel in which almost nothing [was] going on but mourning for Stalin," Salisbury wrote.[15] Writing in *Pravda*, the veteran writer Alexei

Surkov observed that "For three successive days, without running dry morning or evening, there has flowed and flowed, twisting through the streets of Moscow, a living river of the people's love and grief, pouring into the Hall of Columns."[16] Salisbury was stunned at how efficiently the authorities "commandeered" the central streets and squares of the capital, deploying trucks and later tanks according to a pattern of checkerboard parking that physically blocked the main avenues.[17]

But all these measures, which were intended to preserve order, could not prevent tragedies from happening among the mass of humanity, and likely precipitated them. The poet Yevgeny Yevtushenko, like so many of his compatriots, was in the streets of Moscow and saw the panic for himself. "I was in the crowd at Trubnaya Square," he wrote.

The breath of the tens of thousands of people jammed against one another rose up in a white cloud so thick that on it could be seen the swaying shadows of the bare March trees. It was a terrifying and a fantastic sight. New streams poured into this human flood from behind, increasing the pressure. The crowd turned into a monstrous whirlpool. I realized that I was being carried straight toward a traffic light. The post was coming relentlessly closer. Suddenly I saw that a young girl was being pushed against the post. Her face was distorted and she was screaming. But her screams were inaudible among all the other cries and groans. A movement of the crowd drove me against the girl; I did not hear but felt with my body the cracking of her brittle bones as they were broken on the traffic light. I closed my eyes in horror, the sight of her insanely bulging, childish blue eyes more than I could bear, and I was swept past. When I looked again the girl was no longer to be seen. The crowd must have sucked her under. Pressed against the traffic light was someone else, his body twisted and his arms outflung as on a cross. At that moment I felt I was treading on something soft. It was a human body. I picked my feet up under me and was carried along by the crowd. For a long time I was afraid to put my feet down again. The crowd closed tighter and tighter. I was saved by my height. Short people were smothered alive, falling and perishing. We were caught between the walls of houses on one side and a row of army trucks on the other.

When Yevtushenko and others pleaded with the soldiers to move the trucks, where people's heads were being smashed against their steel sides, the soldiers refused. They had no instructions to do so. "For the first time in my life I thought of hatred for the man we were burying. He could not be innocent of the disaster. It was the 'No instructions' that had caused the chaos and bloodshed at his funeral." Yevtushenko did not make it to the Hall of Columns but returned home thinking he had seen Stalin nonetheless. "Because everything that had just happened—that was Stalin."[18] For Yevtushenko, it was only natural to attach symbolic importance to the unrest, connecting official incompetence and inability to anticipate the uncontrollable behavior of such large, emotional crowds to Stalin's personal legacy.

Witnessing the turmoil in Moscow's streets, the writer Andrei Sinyavsky, who was a student in 1953, had similar feelings. "It turned out the dead man had not lost his bite," Sinyavsky wrote in his autobiographical novel *Goodnight!* "He had cleverly worked his death so that a fat slice of his congregation was sacrificed to him. Immolated in honor of his sad departure, a fitting culmination to his reign! As the body of a saint is surrounded by miracles, so was Stalin's surrounded by murder. I could not help admiring it. History had been given a finishing touch." While Sinyavsky explored the streets of Moscow with a friend, they resisted the urge to enter the Hall of Columns. "To gaze upon Caesar with our own eyes had not been our intention."[19]

The family of Nikita Khrushchev was not immune to the tensions of the day. His teenage son, Sergei, tried to approach the House of

Unions with a group of fellow students. Caught up in the crowd they failed to reach their goal, spending most of March 6 and overnight to the following morning being shoved from one block to another by the teeming throngs. Like Yevtushenko, they ended up in Trubnaya Square. But the crowds prevented Sergei and his friends from drawing any closer. His parents did not hear from him, did not know where he was, but with rumors of casualties, his father had contacted police stations and morgues anxious to learn Sergei's fate before his son returned home on Saturday morning, March 7.[20] During the final, nocturnal hours of public viewing before the funeral, "ambulances, police, and military vehicles plied the streets," wrote Dmitrii Shepilov, "transporting their loads of mutilated bodies to the morgues."[21] No one can say for sure how many people died in the streets of Moscow during those days of mourning. There were hundreds, perhaps thousands of casualties. As Sinyavsky wrote, "He would have taken everyone else with him if he'd been able to."[22] Nikita Khrushchev insisted otherwise. Once in power, he clarified on different occasions that 109 people lost their lives in the crush and panic of the crowds. (There were additional casualties in Leningrad and Tbilisi, where large crowds also gathered.)[23]

The constant flow of crowds streaming in the direction of Red Square had another unforeseen consequence. The composer Sergei Prokofiev died on the same day as Stalin. Recognized as one of the century's leading composers, Prokofiev had lived his final years under a cloud. He was twice denounced by communist officials for so-called "formalist" tendencies in his music. Prokofiev had suffered from severe high blood pressure so the assumption is that he succumbed to a cerebral hemorrhage, much like Stalin and also on the evening of March 5, less than an hour before Stalin's demise.

Prokofiev died while he was staying at his father-in-law's apartment near Red Square but the crowds in the street were so pressed together that it was difficult to move his remains. The funeral ceremony was supposed to take place at the House of Composers on Saturday, March 7, but it was impossible to bring a van to the apartment building. Six students volunteered to carry the coffin. They walked up a side street that ran parallel to the main thoroughfare that was seething with people. It took them five hours to walk two kilometers, "at times needing to lower their sorrowful burden to the frozen sidewalk in order to rest."[24]

The memorial service drew a handful of family, friends, and colleagues.[25] There was no public announcement of Prokofiev's death for several days and no flowers were available to adorn the coffin; all flower arrangements throughout the country were being requisitioned for one and only one purpose: to honor Stalin. For Prokofiev a lone wreath leaned against a piano; a neighbor brought some potted plants to adorn the casket. Nonetheless, a way was found for other renowned musicians and composers to demonstrate their regard for him. Tikhon Khrennikov, the notorious head of the Union of Composers who had treated Prokofiev's family with consistent disdain for several years, assured that basic arrangements were in order.[26] Dmitri Shostakovich spoke. The violinist David Oistrakh performed two movements from Prokofiev's 1946 Violin Sonata. The pianist Samuil Feynberg, who was Oistrakh's favorite accompanist, played works by Bach. Prokofiev was buried later that day in Moscow's Novodevichy Cemetery, the country's most famous, where many notable figures, among them Anton Chekhov and Nikolai Gogol, and later Nikita Khrushchev, Dmitri Shostakovich, Boris Yeltsin, and Mstislav Rostropovich were interred.

The House of Composers was near Pushkin Square, a mile or more down Gorky Street to Red Square and the House of Unions. Many of the musicians who had performed in honor of Prokofiev were soon hustled off to pay homage to Stalin. Under normal conditions they could have easily walked, but the crowds were streaming onto Gorky Street from different directions. Officials had to recruit twenty burly policemen to push their way through the crowd, with the musicians behind them clutching their instruments. They were exhausted by the time they reached the stage entrance to the House of Unions.

For three days many of the most prestigious musicians in the country, like David Oistrakh, the Bolshoi Orchestra, and the Moscow Conservatory Orchestra had to offer their talents as crowds streamed past the catafalque. Over and over again, they performed the slow movement from Tchaikovsky's Second Quartet. The violinist Rostislav Dubinsky occasionally dozed off, violin in hand, his colleagues nudging him to be sure he did not fall off his chair. Rostropovich's sister, Veronika, a violinist with the Moscow Philharmonic, was there as well. She cried the whole time. Inconsolable, she resisted her friends' attempts to comfort her. "Just leave me alone," she told them. "I'm not weeping for Stalin, but Prokofiev."[27] Oistrakh had thought to bring a small, traveling chess set. In between performing, Oistrakh and Dubinsky played discreet chess games, using sheet music to cover the pieces and board. Not everyone recognized the unique security arrangements in place. The violinist Pavel Mirsky approached Stalin's bier with his violin case in hand. "Two men in identical suits ran up to him, tore the case away, pinned his arms behind his back and dragged him away," Dubinsky recalled. Other ensembles continued to play. The musicians remained in the Hall of Columns for three days with hardly any food or drink, only able to sleep when public viewing was closed for a few hours each night. Then they had to snatch some time "backstage and in the foyer, in chairs and on the floor, wrapped in overcoats or just in their tuxedos."[28]

* * *

As Stalin's remains lay in state, word of his death reverberated around the world. The American and international press, along with governments on every continent, expressed their own sometimes uninformed and curious reactions. In an initial editorial the *New York Times* struck an expected chord, holding Stalin responsible for the Cold War and for plunging "the earth into the greatest armament race ever known." The editors had no illusions about the brutal nature of his regime. "He wore the mantle of the high priest of utopian communism, but his rule produced a reality most reminiscent of George Orwell's vision of hell on earth."[29] The obituary referred to him as "Genghis Khan with a telephone."[30] But then one news article in the same issue called him a "master military strategist," forgetting that Stalin bore full responsibility for the success of Hitler's surprise attack on June 22, 1941. During the summer and fall, whole Soviet armies were captured or annihilated. Outside of Kiev alone, Stalin would not allow his army to retreat in the face of a hopeless situation, resulting in the avoidable deaths of hundreds of thousands of men in one battle. Such colossal military blunders on his part undercut any claim that he was a master strategist.[31]

This romanticized view of his career seeped into the newspaper's obituary. It would be unfair to judge this obituary based on our present-day access to once-classified documents and an array of scholarly and memoir literature. There is simply no comparison between what was known and acknowledged to be true about the Soviet Union at the time of Stalin's death and what we know now. But still, the *New York Times*—in common with other serious newspapers and journals of opinion—did not adequately address what *was* known at the time. "Stalin took and kept the power in his country through a mixture of character, guile, and good luck," its full-page obituary claimed. In the face of serious setbacks during the war, Stalin, "like Churchill in England, . . . never faltered, not even at moments when everything seemed lost."[32] Stalin, in fact, did falter; he suffered a nervous breakdown in the days following Hitler's betrayal and the German invasion. The fact that Molotov, not Stalin, alerted the population to the invasion over national radio was well known. Even if the full details of Stalin's emotional collapse was not divulged until decades later, the fact that he deferred to Molotov at this crucial moment should have given pause to the idea that he remained steadfast throughout the war. As for the claim that he gained power through a combination of "character, guile, and good luck," such praise hardly matched the brutal game he played against his rivals. Stalin had defeated Trotsky, Kamenev, Zinoviev, and Bukharin even when they enjoyed political advantages over him; he was only finished with them when they were dead. In addition, the words "terror" and "labor camps" failed to appear in the *New York Times* obituary. To neglect to mention his barbaric use of power, the execution of his erstwhile political rivals and their family members, and the brutal programs of dekulakization, collectivization, the Gulag, the Great Terror, and the mass deportations that engulfed and destroyed millions of people marked a failure of serious proportions on the newspaper's part.

The Times of London fell into a similar trap. Reflecting on the arc of both Lenin's and Stalin's careers, the leading British newspaper commented that "Rarely have two successive rulers of a great country responded so absolutely to its changing needs and piloted it so successfully through periods of crisis." It seems hard to understand why a leading, mainstream newspaper in a Western capitalist country should be so deferential and generous toward men who had been responsible for the rejection of democracy following the downfall of the tsar and for the calamitous events that followed. As for Stalin himself, his "sense of timing was on the whole superb," a statement so divorced from reality, so oblivious to the disastrous consequences of his foreign policy toward Nazi Germany that the editors seemed to be doubling over backwards to avoid condemning his callous blunders. It was Stalin's decision to oppose an electoral alliance between the communists and the socialists in Germany that weakened the Left and helped Hitler gain power in January 1933. With typical demagoguery, Stalin had declared that the socialists were not genuine opponents of the Nazis, that they were "not opposites, but twins." And even when *The Times* mentioned the show trials and the broader purge of both the army and the party, the editors could only say that "things probably went a good deal farther than Stalin or anyone else intended at the time."[33] Given that the purges carried off hundreds of thousands of innocent victims, the editors of *The Times* in London were displaying a talent for misleading understatement that did not serve their readers.

By 1953 at least some Western scholars had come to recognize the scale and nature of the Gulag. In their book *Forced Labor in Soviet Russia*, which had come out in 1947, David Dallin and Boris Nicolaevsky included an annotated bibliography of eleven pages where they listed dozens of memoirs which had mostly appeared in Western Europe and the United States. They had been written by people who had survived years in the labor camps and then found themselves liberated from Stalin's kingdom, most often because of the dislocations of World War II. Dallin and Nicolaevsky could not help bemoaning how few people in the West recognized the fundamental role of the Gulag either in the Soviet economy or within the regime's repressive control of the population. "In the face of a resurgence of slavery in Stalin's Russia," they wrote, "the world remains ignorant or skeptical, and usually silent. It knows of purges and mock trials, mass persecutions and executions, but it has not as yet realized the extent and significance of the use of forced labor in the Soviet Union."[34] In their coverage of Stalin's death too many mainstream newspapers made this neglectful omission.

In *Le Monde*, at least, the columnist André Pierre had more subtle and incisive reflections, leaving no doubt that Stalin "was at the same time the most adored and the most detested among men." His followers believed in him with almost religious devotion, while his detractors, including members of the socialist opposition who had been targeted by waves of repression, loathed him. As for the Stalin cult, it "rested for the most part on historical lies,"[35] an accurate reading of how he had manipulated the history of the revolution for his own sinister purposes. In the struggle for power against Trotsky, for example, Stalin had distorted his role in 1917. Stalin, not Trotsky, had worked closely with Lenin to devise the Bolsheviks' military strategy. Stalin, not Trotsky, had dispatched the units who gained control of the Winter Palace. With Stalin and his followers in charge, it was not possible to challenge this new, official, and deceitful account of the revolution.

Official reactions to Stalin's death also reflected routine condolence and some moral confusion. Delegates to the Political and Security Committee of the United Nations observed a moment of silence in his memory. In keeping with UN protocol the only flag on display that day was the UN banner and it was kept at half-mast. The same procedure took place three days later to coincide with the funeral in Moscow. There were also the expected pronouncements and telegrams to the Kremlin. President Juan Perón of Argentina sent a cable expressing his "sincere condolences on the loss of [an] eminent statesman."[36] From Vietnam, Ho Chi Minh sent regrets over not being able to attend "by virtue of the great distance."[37] In Shelton, Washington, just hours after Stalin's death was announced, a mock jet fighter attack staged by pilots from nearby McChord Air Base buzzed the town for twenty minutes at speeds up to 600 miles per hour. The fake air raid caused a panic among hundreds of residents who feared that Stalin's death was leading to a full-scale attack on the United States. They jammed telephone lines to City Hall and the sheriff's office, and, buoyed by curiosity but regardless of the assumed danger, rushed into the streets with their children to watch the start of World War III.[38]

Pablo Picasso ran into trouble with fellow French communists because of his memorial portrait of Stalin in the party journal

Les Lettres Françaises. The image was very youthful-looking and except for the mustache hardly resembled Stalin at all, "which the Party rank and file considered unacceptable homage to the dead," according to Janet Flanner in her *New Yorker* column from Paris.[39] London's *Daily Mail* enjoyed mocking the drawing: "Note the large, melting eyes, the tresses apparently done up in a hair net, and the coyly concealed Mona Lisa smile; it could be the portrait of a woman with a moustache." Animated by their slavish attachment to socialist realism, more conservative leaders of the French Communist Party rebuked both Picasso and the journal's editors, among them the famous writer and poet Louis Aragon. Under pressure from his political masters Aragon backed off, issuing an apology for opening "the gate to counter-revolutionary bourgeois ideas." But Picasso was furious with such narrow-minded taste. "You do not bawl out people who send you condolences, and it is customary to thank people who send wreaths, even if the flowers are somewhat faded. . . . I put all my effort into producing a resemblance. Apparently it was not liked. *Tant pis.*"[40]

Following the news out of Moscow, Communist Party members staged a work stoppage in Rome on the day of the funeral. Street cars and buses were left at a standstill for twenty minutes while here and there varying proportions of workers followed the party line and laid down their tools. *Pravda* still could not help but exaggerate when it claimed that the work stoppage took place "in all factories and plants, all agricultural enterprises."[41] It was said that 47,000 people visited the Soviet embassy in Rome in the days following Stalin's death.

In Eastern Europe the reactions were more pointed and dramatic. Orchestrated public ceremonies dominated life throughout the region as communist rulers did their best to stage spontaneous grief among their people. Albania's megalomaniacal ruler Enver Hoxha was busy creating an extreme version of Stalin's "cult of personality."

As party boss, prime minister, minister of foreign affairs and of defense, and head of the army, he assembled the entire population of Tirana in the capital's biggest square. He then "made them kneel and take a 2,000-word oath of 'eternal fidelity' and 'gratitude' to their 'beloved father,' the 'great liberator' ... to whom they owed 'everything.'"[42]

In Romania, according to American diplomats, Bucharest "was hastily decorated with black bordered Soviet and Romanian flags and portraits of Stalin, as was the rest of the country." Crowds lined up "4 to 8 abreast as far as one-half mile" from the Soviet embassy from March 6 to 8, waiting for their turn to sign the official condolence book. Churches held special services. On March 9, a parallel funeral ceremony was held in the center of Bucharest; 400,000 people were said to be in attendance.[43]

Underneath this public display, however, both officials and ordinary people responded with different types of emotions, ranging from anxiety to drunken celebrations. The Swedish chargé d'affaires was living next to Romania's premier, Gheorghe Gheorghiu-Dej, and observed cars pulling in and out of the house incessantly during the nights of March 4, 5, and 6. The regime deployed tighter than usual security measures: uniformed police were now carrying rifles instead of revolvers, while auxiliary police patrolled streets with "long pointed wooden staves."[44] Travel around the country by foreign diplomats was summarily restricted. And there was an "acceleration of secret arrests." As the US embassy noted in a confidential cable, "The Israeli legation reports that three of its employees were seized on March 13 (bringing the total to 13 in 2 years) and that more 'Zionists' than usual have been jailed in the past 10 days." The embassy also heard of many private drinking parties lasting well into the night. Such spontaneous celebrations so unnerved the regime that it halted the sale of liquor.[45] (Similar, private parties were reported out of Poland where "excessive alcoholic celebrations" could not be suppressed and where the US embassy confirmed "general rejoicing" and "excitement" over Stalin's illness and death.[46]) But there was nothing the regime could do to stop Romanians from circulating jokes to mark the occasion. What was the real reason for Stalin's death? Stalin did not want to meet with Eisenhower, but with Roosevelt.[47]

There was a similar range of reactions in Hungary. An official period of national mourning was declared, with all theaters closed and sporting events suspended for several days. The official press outdid itself with eulogies for Stalin, even making the preposterous claim that factory workers were pledging to increase their output as a sign of respect. The entire diplomatic corps attended a memorial session inside the Hungarian parliament on Sunday, March 8. In the eyes of the US embassy, the proceedings were "uneventful and public interest nil." But the next day, when there would be a public ceremony and a five-minute work stoppage around the time of the funeral in Moscow, Western diplomats unanimously refused to lay a wreath at Budapest's Stalin monument, except for the Turkish ambassador who gave in after four telephone calls from the Hungarian foreign office. The Turkish government felt a need to respond with greater respect than other European powers; on Stalin's orders, the Soviet Union had sent a full delegation in November 1938 to the funeral of Mustafa Kemal Atatürk, the founder of the Turkish republic.[48]

Not surprisingly, officials in East Berlin went into full mourning, tying thousands of yards of crepe above the Soviet and German flags that normally flew in the Soviet sector. "They are draped from cornices, they flap atop hot dog stands on subway platforms," the New York Times reported. Crowds gathered around the statue of Stalin, which stood two stories high in the city. "This statue and its pedestal took on some of the atmosphere of Lenin's tomb in Moscow's Red Square. Tier upon tier of huge floral wreaths were stacked against it and laid on the surrounding lawns." An East German labor union newspaper tried to reflect its government's sentiments. But when it published the cable of condolence sent by the East German Communist Party to Moscow, the wording came out wrong, referring to Stalin as "the great fighter for the preserving and consolidation of war in the world." Over in West Berlin, the mood was starkly different. Hawkers for an afternoon newspaper were encouraged to shout: "Stalin responds to cry of the people—he dies."[49]

Chinese leaders arranged for more suitable tributes. Mao Zedong, accompanied by members of his Politburo, including Premier and Foreign Minister Zhou En-lai, visited the Soviet embassy to express their "profound anxiety." Mao "tried to maintain his self-control and not display any emotions, but he did not succeed," one Soviet diplomat recalled. He had tears in his eyes, while Zhou En-lai broke down and cried with the new Soviet ambassador, Aleksandr Panyushkin. Stalin's death was turned into an occasion for further ideological indoctrination. Nearly 50,000 Chinese communist cadres were said to be studying Malenkov's report to the Nineteenth Party Congress the previous October as well as concentrating on Stalin's last theoretical essay about the Soviet economy. And Zhou En-lai himself led an eighteen-member delegation to Moscow, all to demonstrate Chinese solidarity with their grieving comrades.[50]

But Mao Zedong did not travel to Moscow, the only communist leader in the Soviet bloc to stay home. His wife, Jiang Qing, happened to be there for medical treatment that March. Constrained by her illness and not knowing Russian, she could only discuss Stalin's death with other patients and the medical staff in the government sanatorium where she was being treated by relying on her official translator. Everyone around Jiang Qing advised her that Mao must come to Moscow for the funeral. She knew better than to offer her own opinion, making clear that such a decision could only be made by Chinese leaders themselves.

Mao may have decided to stay in Beijing for reasons other than the cold weather. In January 1953, Mao learned that Stalin had been monitoring his conversations with other Chinese leaders. Soviet secret police assigned to Beijing had installed microphones in Mao's bedroom, no doubt with the assistance of Chinese agents. Once he discovered the listening devices, Mao was furious and complained to Stalin in writing. Stalin adopted a pose of innocence, insisting that he had "no idea what sorts of unseemly activities these MGB agents were up to in China."[51]

Anxious to see Stalin honored properly, the Kremlin approached several countries with pointed requests to send delegations. According to the American embassy in Tehran, the "Iranian government was placed in an embarrassing position when the Soviet Embassy ... asked ... to inform it 'before the end of the day on March 8' if it planned to send a special mission to Moscow to participate in Stalin's funeral." In response, Iran agreed to send four government and military officials, who were dispatched aboard a special Soviet aircraft. Iran's prime minister Mohammad Mossadegh ordered all flags flown at half-mast, a decree that foreign embassies were also obliged to accept. When the American embassy neglected its diplomatic duty, a Soviet representative called on embassy officials to correct their oversight, a request it dutifully, if reluctantly, satisfied.[52]

The Indian parliament also made an unprecedented gesture of mourning by standing in silence for two minutes and then adjourning in memory of a foreign leader for the first time since the country's independence. Flags were lowered on all government buildings in Delhi and in the capitals of the Indian states. In his official eulogy, Prime Minister Jawaharlal Nehru claimed that "Stalin's weight and influence had been cast in favour of peace." He was "a man with a giant's stature and indomitable courage. . . . I earnestly hope that his passing will not mean that his influence . . . will no longer be available."[53]

As individuals and governments expressed their regrets, there were even references to religion on Stalin's behalf. "My first reaction," said Muhammad Naguib, the prime minister of Egypt, "was to pray to Allah to give mercy to a great man."[54] The Vatican called on Roman Catholics to pray for Stalin's soul. "[He] has arrived at the end of his arid life and must account to the Almighty for his actions," was how it voiced concern for his prospects in the hereafter. "One cannot feel anything but profound commiseration."[55] Italian communists could not put aside their childhood habits; inside the Soviet embassy in Rome, they crossed themselves and genuflected as they approached Stalin's portrait. At a moment of deep mourning their Catholic upbringing trumped their devotion to an atheist.

Jews throughout the world pondered a different kind of religious epiphany. Stalin had taken ill on Sunday, March 1, a date corresponding to Adar 14 on the Hebrew calendar—the date of the Purim holiday. According to the biblical Book of Esther, Purim celebrates how the Jews of the Persian Empire were saved from Haman, the chamberlain of King Ahasuerus who had been plotting their destruction; for Jews, Haman personifies the image of a relentless antisemite. But the courageous intervention of the Jewish Queen Esther and her uncle Mordechai saved the day and led to Haman's disgrace and execution. So in Jerusalem in March 1953, beggars rattled their tin cups and shouted, "Haman is dead." Israeli officials were more circumspect. Diplomatic relations between the two countries had been broken off by the Kremlin in February; in addition, the Doctors' Plot was still unfolding. Fearful of provoking Stalin's heirs, they kept silent. Following Ben-Gurion's ongoing caution, the Ministry of Foreign Affairs instructed the remaining Israeli embassies in Eastern Europe to "fly the flag at half-mast in mourning for Stalin, as do the Western missions." But they should "not pay condolence calls" or sign the condolence books, and only "attend memorial ceremonies if invited to do so by the government." As for Israeli missions in the West, they were instructed "not to participate in any . . . official display of mourning."[56]

On the day of the funeral, tributes to Stalin in Western Europe reached their peak in France. Premier René Mayer's government had declared three days of official mourning, ordering the tricolor lowered on military posts. According to the government, it was "a matter of courtesy" for a fallen allied leader.[57] But civil authorities were under no such obligation, creating the inconsistent picture of flags on public buildings continuing to fly at full-mast in contrast to military facilities. The popular, conservative newspaper, *Le Figaro*, protested, pointing to French soldiers fighting communist troops in Indochina and Korea. "Have our authorities thought of the effect which [lowering the flag] will have on the morale of our combat units?"[58] Nevertheless, Russian-language broadcasts permeated French national radio, with mournful singing by a Russian male choir preceding repeated announcements from Radio Moscow. *Pravda* reported that 15,000 people visited the Soviet embassy in Paris to express their condolences, while French factories remained silent for fifteen minutes at the moment of Stalin's interment.

What are we to make of these respectful tributes? A handful of years after the defeat of Nazi Germany, it is understandable that there would be a modicum of respect in how the world covered Stalin's death, including Western democracies. France, in particular, had been occupied by the Germans and many Communist Party members had played a major role in the Resistance (after the Soviet Union was invaded). Paris, after all, had a subway station and public square named "Stalingrad." His death was a momentous occasion. It marked the end of an era and opened his country and the world to a new, more hopeful direction. But any gesture of reverence, particularly in a country like France, was a mark of obliviousness to all that Stalin's subjects had endured.

CHAPTER FIVE

THE SURPRISE OF REFORM

Stalin's funeral on Monday morning, March 9, was stately and dignified. Red Square was mostly filled by 8 a.m., with civilian units taking up their positions, an impressive crowd that soon reached 50,000. Black and red mourning banners decorated buildings across from the Kremlin, while civilian mourners carried still more banners and hundreds of black-draped portraits of Stalin. The funeral began at 10 a.m. when the pallbearers, led by Malenkov and Beria, joined by seven other honorary pallbearers, including Zhou En-lai, who was the only non-Soviet pallbearer, carried the coffin out of the Hall of Columns two blocks away. The sound of the funeral procession reached Red Square about twenty minutes later, highlighted by Chopin's Funeral March. At 10.30 all troops in the square turned eyes-right and a second band continued the funeral cadence.

It was then that Lieutenant General K. R. Sinitin, commander of the Moscow garrison, came into view, walking slowly at the head of the procession. Behind him came the flower bearers, with hundreds of green, pink, and purple wreaths, bringing color to an otherwise cold, dreary winter day; they were deposited around the base of Lenin's Mausoleum. Next came fourteen marshals of the Soviet Union, led by the legendary Semyon Budenny, who was famous for commanding a cavalry unit during the Russian Civil War. Each marshal carried a medal or military decoration issued to Stalin, on a cushion of crimson velvet. Behind them came a single black horse and then six more black horses drawing an olive-drab gun caisson bearing the coffin. It was "framed in red for revolution and black for death," *Time* observed. "The dead man himself visible through its glass dome."[1] Behind the caisson came Malenkov, walking with Zhou En-lai, and then other leading party and government dignitaries, family members—including Stalin's daughter Svetlana—and other relatives. A large group of diplomats followed, with officials from Eastern Europe walking with Moscow-based diplomats.

The Kremlin had requested that the United States send a hand-picked delegation, even asking for details about its composition and travel arrangements, and who would be "quartered" in the embassy, with the unspoken hope that President Eisenhower would come to Moscow.[2] But the White House designated chargé d'affaires Jacob Beam to represent the president instead, elevating him temporarily to the position of special ambassador; three military attachés from the embassy staff joined Beam on the delegation. Disappointing the Kremlin, no officials flew in from Washington.

Once the casket was placed on a simple dais in front of the Mausoleum, leaders of the Soviet Communist Party took their place on the balcony of Lenin's tomb. Zhou En-lai stood among them and not among the other foreign leaders. As head of the organizing commission for the funeral, Khrushchev introduced only Malenkov, who delivered the principal eulogy; Beria and Molotov followed. Malenkov stressed the need for the Soviet Union to live in peace with all countries and for the population to enjoy a higher standard of living, two noteworthy declarations. Beria, to the surprise of many, declared that the Soviet people could "work calmly and with conviction, knowing that the Soviet Government will maintain their rights guaranteed under the Soviet Constitution." At the time it must have struck some that Beria was either making a bad joke or had something else in mind. And it was Beria who referred obliquely to the chaos in nearby streets when he said that "The enemies of the Soviet state calculate that the heavy loss we have borne will lead to disorder and confusion in our ranks." Listening closely to their remarks, Konstantin Simonov was struck by the cold, officious tone of their voices, that both Malenkov and Beria lacked any "reference to their own relationship with [Stalin], lacked even a shadow of personal sorrow." And they both sounded like "people who had assumed power and were satisfied by that fact."[3]

Only Molotov offered a more personal remark, referring to Stalin as "a close friend and our own infinitely dear man."[4] There was a moment of silence and then, as the noon hour struck, the chimes of the clock in the Spassky Tower began to be heard along with the salute guns of the Kremlin, thirty salvos, ten to a minute, joined by all of Moscow's factory whistles. Similar artillery salutes sounded in all the capitals of the union republics, in the "hero cities" of Leningrad and Stalingrad, Sevastopol, Odessa, and four others. A five-minute work stoppage was observed throughout the country. "Every train, every tram, every car had stopped," Harrison Salisbury wrote.[5] At the same time, Stalin's successors lifted the coffin and carried it into the Mausoleum, placing it alongside Lenin's mummified corpse. With Stalin laid to rest, the Soviet flag—the hammer-and-sickle banner—which had flown at half-mast above the Mausoleum since Friday, was raised to its peak.

As the noise subsided, General Sitinin gave the order for the march past the Mausoleum to begin. Young soldiers marched smartly across Red Square, followed by elements of the Moscow garrison—heavy guns, weapons carriers, and armored cars. Military aircraft flew overhead.

And then it was over. Within hours, truck barricades and police and army cordons all disappeared from the center of Moscow with the exception of Red Square. By Tuesday, ordinary citizens could now walk into its great expanse, to view the wreaths and imagine the direction the country would take now that Stalin was gone.

Immediately after the funeral the Kremlin took on some urgent business behind the scenes: a team of scientists and doctors set to work embalming Stalin's corpse. Within two days, Minister of Health Tretyakov—the same man who had officially issued the medical bulletins about Stalin's collapse—reported to Khrushchev that the initial process of embalming had concluded successfully. He promised that the entire procedure would be finished by September 15, "after which [the corpse] could be transferred to the mausoleum hall and be available for viewing." But the hall now required a new lighting apparatus and other technical equipment in addition to an opulent sarcophagus to accommodate Stalin's body next to Lenin's. With all that needed to be done, Stalin's mummified remains were not placed on public view until November 17, 1953.[6]

* * *

Quietly, behind the official pomp of the funeral, the reactions to Stalin's death among the population were as varied as the people themselves. Under Leonid Brezhnev in the 1960s and 1970s, Ludmilla Alexeyeva first came to public attention as an outspoken human rights activist who signed petitions on behalf of political prisoners and helped circulate *samizdat* reports. In 1953, she was twenty-six years old, working as a high school teacher while also serving as a lecturer for the Communist Party. She had joined the party out of naïve idealism, hoping to reform it from within. Like many, she "broke into tears" when she heard the news over the radio. "We cried because we were helpless; we cried because we had no rational way of predicting what would happen to us now; we cried because we sensed that, for better or for worse, an era had passed."[7]

The soprano Galina Vishnevskaya also broke down. Newly appointed to the prestigious Bolshoi Opera, she experienced the same feeling of panic and loss. "Life had come to an end," was how she recalled her feelings. "The nation was seized with a panic, full of confusion, and fear of the unknown. For thirty years we had heard only Stalin, Stalin, Stalin. . . ."[8] As the scholar Juliane Fürst has written, "The sense of 'being orphaned' pervaded all sectors of society."[9] Looking back on that time, Aleksandr Solzhenitsyn sarcastically observed that "To judge from the widespread tears, you would think that a crack had appeared in the universe rather than that one man had died."[10] One man *had* died, but his death provoked a deep psychological shock, a mood of disorienting anxiety that overtook virtually the entire population. Two generations had heard nothing but lies and propaganda about the virtues of a single man; then, suddenly, he was gone.

The poet Yevgeny Yevtushenko was nineteen that March. Like Alexeyeva, he sensed that "a sort of paralysis came over the country. Trained to believe that they were all in Stalin's care, people were lost and bewildered without him. All Russia wept. And so did I. We wept sincerely, tears of grief—and perhaps also tears of fear for the future."[11]

The historian Aleksandr Nekrich was working under a cloud of suspicion at the Institute of History in Moscow. His research into the outbreak of World War II and the post-war period was troubling his superiors. The events were much too recent, their ideological dimensions too ambiguous, too subject to abrupt changes in the party line. So it was clear to him that "Stalin's death was tantamount to salvation." He also saw the required grieving that unfolded in the institute. "Fortunately," he wrote, "there were enough false notes struck in the statements to have a sobering effect, somehow neutralizing the heightened emotion." One middle-aged father of three children, a professional party official, shared his daughter's supposed sadness with his grieving colleagues. "Papa," she reportedly had asked him. "How are we going to live now that Comrade Stalin is gone? He was a best friend to all children!" Nekrich was relieved to witness "such cheap histrionics." For him, it meant that people were not as emotionally devastated as they pretended to be, only playing along with the enforced hypocrisy.[12]

The physicist Andrei Sakharov also remembered those March days with vivid emotion. "People feared the situation would deteriorate—but how could it get any worse? Some, including those who harbored no illusions about Stalin and the regime, worried about a general collapse, internecine strife, another wave of mass repressions, even Civil War." His colleague, Igor Tamm,[13] brought his wife to the secret location where they were working, a military facility 300 miles east of Moscow—the Installation, as they called it, where scientists and engineers devoted themselves exclusively to the development of nuclear weapons—"in the belief that at such times it was safer to be as far from Moscow as possible." Sakharov wrote to his wife that March: "I am under the influence of a great man's death. I am thinking of his humanity." Writing in his memoirs decades later, he had to admit that he had gotten "carried away, . . . affected by the general mourning and by a sense of death's universal dominion." Sakharov felt a need to apologize to his readers, to justify a reaction that was altogether common throughout the country.[14] As Yevtushenko wrote, "All Russia wept"—half out of sorrow, half out of relief.[15]

Aleksandr Solzhenitsyn was living in exile in a remote corner of Kazakhstan. Following his arrest at the front in February 1945 (he was serving in an artillery unit in East Prussia), he was convicted of "anti-Soviet propaganda" and of "founding a hostile organization" because of derogatory remarks about Stalin he had included in private letters. After eight years in the labor camps he had just been transported to Kazakhstan that March and was renting a small room in a mud hut. It was his landlady who urged him to go to the town square and listen to what the loudspeakers were relaying. She was too frightened to tell him herself. "Solzhenitsyn found a crowd of about 200 people listening to a radio announcement that Stalin had died," his biographer Michael Scammell wrote. "The old men had bared their heads and were openly grief-stricken. Others looked mournful, and only a few of the younger men seemed unconcerned. . . . Women and girls wept openly on the street, dabbing their eyes with their handkerchiefs." Solzhenitsyn knew to keep his joy to himself, "setting his face in a suitably solemn expression." He returned to the hut and spent the remainder of the day writing a commemorative poem, "The Fifth of March."[16]

Another prisoner, Eugenia Ginzburg, was also living in exile in far-off Kolyma, having spent the previous eighteen years in various labor camps. She later wrote in her memoir *Within the Whirlwind* that for the "Kolyma bosses . . . [they] could not accept the vulgar notion that the Genius, Leader, Father, Creator, Inspirer, Organizer, Best Friend, Coryphaeus, etc., etc., was subject to the same base laws of biology as any prisoner. Moreover, they had all become used to the idea that persons of note could die only if Stalin personally gave the order." For prisoners, as well, there were "not a few heart attacks and nervous breakdowns. . . . Deprived of hope for decades on end, we were bowled over by the first flicker of distant lightning. Accustomed as we had grown to slavery, we almost went into a dead faint when the thought of freedom first dawned on us."[17]

Even in death, Stalin dragged people into a netherworld. Elena Bonner, who decades later would become a prominent human rights activist and the wife of Andrei Sakharov, was a student in the First Medical Institute of Leningrad that March. Somewhat older than her classmates, she had served in World War II, suffered severe damage to her eyes, and had begun her medical studies as a disabled veteran in 1948 at the age of twenty-five. As the Doctors' Plot continued to ensnare its victims, one of her favorite professors, Vasily

Zakusov, a leading pharmacologist, was arrested along with his wife, Irina Gessen. Zakusov, in fact, was not Jewish, but in a case like this it was necessary to rope in some non-Jewish doctors in order to deflect attention from the obvious fact that the Doctors' Plot was an explicitly antisemitic campaign.

As often happened, an all-institute meeting was assembled where the entire student body was expected to denounce Professor Zakusov and call for his execution. He was now "an assassin in a white coat," accused of trying to hasten the deaths of Soviet leaders. Because of her high academic standing and seniority among the students, Elena Bonner was asked to lead the meeting on Wednesday, March 4, the day on which Stalin's illness was announced. But she confounded the party leaders on hand. "Have you gone crazy?" she challenged her fellow students. "You are demanding the death penalty for our own Vasily Vasilievich?" Her remarks provoked a sharp reaction from party and Komsomol leaders who were monitoring the assembly; they expressed their angry disappointment in front of everyone. Bonner hurried home after the meeting. It would not have been surprising if she had been immediately arrested.

When Bonner returned to campus the next day her presence surprised her friends. Didn't she know she had been summarily expelled? Scared to see her and scared to be seen with her, they told her that the secretary to the dean was looking for her. Known as a woman of intelligence and integrity, the secretary urged Bonner to quickly leave the city. Two students at the institute had been arrested a year or two earlier because of their enthusiastic support for the establishment of Israel. Too much was at stake for Bonner to stay in Leningrad.

She decided to leave the following day. That morning she and her neighbors learned about Stalin's death. But Bonner did not change her plans. Together with her three-year-old daughter, Tatiana, she traveled to Gorky to see her mother, Ruth Bonner. (In an ironic turn of fate, Sakharov would be exiled there in January 1980.) Her mother had already spent years in the labor camps and was now serving out a term of exile. Elena Bonner remained in Gorky for several weeks. Fortunately, the trouble passed her over. When the Doctors' Plot was publicly disavowed in April—a step that signaled major reform was underway—her expulsion from medical school was invalidated.[18]

Other people did not get off so easily. For months, the police and prosecutors dragged off anyone who exulted in Stalin's demise. There were many cases of open grumbling, crude or obscene jokes, minor acts of vandalism, or isolated, drunken outbursts from people who were already on the margins of society. Such remarks were regarded as seditious and deserving of prosecution by a skittish regime. Upset by this lack of respect, their neighbors or colleagues—or perhaps a stranger passing by—thought it best to denounce them, then testify to their blasphemous utterances. A prosecutor in the Department for Special Cases of the Krasnoyarsk region, for example, went after a certain B. A. Basov, who was working as a technician in a hospital. "On March 5," it was claimed, a witness was discussing "the health of one of the leaders of the Party and the Soviet government, on which Basov commented, 'Let him die. There will be dozens of people to take his job.'" When someone objected, saying that millions would cry over his passing, Basov responded, "Millions of people will rejoice, they won't cry." Basov was detained by two witnesses to his remarks. For this act of subversion, Basov was sentenced to ten years' imprisonment and a further three-year suspension of his rights.[19]

There were an untold number of similar cases. On March 6, a drunken, middle-aged man openly declared in a tramway, "What a lovely day. We buried Stalin today. One less swine. Now we can go on living." Another man who was attending a memorial meeting for Stalin was seen ripping his portrait, declaring "so I don't have to look at you anymore." Upon hearing the news of Stalin's death, a worker pointed to the radio loudspeaker and said, "Listen, his corpse already stinks." An employee in a movie theater was watching a newsreel when Stalin's image crossed the screen. "For Stalin's death, hooray!" he shouted. Another worker, upon hearing a radio announcement about Stalin's condition, said out loud: "Dark, illiterate jackasses also have hemorrhages in the brain." On March 6, a sailor declared, "Today is my holiday, so I'm getting drunk." During a memorial meeting with 200 people at a store, the director said, "We have lost a dear and beloved enemy." Another man in a brick factory explained that due to his being upset and a speech defect, he had accidentally said the word *vrag* ("enemy") instead of *vozhd* ("leader"). The prosecutors rejected his plea.

Most of the cases were prosecuted "for cursing one of the leaders of the Communist Party of the Soviet Union in a vulgar manner"; the courts preferred to avoid invoking Stalin's name as they sentenced these hapless individuals to ten years of confinement.[20] Fortunately, the defendants in all these cases were released within two years when the regime was already committed to releasing hundreds of thousands of long-term political prisoners. But even in 1953 some reforms began to percolate through the system. During an assembly in Lvov to mourn Stalin, an eighteen-year-old Jewish high school student muttered, "Let him rot." Her classmates proceeded to hit and denounce her. Within weeks, she was arrested, convicted, and sentenced to ten years of confinement. By June, however, the situation was changing in the country; she was released "as part of the populist effort to 'restore justice.'" With Stalin gone, officials were beginning to show a semblance of humanity.[21]

No single incident can best exemplify the full range of emotions that emerged in those unsettling days. Perhaps a quiet story from Andrei Sinyavsky's novel *Goodnight!* catches the fear and cautious relief that engulfed the country after Stalin's death.

The doorbell rang. ... A close friend of mine was at the door. Without saying a word, the key in my pocket, I led him away from my neighbors' eyes and down to the basement. No one could spy on us there. I double-locked the door. We stood facing each other, our eyes radiant. We embraced silently. We smiled. . . . Secret conspirators. Exchanging happy smiles when everyone else was in tears. Was it a holiday? A masquerade? A last salute, then he left quietly, still silent.[22]

A celebration of survival. However uncertain, what would follow could only be better.

* * *

With Stalin out of the way, Georgy Malenkov seemed to be securing the three most important positions within the Soviet hierarchy: the premiership of the government (as chairman of the Council of Ministers), the head of the Party Presidium, and the Secretariat of the party itself. But he was not able to hold onto all three for very long. Following the appearance of the doctored photograph with Stalin and Mao on March 10, Malenkov's build-up ceased. His photograph stopped appearing, quotations from his "works" grew fewer. The writer Isaac Deutscher, always a well-informed if not accurate reader of Soviet affairs from his perch in London, observed that Malenkov was starting to overstep his prerogatives, that "the men of the old guard . . . expected Mr. Malenkov to act deferentially on their advice and to behave more timidly or discreetly than he has already behaved."[23] On March 21, the public learned that Malenkov had resigned as secretary of the Central Committee a week before. A five-man Party Secretariat was also being appointed: Malenkov would no longer be a member, while the still relatively unknown Nikita Khrushchev was listed first and out of alphabetical order.[24] The new leadership was taking shape. Malenkov remained premier and thereby first among equals, but he no longer exercised leadership

1 Stalin and his "comrades-in-arms" in January 1947. From left to right: Beria, Kaganovich, Malenkov, Molotov, Alexei Kuznetsov, Stalin, Alexei Kosygin, Nikolai Voznesensky, Voroshilov, Matvei Shkiryatov. Two years later, Kuznetsov and Voznesensky were arrested and then shot.

2 Entitled "Traces of a Crime," this anti-semitic caricature appeared in the Soviet satirical journal *Krokodil* on January 30, 1953. The text denounces the combined intelligence work of the Americans, the British, and the "Joint."

3 Stalin stands between Malenkov and Molotov and others to commemorate the twenty-eighth anniversary of Lenin's death in January 1952.

4 Stalin addresses the Nineteenth Party Congress in October 1952, his last public speech.

5 Stalin at the Nineteenth Party Congress. Unflattering photographs like this were never published. In five months' time, Stalin would be dead.

6 The front page of *Pravda*, March 6, 1953, with the announcement of Stalin's death.

7 Eileen Keenan, a waitress at the 1203 Restaurant in Washington, D.C., puts up a sign inviting the public to enjoy a free serving of borscht to celebrate Stalin's death, on March 6, 1953.

8 *Pravda*, March 7, 1953, the first time a photograph of Stalin's corpse is published. Members of the Presidium stand by the bier in the Hall of Columns in the House of Unions.

9 Stalin's heirs form an honor guard while he lies in state. The photograph appeared in *Pravda* on March 9, 1953, the day of his funeral.

10 Stalin's body lying in state among a sea of flowers.

11 An enormous column of people moves slowly down Gorky Street in central Moscow to view Stalin's body in the Hall of Columns.

12 Lines of people waiting to pay their respects to Stalin. The Bolshoi Theater is visible behind them.

13 Svetlana Alliluyeva in the Hall of Columns while her father's body lies in state. Her husband, Yuri Zhdanov, stands to her right.

14 Vasily Stalin and his wife, Yekaterina Timoshenko, sit in the Hall of Columns.

15 Party and government leaders carrying Stalin's coffin. Beria and Malenkov lead the pallbearers on each side.

16 The funeral procession through the streets of Moscow, March 9, 1953. In the first row directly behind the casket are, from left to right, Molotov, Bulganin, Kaganovich, Voroshilov, Malenkov, Zhou Enlai, Beria, and Khrushchev.

17 The officially assembled crowd in Prague's Wenceslas Square on the day of Stalin's funeral, March 9, 1953.

18 The doctored photograph of Malenkov, alongside Stalin and Mao, as it appeared in the Soviet press on March 10, 1953.

19 The original photograph of the signing ceremony for the Sino-Soviet Treaty of Friendship, Alliance, and Mutual Aid, taken on February 14, 1950. Stalin, Mao Zedong, and Malenkov are standing among a large group of Soviet and Chinese officials. It appeared in *Pravda* the next day.

20 President Dwight D. Eisenhower delivering his "Chance for Peace" speech in Washington, April 16, 1953.

of the party. Beria was first deputy premier and head of the internal police, but he too had no formal role among the party leaders. Khrushchev was emerging as head of the party. Molotov was restored to his role as foreign minister, while Bulganin would serve as defense minister. The old Politburo, or the Presidium as it was now called, but without Stalin, remained the ruling group, and appeared to be exercising collective leadership. For Isaac Deutscher, the men in charge looked "more like a council of elders than like the effective seat of power."[25] Convinced of Malenkov's unquestioned preeminence, *Time* featured his portrait on its cover for the issue of March 23. "The face that Moscow turned to the world this week was, except for the missing mustache, disconcertingly the same—fat, inscrutable, steelyeyed." This was how it described Malenkov, "the Cossack with the shady past and forbidding presence who stepped from Stalin's shadow into the role of No. 1."[26] Stalin's lieutenants were now officially his heirs.

As for Stalin, the pages of *Pravda* reflected his gradual public decline. To provide some historical perspective, when *Pravda* marked Aviation Day and the opening of the Volga–Don Canal with a special four-page issue on July 28, 1952, Stalin was mentioned no less than 123 times. After his funeral, reports about memorial meetings throughout the country dominated the issues of March 11 and 12. But already on March 11, non-Stalin news made its way back into the paper; a single, short column appeared on the last page with reports about developments in Korea and at the United Nations. There was also a list of theatrical productions that were resuming in the capital. Similar reports gradually began to expand as the days progressed, and then finally on March 15 non-Stalin-related news returned to the front page. For five more days commentary about his death continued to diminish until March 20 when *Pravda* failed to feature a single headline devoted to its deceased leader. Any seasoned reader of the Soviet press would have understood the meaning of this gradual decline in official obeisance.[27] Certain news-papers and institutions, though, kept to their old habits; on March 19, *Literaturnaia gazeta*, the official organ of the Writers' Union, instructed its members in a front-page editorial "To portray in Soviet literature, for their contemporaries and for future generations, the greatest genius of all time and all peoples—the immortal Stalin."[28] Two weeks after Stalin's death, this kind of rhetoric was already growing stale. Khrushchev knew that the newspaper's editor, Konstantin Simonov, had written it, and threatened to dismiss him.[29]

* * *

As the new leaders consolidated their power, Lavrenti Beria began pushing them to adopt startling reforms. "Beria was not a closet liberal," the political scientist William Taubman once noted. "He played the role of reformer just *because* he was drenched in blood. The way to improve his reputation and taint that of others was to incrimi-nate Stalin, whose orders all of them had carried out."[30] Beria had relinquished his formal role as head of internal security in August 1945 when he took on the responsibility to organize the atomic bomb project. Following Stalin's funeral, he quickly organized five commis-sions to review cases and incidents from Stalin's final years, including the death of Solomon Mikhoels and the Doctors' Plot. By confining these reviews to the post-war period he was trying to avoid casting attention on the 1930s—the period of the Great Purge, the famous show trials, and the roundup of millions of innocents—and the war years, as well, which saw the deportations of whole peoples. Perhaps he thought it would be easier to pin all the blame on Stalin alone.

By the end of March, the public began to learn about significant and surprising reforms. Beria insisted that industrial and construc-tion projects being run by the Ministry of Internal Affairs—including logging, mining, and manufacturing enterprises that dotted the

Gulag landscape—be transferred to ordinary, civilian economic ministries, and that forced labor no longer be deployed at construction sites, a practice Stalin had relied upon for many large-scale projects. Under orders from Beria, several canals, tunnels, and railroad lines that were being built by forced prison labor were abandoned. Work on the Salekhard–Igarka railway in northern Siberia, for example, had begun in 1949 and involved over a 100,000 such workers. But Stalin's lieutenants knew there was little economic need for the rail line and called off the project within days after his death. Taking on the issue of what to do with the vast network of forced labor—the infamous Gulag—Beria reported to the Presidium that 2,526,401 political and non-political prisoners (including 438,788 women, 35,505 of them with children and 62,886 pregnant) were being held in prisons, colonies, and labor camps. Only the mass executions and the famine that followed collectivization exceeded the scale and cruelty of the forced labor system. Beria convinced his colleagues to approve a broad amnesty for prisoners who were believed to pose no serious threat to society. On March 27, the new regime announced a sweeping revision of the Criminal Code and an amnesty for over a million prisoners, the largest such release in the history of the Gulag. The amnesty provided for the release of all prisoners serving terms of five years or less; all pregnant women; juveniles up to eighteen years old; women over fifty and men over fifty-five; and the incurably ill. It was also extended to include prisoners being held for unspecified "official and economic crimes," while cutting in half all sentences of more than five years, except in cases involving counter-revolutionary crimes, and other serious criminal offenses. With this one decree, the new leaders radically changed the scale of the forced-labor system.

But the decision to release so many prisoners had unforeseen consequences. In the weeks following the decree, as hundreds of thousands of released prisoners, many of them hardened and unreformed criminals, made their way across the country, they unleashed a wave of violent crime. The archives contain many accounts of terrifying incidents, including assaults, stabbings, killings, even mass rapes carried out on trains by newly released prisoners. In April, a secret report described how fifteen amnestied prisoners entered a train carriage reserved for women and raped almost all the forty women inside. An American named John Noble was serving a term in Vorkuta when the amnesty decree was announced.[31] He recalled how 5,000 were released but that 800 were soon "back in camp after they had started a murderous wave of robberies and knife stabbings in town, killing 1200."[32] On June 19, Khrushchev was informed about letters to *Pravda* in which ordinary citizens complained about "a significant increase in petty crime, in burglaries and murders in numerous cities and towns." A group of party activists in Leningrad described a frightening rise in thefts on the streets of the city. "It is characterized by the impudence of the criminals who even act in broad daylight and with barely any reaction on the part of the police." Several letters to *Pravda* even urged that the fingers or hands of thieves be chopped off. The regime had assured the public that only prisoners who no longer posed any danger were being let go. But their assurances did not comfort local officials, who felt helpless over what to do.[33]

In general the amnesty did not apply to political prisoners. The "special camps" holding them remained under the jurisdiction of the Ministry of the Interior, not the Ministry of Justice, which was taking over administration of the labor camp system as a whole. But unbeknownst to the public, the very first political prisoner had already been released: Polina Zhemchuzhina, the wife of Molotov, was reunited with her husband in Stalin's Kremlin office on March 10, the day after the dictator's funeral, which was Molotov's birthday as well. It is believed that Zhemchuzhina was already in Moscow at the time of Stalin's collapse, undergoing interrogation in connection with the Doctors' Plot; the questioning ceased on March 2 as word of Stalin's condition began to permeate security circles. According to one story, Zhemchuzhina was not aware that Stalin had died; upon learning of his demise, she fainted. Nonetheless, given the recent anti-Jewish measures associated with the Doctors' Plot and Molotov's own vulnerability, it is especially ironic that it was Zhemchuzhina who was the first to gain her freedom and that it was Beria who personally arranged for her release.[34]

Other reforms quickly followed. On April 1, the regime announced a substantial lowering of retail prices for food and manufactured goods. Since Stalin's death only three weeks earlier, there had already been promises to improve the standard of living, to upgrade the country's housing stock, and to broaden the availability of consumer goods. Malenkov himself had emphasized the need to address such shortcomings in his eulogy for Stalin. His heirs seemed determined to address the country's misery. It had been their job "to keep the country afloat," as Oleg Khlevniuk observed in his biography of Stalin. As his lieutenants they "were keenly aware of the urgent need for change to which he seemed willfully blind."[35] Khrushchev later admitted that "We were scared, really scared. We were afraid the thaw might unleash a flood, which we wouldn't be able to control and which would drown us."[36] But with Stalin gone they did not hesitate to act.

The next day Beria pushed for another extraordinary step: he reported the circumstances of Solomon Mikhoels' death to the full Presidium. As Beria confirmed, Stalin had personally ordered the killing, assigning Lavrenti Tsanava, the head of the MGB in Minsk, along with Sergei Ogoltsov, a secret police official in Moscow, to carry it out. Beria added that Tsanava and Ogoltsov had been quietly awarded state medals in late 1948 as a reward for the crime. Beria urged that they be arrested and their medals withdrawn; the Presidium agreed, ordering the (posthumous) rehabilitation of Mikhoels and the arrest of Tsanava and Ogoltsov. The Presidium also voted to revoke the bestowal of the Order of Lenin on Lidia Timashuk—the Moscow cardiologist whose claims about the death of Zhdanov had been used to initiate the Doctors' Plot—"in view of the state of affairs which had now been discovered."[37]

Acting quickly, the Kremlin publicly disavowed the Doctors' Plot on April 4 and announced the release of the falsely accused physicians. Eighty-two days had passed since the alleged conspiracy had been exposed, nearly three months of unabated anxiety and fear over the fate of the doctors and the broader fate of the country's Jews. Only now did the Kremlin lift the sword of Damocles. Under the bland, official-sounding headline "A Communiqué of the USSR Ministry of Internal Affairs" and consigned to a corner of the second page of *Pravda*, the brief announcement credited the Ministry of Internal Affairs for carrying out "a thorough verification of all the preliminary investigation data and other material in the case of the group of doctors accused of sabotage, espionage and terrorist acts against active leaders of the Soviet State." The accused had been arrested "without any lawful basis." The accusations had been "false," documentary evidence against them was "without foundation." In the communiqué's most explosive sentence, "It was established that the testimony of the prisoners, allegedly confirming the accusations against [the accused], was obtained by the officials of the investigatory department of the former Ministry of State Security through the use of means which are impermissible and strictly forbidden under Soviet law." In plain language, they had been tortured. They were now being released. "The persons accused of incorrect conduct of the investigation have been arrested and brought to trial," the article concluded, while the true culprits—Stalin who was dead and his "comrades-in-arms" who had applauded his every move—were not held accountable.

Two days later, on April 6, *Pravda* carried another column about the Doctors' Plot. But this time it was a prominent editorial on the front page, an unmistakable message that Stalin's heirs felt the need to elaborate on the earlier disavowal. Entitled "Soviet Socialist Law is Inviolable," it repeated the retraction of the libelous charges and expanded on the previous communiqué which had noted the arrest of unnamed officials. Now it held the deputy minister for state security, Semyon Ignatiev, and the ministry's director of the Department of Investigation, Mikhail Ryumin, responsible for the entire case. Ignatiev had "displayed political blindness and heedlessness" for having been manipulated "by such criminal adventurers as Ryumin."

The column then added startling observations. It indirectly admitted that the Doctors' Plot had been fabricated for the broader purpose of inciting hatred against the Jews: "Despicable adventurers of the Ryumin type tried . . . to inflame in Soviet society . . . feelings of national antagonism, which are profoundly alien to socialist ideology." And it then cleared Solomon Mikhoels of any wrongdoing, announcing that he was "an honest public figure" whose memory had been "slandered."[38] (Still, the regime required three more weeks before it released his son-in-law, the composer Mieczysław Weinberg, who had been arrested in the first week of February.) Ilya Ehrenburg read the article so often that morning that he came to know it by heart. "I understood that history was beginning to unravel the tangle in which the clean and the unclean had been mixed up, and that the story would not end with Ryumin." It was fair to wonder "whether it was likely that things would stop at so relatively insignificant a figure."[39]

In the context of Soviet history the disclosure was an unprecedented gesture of regret on the part of a regime that never made mistakes and never admitted being wrong. Nothing like this admission of an official crime had ever before appeared in the Soviet press. For *Newsweek*, it was "a staggering reversal."[40] *Le Monde* called it "an event without precedent in the history of Soviet justice."[41] The *New York Times* noted, "What is astonishing is that the Kremlin should so dramatically repudiate one of the biggest of its big lies and lay so open before the world the corruption and the brazen disregard for the truth which are so basic to Soviet power."[42] As Jacob Beam reported to the State Department, "This startling event, perhaps more than any other, provides most concrete evidence thus far of present regime's break with Stalinism."[43] The Israelis, too, expressed "deep satisfaction" over the doctors' exoneration, along with the hope that "the accusers of yesterday would become the accused of tomorrow."[44]

There were limits, though, to the Kremlin's candor. At least two of the doctors were no longer alive: Professors M. B. Kogan and Y. G. Etinger had been among those publicly denounced. Now their names were not on the list of those exonerated, a conspicuous and unexplained absence. (Etinger had died in prison after prolonged mistreatment and interrogations in March 1951; Mikhail Kogan, according to Yakov Rapoport, had already died of cancer "several years" before he was publicly accused of espionage. The Kremlin failed to explain why two dead doctors had been implicated in the plot.)[45] And there was no mention of the crackdown on the Jewish Anti-Fascist Committee, the execution of its members, or the widespread purge of Yiddish culture. There was never any full accounting for the harassment, threats, dismissals from work, and general atmosphere of dread that had enveloped the country during the many weeks of antisemitic abuse. There was no mention of the broad propaganda campaign that had gone on for several years. No apology for the hysteria in the hospitals, for the panic within Jewish households, for the vehement denunciations of Zionism and Israel. The words "Jew," "Zionist," "Joint," and "American imperialism" which had so highlighted the accusations in January did not appear in the disavowals in April; the Kremlin could accuse Ryumin of "inflaming feelings of national antagonism" and still refuse to specify that he had been targeting Jews. The entire antisemitic campaign had been so public and pervasive that to treat the arrest of the doctors as an isolated miscarriage of justice meant that the regime, in spite of its unprecedented admission, was engaging in a kind of cover-up at the same time that it was releasing the (surviving) doctors and disavowing the accusations against them. Even when the regime "rehabilitated" Solomon Mikhoels, in the sense that it cleared him of any accusation of treason or espionage, it failed to say how he had died or who had ordered his murder. But on the occasion of these spectacular, though limited, admissions, the regime felt the need to reassure the public that "Nobody can be arrested without the decision of a court or state prosecutor." With such a statement, it was inviting the Soviet people to wonder how arrests had taken place before, on what scale, and on whose authority.

If the doctors were innocent, then Stalin was guilty, and his crime was worse than the alleged crimes of the doctors. But the regime was not ready to denounce Stalin. As Charles Bohlen could sense from his office at the US embassy, "It would have been too risky to the Communist Party for the Soviet people to learn suddenly that their idol had not only feet of clay but also bloodstained hands."[46] Almost three full years would have to pass before Khrushchev could deliver his famous "secret speech" and denounce Stalin for the tyrant that he had been. But the dramatic disavowal of the Doctors' Plot was as forceful a message as could be imagined for the new Kremlin leaders—and it confused many citizens. Within weeks, the editors of *Pravda* reported on the scores of letters they were receiving about the released doctors. Only a small portion congratulated the party for admitting its mistake. Others asked for clarification, insisting that this reversal of fortune required further explanation over how people who had been so denounced in January could prove to be so innocent in April.

Others, writing anonymously, took a distinctly antisemitic tone. One pointed out "how many innocent victims of repression from 1933–34 and 1937–38 remain in the camps, but they are not the first to be rehabilitated, unlike this small group of Jews." Another wrote that "the article smells of the Jewish bazaar." Or: "You think you can change our thinking about the Jews. No, you cannot change this. Jews were parasites in our eyes and will remain so." And: the release of the doctors meant that "after Stalin's death, Jews were taking power into their hands."[47] For a population schooled to accept official signals, learning what to endorse and what to denounce, such letters exposed a deep vein of anti-Jewish prejudice. At least for a time, the Kremlin seemed embarrassed by the wave of anti-Jewish demagoguery that Stalin had unleashed and was looking for ways to counteract it. On April 17, Soviet Minister of Justice Konstantin Gorshenin reinforced this theme. *Pravda* reported his warning that "preaching of racial hatred or scorn in the Soviet Union would be punished."[48]

The official disavowal of the Doctors' Plot raises the perplexing question of why the country's new leaders made this admission so quickly and so publicly. We can dismiss the possibility that it was an act of conscience. While they knew many, if not all, of the imprisoned doctors because they and their families had been under their care, the Presidium members were not men who based their political judgments on ordinary categories of good and evil. They had survived years of working closely with Stalin and collaborated in his crimes. When they released a million prisoners from the Gulag, it was because they understood that the forced labor system was wasteful and unnecessary. And if they decided not simply to release the innocent doctors but to publicly bemoan the abuses associated with their case, it was because they saw a pragmatic advantage to doing so. Perhaps it was meant as a signal to the West: to offer a new, more benign face to the world. Perhaps they understood the need to distance themselves from Stalin's rule and focused on the Doctors' Plot as an official conspiracy they could expose without incriminating themselves. Perhaps the anti-Jewish unrest that followed the announcement of the Doctors' Plot unnerved them to the point where they saw a need to "push back," to repudiate Stalin's ever more explicit campaign against the Jews because it was disrupting social relations within the country. Whatever their reasoning and without making an explicit promise, the new leaders were assuring the public that arbitrary terror would no longer be the basis of state policy.

And they were far from done. On April 16, *Pravda* published an outspoken criticism of one-man rule. "It is impossible to provide genuine leadership if inner Party democracy is violated in the Party organization, if genuine collective leadership and widely developed criticism and self-criticism are lacking." In case any reader needed prompting about what the article was really about, the newspaper observed that "Leaders cannot consider criticism of themselves as a personal affront." Otherwise, an atmosphere of "unprincipled, alien habits of kowtowing and flattery" would develop.[49]

A month later, *Pravda* repeated its repudiation of one-man rule, citing the case of obscure party officials in Chernovtsy Province who were grossly violating the principle of group decisions.[50] Such articles in the party's most authoritative organ delivered an unmistakable signal: the new leadership was repudiating Stalin's personal dictatorship and, at least publicly, rejecting any expectation that one of them would inherit undisputed control of the levers of power.

CHAPTER SIX

A CHANCE FOR PEACE?

American officials had long assumed that Stalin's death would expose the fragility of his regime. As far back as February 1946, George Kennan advised that the stability of the Soviet state "is not yet finally proven. ... [It would need to demonstrate] that it can survive [the] supreme test of successive transfer of power from one individual or group to another. Lenin's death was first such transfer, and its effects wracked Soviet state for 15 years after."[1] For Kennan, "Stalin's death or retirement will be second" and could well lead to another protracted convulsion. Such advice governed American understanding of Kremlin politics.[2] And if Soviet leaders—within the party, the government, or the army and security services—turned on each other then they might lose control of their own country and the satellite states in Eastern Europe. The United States could exploit such instability for its own advantage, or at least that was the hope.

Nearly seven years later the United States dreamed of disrupting succession plans in the Kremlin. After the announcement of the Nineteenth Party Congress in August 1952, when it was believed that Stalin might appoint a successor, State Department officials prepared "a script conjuring up a 'Stalin Testament' hoping to sow confusion within the Kremlin leadership by floating a false statement of its own." The plan went nowhere.[3] (The idea was to mimic Lenin's earlier political testament. Following a series of debilitating strokes, Lenin had evidently dictated his famous Testament over the winter of 1922 and 1923 in which he criticized other Bolsheviks, including Stalin and Trotsky; he did not endorse any of them as his successor.) And just days before General Dwight Eisenhower's election to the presidency, in November, 1952, the Psychological Strategy Board outlined a contingency plan in the event of Stalin's death. It offered vague proposals, recognizing that "many uncertainties" were bound to arise and concluded that "strains must be presumed to exist between individuals and groups closely connected with the problem of succession."[4] Here again the US was hoping to aggravate tensions in a post-Stalin Kremlin. Echoing Kennan's views, the logic was simple: a political crisis was likely to unfold in the Kremlin once Stalin died, allowing the United States to exploit the turmoil for its own advantage. But there were still no concrete ideas of what to do.

Eisenhower came into office after a campaign in which he and his principal foreign policy adviser, John Foster Dulles, who would soon become secretary of state, had emphasized their determination to "roll back" Soviet control of Eastern Europe and "mark the end of the negative, futile and immoral policy of 'containment,'" as the Republican platform of 1952 declared.[5] They were rejecting Kennan's famous policy of containment, finding it too accepting of Soviet gains which, they argued, both Roosevelt and Truman should have resisted. They wanted to replace what Foster Dulles called the "treadmill policies" of the Truman administration with a "policy of boldness."[6]

Probably no secretary of state in American history has come to office with greater experience or sense of purpose than John Foster Dulles. He was the grandson and nephew of two previous secretaries: John Foster, who served under President Benjamin Harrison, and Robert Lansing, who served under President Woodrow Wilson. A graduate of Princeton, Foster Dulles studied in Paris for a year before earning his law degree and joining the famous New York firm of Sullivan and Cromwell. His uncle, Robert Lansing, was secretary of state during World War I. Foster Dulles joined him in Washington where he worked in the department's Russia Bureau and was part of the effort to oppose the Bolsheviks once they seized power. With the end of World War I, Foster Dulles took on even greater responsibilities. Appointed legal adviser to the US delegation to the Paris Peace Conference in 1919, he worked closely with Wilson and Lansing as they sought to limit French and British demands for onerous postwar reparations from a defeated Germany.

For years Foster Dulles contributed to a bipartisan approach to foreign policy. He served as foreign policy adviser to New York's Republican governor Thomas Dewey when he sought the presidency in 1944 and 1948, and accompanied Republican Senator Arthur Vandenberg to San Francisco for the founding of the United Nations, where he helped to draft the preamble to the UN Charter; Foster Dulles subsequently attended several sessions of the General Assembly as a member of the US delegation appointed by President Harry Truman. But Foster Dulles grew disillusioned with Truman's policy of containment and became famous for advocating the more aggressive stance of "rollback" on behalf of the Soviet-controlled nations of Eastern Europe. As he wrote during the election campaign of 1952, "liberation from the yoke of Moscow will not occur for a very long time, and courage in neighboring lands will not be sustained, *unless the United States makes it stubbornly known that it wants and expects liberation to occur.* The mere statement of that wish and expectation would change, in an electrifying way, the mood of the captive peoples. It would put heavy new burdens on the jailers and create new opportunities for liberation."[7] With this kind of unsparing anticommunist rhetoric Eisenhower and Dulles wrested control of US foreign policy after two decades of Democratic administrations.

Stalin did not hesitate to bait them. On Christmas Day, 1952, seven weeks after Eisenhower's election, Stalin offered a meager olive branch in response to questions from James "Scotty" Reston, the diplomatic correspondent of the *New York Times* and one of its star reporters. A front-page headline carried the startling news: "Stalin For Eisenhower Meeting; Tells the Times That He Favors New Approach To End Korea War."[8] While the statement was hailed throughout the world, the coverage infuriated Eisenhower's adviser, C. D. Jackson, who was a staunch anti-communist and promoter of psychological warfare. He was appalled by "the shocking stupidity and/or irresponsibility of Scotty Reston, aided and abetted by the high priests of the *New York Times*, who should know better, which permitted the front page of that paper on Christmas morning to be given over to a photograph of Stalin and his phony peace proposal."[9] Jackson was over-reacting, fearful that a holiday gesture from Stalin could sway public opinion in the West. Observing from Moscow, Harrison Salisbury noted that Stalin was offering Eisenhower "an excellent opportunity of making an important and practical test of what so often is referred to by Western diplomats as 'Soviet good intentions.'"[10] But Eisenhower decided not to "test" what Stalin had in mind. Such reassuring words out of Moscow did not placate him.

During the election campaign he had made two promises: to visit Korea should he be elected—a trip he made in early December—and to end the war as promptly as he could. Eisenhower had met Stalin in Moscow in August 1945 and had no illusions about his character: he was the "iron-handed boss of the Soviet Union," Eisenhower wrote in his memoir. He "doubted whether much that was productive could come out of meeting such a man."[11] Eisenhower's chief of staff Sherman Adams understood that "Eisenhower never felt that he would be able to negotiate successfully with Stalin."[12] But when Eisenhower saw Winston Churchill in New York on January 7, 1953, he referred to an idea he was thinking to propose in his inaugural address: "to meet anyone to promote peace and even volunteer to travel to a neutral country for such talks." This would entail seeing Stalin, perhaps in Stockholm. Although Churchill had no objection, he warned Eisenhower that such a meeting could raise "vast hopes" and that it would be better to wait several months before such a "momentous adventure" should take place.[13] By the time the president delivered his address two weeks later he had decided to drop a reference to a meeting with Stalin. He remained determined not to see the Kremlin leader until the fighting in Korea came to an end.

The first Republican president in twenty years (since Herbert Hoover had left office in 1933), Eisenhower, along with Foster Dulles, was determined to show that Republicans "could prosecute the Cold War harder and more effectively than the Democrats had done."[14] In his first State of the Union Address in early February, the president insisted—consistent with the rhetoric of his presidential campaign—that his administration wanted to see "liberation of the 800,000,000 living under Red terror."[15] But the idea of a meeting between Eisenhower and Stalin persisted. At a press conference on February 25, Eisenhower was asked about a summit. "I would meet with anybody anywhere, where I thought there was the slightest chance of doing any good."[16] And the Kremlin too was not above floating such a possibility. Just days before Stalin's death, *Newsweek* claimed that the "Russians are reported suggesting a Stalin–Eisenhower meeting in Berlin or Vienna. They are offering to end the Korean War and withdraw their troops from Germany and Austria. In return they are asking an American commitment 'not to rearm Germany.'"[17]

At that time Foster Dulles was eagerly trying to assemble the European Defense Community (EDC) which would include a newly sovereign and rearmed West Germany along with France, Italy, Belgium, the Netherlands, and Luxembourg.[18] Creation of the EDC had been a fundamental priority of President Truman and now it was up to Eisenhower and Foster Dulles to make it a reality. By anchoring West Germany in a military alliance linked to NATO, the Americans intended to end the Allied occupation and integrate the Federal Republic into the West. The EDC represented "the acid test of Western cohesion and readiness to stand up to the Soviet threat," as the scholar Vojtech Mastny once concluded.[19] But the French were nervous about rearming West Germany—Germany had invaded France on three occasions in the not-so-distant past, in 1870, 1914, and 1940—and French support would be necessary for German rearmament to go forward. For the Kremlin the proposed Stalin–Eisenhower meeting may have been nothing more than an attempt to confuse European policymakers and forestall if not prevent Foster Dulles' plan. Stalin's death brought an end to this ploy.

His collapse also created the first severe test for the new administration. When word of his illness reached Washington, one high-ranking US intelligence official was wary of any precipitous action. Frank Wisner was in charge of covert CIA operations in Eastern Europe where, beginning in 1949, the United States had been air-dropping agents into the Soviet Union to assist resistance forces in Lithuania and Ukraine and mounting even more aggressive covert actions in Poland, including the supply of agents and arms to an anti-communist resistance movement.[20] As soon as Wisner heard the news early on the morning of March 4 he rushed to see CIA director Allen Dulles and urged him to counsel restraint. Dulles brought Wisner to the home of his older brother, Secretary of State John Foster Dulles, who accepted Wisner's advice: If the United States tried to provoke a revolt, the Red Army would ruthlessly intervene. The anti-communist underground was "unarmed and not prepared. The CIA needed time to organize its clandestine forces and get arms dumps and commando forces ready to exploit the situation."[21] The United States would not do anything rash.

Within hours Eisenhower chaired a meeting of the National Security Council where he sought advice from senior officials. No one anticipated that Stalin's heirs might be easier to negotiate with. Vice President Richard Nixon, prompted by longstanding Congressional pressure to reduce military expenditures, saw the need to caution Congress that "Stalin's successor might very well prove more difficult to deal with than Stalin himself." Foster Dulles quickly voiced his agreement. But Eisenhower, while agreeing with Nixon and Foster Dulles, went even further by making the astonishing and altogether baseless statement that "it was his conviction that at the end of the last war Stalin would have preferred an easing of the tension between the Soviet Union and the Western powers, but the Politburo had insisted on heightening the tempo of the cold war and Stalin had been obliged to make concessions to this view."[22] Inspired by a well-placed source, *Newsweek* reported that the White House "considers [Malenkov] to be just as tough as Stalin, more suspicious, and probably even harder to deal with."[23] It was this commonly held assumption and the strategic need to resist calls for a relaxation of tension that cast a shadow on American policymakers in the months to follow. As the historian Klaus Larres wrote, many Western statesmen worried "that Stalin's death had deprived the West of a formidable enemy image. This would make the unity of the western alliance and the continuation of the western world's expensive military build-up much more complicated to maintain."[24] Stalin was gone but the threat of communist aggression remained and had to be resisted.

In the wake of Stalin's illness, American officials also assumed that his lieutenants would need to consolidate their power and would feel too insecure to fashion a new foreign policy. A State Department Intelligence Estimate issued on March 4 assumed that "the policy decisions taken by Stalin will tend to be frozen for a more or less prolonged period with no one Soviet leader strong enough, or daring enough, to attempt changes."[25] The American chargé d'affaires in

Moscow, Jacob Beam, reinforced this view. Writing from Moscow that same day, he was "inclined to see picture as one of confusion, uncertainty, and temporary restraint in ruling group."[26] As Klaus Larres wrote, officials in Washington assumed that Stalin's heirs "would be glad if the capitalist world would leave them alone for a while."[27] They were facing the "greatest crisis since the Hitler attack of 1941," the veteran diplomat Charles Bohlen later observed, and so needed time and a more relaxed international atmosphere to consolidate their control.[28] This was the presumed mood US officials sought to exploit. William Morgan, the acting head of the Psychological Strategy Board, wrote at the time, "Our strategic guiding principle, as well as our secret goal, should be to do everything to encourage and promote chaos within the USSR."[29] At least some members of the administration were not looking for ways to lessen tensions with the Kremlin. They were hoping to gain a propaganda advantage in the Cold War—if not outright victory.

Later that morning Under Secretary of State Walter Bedell Smith—who had served as chief of staff to Eisenhower during the war, as US ambassador to Moscow between 1946 and 1948, and as director of the CIA from 1950 to early 1953—appeared before a closed executive session of the Senate Foreign Relations Committee. Under instructions from Foster Dulles, Bedell Smith asked the committee to quickly confirm Charles Bohlen's appointment as ambassador to Moscow. "The sooner we get him there, the better, because there is going to be a very unusual series of developments, one way or another."[30] The Kremlin had forced out George Kennan from his role at the Moscow embassy almost six months before, leaving the post of ambassador open.

To the relief of American foreign-service officers the president was sticking by Bohlen, provoking an ugly fight with right-wing Senators led by Joseph McCarthy, Styles Bridges, and Herman Welker. Bohlen was a close friend and colleague of George Kennan and, like Kennan, was an experienced diplomat, one of the most respected members of the Foreign Service, whose life's work was the study of Soviet affairs. He had served as an interpreter for Roosevelt at the Tehran and Yalta conferences and for Truman at Potsdam where, Republican senators clamored, the Western Allies had conceded too much to the Kremlin. For McCarthy all this added up to treason. With Roosevelt dead and Truman out of office, he and his Senate allies were still looking for scapegoats, even at the risk of embarrassing a new Republican president. In London, *The Times* observed with some regret that "the trouble [Foster Dulles] is having over Bohlen" was making it harder for him to employ "the far more controversial Mr. George Kennan again. . . . Thus it is possible that the new Administration will be unable to use at this moment the two men in the country who know most about Russia."[31] In spite of the pressure from McCarthy, who was at the height of his influence and happy to pursue "the politics of suspicion" even after Eisenhower came into office, the president refused to back down.[32] Cooler heads prevailed; Bohlen gained Senate approval three weeks after Stalin's death.[33]

Bohlen aside, the Senate Foreign Relations Committee was more interested in hearing Bedell Smith's views about developments in the Kremlin. For Bedell Smith the succession crisis after Lenin's death provided the only useful model for how things were likely to unfold. Bedell Smith assured the committee that Stalin "knows better than anybody else what happened after Lenin's death. . . . It is probable that we will see some sort of a testament by Stalin, similar to Lenin's testimony, either actual or post-fabricated, which will more or less line up the succession." But no such political testament emerged following Stalin's death. From the Senators' questions and comments it was clear that they were looking for signs of an implosion: a revolt in the satellite states, a palace coup, the collapse of communism altogether. But Bedell Smith advised caution. "This is not a short-term thing," he concluded. "We do not have an exploitable situation, and it would be wrong for us to expect anything in the way of change of any significance."[34] Stalin died later that night and still the United States had no contingency plan for what to do.

American officials joined Eisenhower in continuous discussions over how to respond to Stalin's sudden demise. Eisenhower had come into office with a promise to support the peoples of Eastern Europe as they endured Soviet domination. But now Stalin had died, giving Eisenhower and Foster Dulles an opportunity of profound dimensions to capitalize on Stalin's death in the interests of peace and do something to alter the trajectory of the Cold War. In spite of this opportunity, though, their discussions frustrated the president. According to his principal speechwriter and close assistant, Emmet John Hughes, Eisenhower told his advisers on March 6, "For about seven years, ever since 1946, I know that everybody who should have been concerned with such things has been sounding off on what we should do when Stalin dies—what difference it would make, how it would affect our policies. Well, he died—and we went to see what bright ideas were in the files of this government, what plans were laid. What we found was that the result of 7 years of yapping is exactly ZERO. We have no plan. We don't even have any agreement of what difference his death makes. It's—well, it's *criminal*, that's all I can say." As Emmet Hughes acidly observed, "No one felt like contradicting."[35]

To Eisenhower's embarrassment, the administration's lack of planning quickly became public knowledge. Just as Eisenhower was berating his staff on March 6, Anthony Leviero of the *New York Times* described how Stalin's fatal illness "caught this country's psychological warfare strategists virtually unprepared to exploit a situation that is regarded as holding great potential advantages in the 'cold war.'" He believed there was "slack, . . . inertia and lack of self-starting drive" within various government agencies. And since psychological warfare typically involved "sabotage, the training, arming and disposition of spies, saboteurs and guerrillas . . . within and without the Iron Curtain," according to Leviero, the administration was clearly not prepared to carry out such actions. Instead, the actions that were taken were "mostly in the nature of improvizations," like Eisenhower's religious-tinged message to the Soviet people, cited in Chapter One.[36]

During the meeting on March 6, C. D. Jackson was instructed to draft a message for the new Soviet leaders to be delivered after Stalin's funeral. By that time Jackson was working with the economist Walt Rostow who had been summoned from his academic post at the Massachusetts Institute of Technology to help outline possible actions. In line with their instructions, they began preparing a major speech for Eisenhower where he would invite Soviet leaders to join him in reducing tensions in Europe and taming the burgeoning arms race. The idea was "to hold up to the new Soviet leadership the option of ending the confrontation in the center of Europe and else-where, even though the chance of its acceptance was slight," and "that the initiative should be taken promptly for maximum effect." According to Rostow, they already understood the need "to pre-empt a possible Soviet peace offensive."[37]

On the surface, such proposals were measured and reasonable, designed to address the principal issues dividing the two countries with the hope that a message from Eisenhower to the Soviet people could lead to productive negotiations with the Kremlin. But Jackson was also looking to unnerve Stalin's heirs. He thought of the proposals as a form of psychological warfare, designed to put the Kremlin on the defensive. As Rostow himself explained, the speech they were preparing for Eisenhower was based on the desire to "[seize] a general initiative in the cold war. . . . It is essential that the initiative have serious diplomatic substance, and be developed with full professional diplomatic skill, even if the chances of immediate success in negotia-tion are rated nil. Nothing would destroy its effect more thoroughly than the conviction inside the Kremlin and in the Free World that we were *merely* playing psychological tricks."[38] But the administration was having difficulty coming up with the kind of "serious diplomatic substance" that might engage Stalin's heirs.

Writing about those days, Emmet Hughes remembered how news of Stalin's illness "quickly excited, and soon obsessed, official Washington." However, "As the capital began rather loudly to speculate on what might follow within the Soviet Union, . . . the American response to the reasonably predictable occasion ignited no flame that could be seen a foot away." For Hughes, the lack of a forward-thinking plan created a void in the political discourse that was soon filled with the fantasies of "prophets and dreamers, alarmists and zealots."[39]

Individual officials, various executive agencies and task forces put forward an array of actions, some cautious, others so outlandish in their desire to undermine Soviet rule that they exposed how little Americans understood about the type of dictatorship they were facing. In the final month of Stalin's life, Charles E. Wilson, who had served as chairman of the powerful Office of Defense Mobilization, urged the White House to prevail upon the Kremlin to allow the president to broadcast a "world wide message" of peace for a full hour directly to people behind the Iron Curtain. For Wilson, such an action could "mean more to the world's people than any event since the Prince of Peace came 2000 years ago."[40] Wilson's celestial sincerity was not enough to convince the State Department to take up his idea.

After Stalin's death the Mutual Security Agency advanced several aggressive proposals. Headed by Harold Stassen, a leading figure in the Republican Party and president of the University of Pennsylvania, it urged "covert" and "unconventional activities" hoping to rattle Kremlin leaders and provoke divisions in their ranks. Coming on March 9, the day of Stalin's funeral, the range of its suggestions was broad and ambitious. As others had done before, Stassen advocated a meeting of foreign ministers with the hope that it would lead to a summit meeting between Eisenhower and Malenkov. But Stassen's real intention was to manipulate Soviet leaders. He argued that Malenkov would be reluctant to let Molotov out of the country. "Presumably, Molotov's recommendation ... would be sought and there would tend to be suspicion of him whichever way he recommended." Stassen also thought the White House could manipulate Beria by inviting him to a meeting in Berlin with Walter Bedell Smith and with himself to arrange "the safe conduct and orderly passage of those who wish to leave the Soviet Union to come out into the Western world." Stassen believed that luring Beria to a meeting about refugees would create unease and suspicion in the Kremlin. But he was not done. He also wanted to see the White House plant false information with sympathetic columnists, claiming that Malenkov was targeting other communist leaders, like Mao Zedong, for liquidation, and that escapees from behind the Iron Curtain knew about "plots against each other between the four top Kremlin men."[41] Evidently, Stassen felt confident that his plans would sow sufficient unease and suspicion throughout the Soviet bloc that officials would seek to escape with their lives rather than become victims to a purge at the hands of the Kremlin's new leader; Stassen was ready to offer them sanctuary in the West. His plans were rejected out of hand.

Two days later, Eisenhower's senior advisers held a pivotal meeting of the National Security Council. C. D. Jackson presented his ideas. He called for a meeting of foreign ministers from the United States, the Soviet Union, Great Britain, and France, and for a major foreign policy address by the president to "the Soviet Government and the Russian people."[42] But both Eisenhower and Foster Dulles had objections of their own. The president was now changing his mind, "remembering his experience with previous four-power meetings" and how the Soviets had used them as platforms for their own propaganda; he would not endorse a four-power summit. Foster Dulles feared that a unilateral initiative of this kind would damage relations with both France and Britain and even topple allied governments in Rome, Bonn, and Paris. "The Soviet Union [is] now involved in a family funeral and it might well be best to wait until the corpse is buried and the mourners gone off to their homes to read the will, before we begin our campaign to create discord in the family. If we move precipitately we might very well enhance Soviet family loyalty and disrupt the free world's."[43] He also feared that support for the EDC would collapse should Moscow and Washington open negotiations because it would create the possibility, however remote, that the Kremlin would allow the reunification of Germany in return for a guarantee of neutrality. For Foster Dulles, according to Rostow, "the bargaining position of the West in a negotiation with Moscow about Germany would be stronger with EDC in hand than without it."[44] The group then put off the idea of a major presidential speech, believing it "should be postponed 'until an important opportunity arises,'" *as if Stalin's death alone were not opportunity enough.*[45] C. D. Jackson, his disappointment palpable, left the meeting not knowing whether he was a man "carrying a shield or being carried upon it."[46] The administration remained caught between competing impulses: wanting to find a way to unnerve the Kremlin at a moment of profound uncertainty while not taking an initiative that might disrupt its alliance with the Western Europeans. At the same time Eisenhower remained mindful of the opportunity created by Stalin's death and open to saying publicly that "he would be ready and willing to meet with anyone anywhere from the Soviet Union provided the basis for the meeting was honest and practical."[47] For now, though, the president would not make a major speech and would not countenance the idea of a meeting with the new Soviet leaders.

Foster Dulles urged Eisenhower to remain cautious. With the opportunity to rearm West Germany and invigorate a Western military alliance, Foster Dulles did not want to engage directly with

Stalin's heirs. He assumed that an initiative by the United States would undercut Western European governments and believed that only a ratified treaty to establish the EDC would provide the United States with necessary leverage during any subsequent negotiations with the Kremlin. Rostow later claimed that he and his colleagues expected a Soviet "peace offensive" and so wanted to forestall its advantageous diplomatic consequences by having the president offer proposals of his own. But neither Foster Dulles nor Eisenhower was prepared to take the first step, a reluctance that Eisenhower would soon regret. As Rostow later observed, Foster Dulles was so committed to the establishment of a new defense structure for Western Europe, which would include a rearmed West Germany, that "Stalin's death, and all the attendant fuss, was intruding on serious business."[48] Establishing the EDC was the cornerstone of Foster Dulles' policies. As long as the president shared the priorities of Foster Dulles, there would be no fresh attempt to reduce the dangers of the Cold War by negotiation.

Winston Churchill saw things differently. He had long believed that it would be worthwhile to hold a summit with Kremlin leaders. In March 1950, while Stalin was still alive (and Churchill was leader of the Opposition in the British Parliament and on the campaign trail in a general election), he called for such a meeting. "I cannot help coming back to this idea of another talk with Soviet Russia upon the highest level. The idea appeals to me of a supreme effort to bridge the gulf between the two worlds so that each can live their life, if not in friendship, at least without the hatreds and manoeuvres of the cold war."[49] But Truman was in no mood to reach out to Stalin. Churchill, who was again prime minister after October 1951, renewed his appeal once Eisenhower was in office. He dispatched Foreign Secretary Anthony Eden to Washington in early March 1953 to urge the president to meet with Stalin. (Eden was crossing the Atlantic by ship when the news out of Moscow reached him.)

With Stalin dead, the opportunities were too tangible to ignore. "Great hope has arisen in the world," Churchill wrote to Eisenhower on March 11. "I have the feeling that we might both of us together or separately be called to account if no attempt were made to turn over a leaf so that a new page would be started." Churchill was suggesting some kind of "collective action," a multi-party conference where British, French, and American leaders could meet their Soviet counterparts and iron out a new arrangement for Europe. The president responded the same day, assuring Churchill that he was "convinced that a move giving to the world some promise of hope . . . should be made quickly."[50] But Eisenhower, as respectful as he could be toward Churchill, was reluctant to make any dramatic gestures toward the Kremlin. Indeed, Churchill's idea "horrified" him.[51] Churchill, with his sense of the dramatic and the urge to continue to play a major role in international affairs—in spite of his own infirmities and the diminished power of Great Britain—insisted on the need to seize the moment. But Eisenhower could not set aside his loathing of the regime and its many crimes.

Just at that sensitive moment four incidents involving military aircraft threatened to disrupt East–West relations. On the day of Stalin's death a Polish pilot landed a Soviet MiG-15 jet fighter on the Danish island of Bornholm, then promptly demanded political asylum; his request was granted over the objection of Polish officials. Five days later, on March 10, two Czechoslovak aircraft shot down an American F-84 Thunderjet fighter over West Germany. The American government claimed that the Czechoslovak planes had entered the US occupation zone and fired on the American plane without warning. Luckily, the pilot parachuted to safety in northern Bavaria.

Two days after that, Soviet aircraft brought down an unarmed British bomber over Germany, killing six of her seven-man crew. And again on March 15, two Soviet jet fighters fired on a US Air

Force weather patrol plane off the coast of the Kamchatka Peninsula in the North Pacific. The Americans returned fire before escaping unscathed.

These incidents roiled public opinion in the West and hardly boded well for the attitudes of the new Kremlin leaders. The *New York Times* carried front-page articles about the incidents for several days, quoting official denunciations for the downing of the F-84; it was an "outrage," they declared, as American diplomats lodged "the strongest possible protest" with authorities in Prague.[52] In editorials on succeeding days, the *New York Times* called the incident a "crime" as "the tempo and savagery of these provocations seem to be increasing."[53] British officials were no less angry. Foreign Secretary Anthony Eden was still in the United States when he called the downing of the British airplane a "barbaric" attack, while the British High Commissioner for Germany, Sir Ivone Kirkpatrick, denounced it as a "deliberate and brutal act of aggression involving the murder of British airmen." In an editorial, *The Times* of London labeled the attacks "brutal and unnecessary," "cold-blooded," and "indefensible."[54] The Kremlin was acting with the same militant vigilance that Stalin had demonstrated against any airplane that appeared to violate Soviet airspace. The incidents suggested that the new Kremlin leaders were not ready to initiate changes in their relations with the West, an impression that soon proved to be wrong.

To Eisenhower's chagrin it was Moscow that made the first invitation to a dialogue. On March 15, Malenkov startled Washington with a statement of his own, declaring that the Soviet Union believed in "a policy . . . of prolonged coexistence and peaceful competition of two different systems, capitalist and socialist. . . . At the present time there is no disputed or unresolved question that cannot be settled peacefully by mutual agreement of the interested countries. This applies to our relations with all states, including the United States of America."[55] While Malenkov had made a similar statement during his eulogy for Stalin, the West had ignored him at the time. In the wake of Stalin's death, the new Kremlin leaders seemed intent on lessening tensions with the West.

They had no illusions over how Stalin had contributed to the threat of an all-out conflict. When the Soviet Union detonated its first atomic bomb in August, 1949, it broke the US monopoly on weapons of mass destruction. Two months later communist forces under Mao Zedong captured Beijing and established the People's Republic of China, creating a new and formidable partner to the Soviet bloc. All this gave Stalin confidence that the momentum of international forces was moving in his favor. As he told Chinese leaders in October, 1950, the United States "was not prepared at the present time for a big war" in part because Germany and Japan had not sufficiently recovered to provide America with military support. "If war is inevitable, let it happen now."[56] In January, 1951, the Kremlin called a secret meeting of Soviet-bloc party leaders and defense ministers. Stalin, Molotov, Malenkov, and dozens of Soviet marshals and generals were included in the gathering to hear reports about the armed forces in the satellite countries and to insist on an all-out program to greatly expand the size of each country's military in expectation of a war with the United States. The Soviet armed forces, too, doubled in size over the next two years. Spurred by the Korean War, the United States carried out a similar expansion of its military, vastly increasing the defense budget and doubling the size of the armed forces to 3 million. The United States, moreover, detonated the first hydrogen bomb on November 1, 1952. By then US air bases encircled Soviet territory making it possible for American bombers to reach Soviet soil. The Kremlin had no such capacity. According to Khrushchev, as Stalin lay dying Soviet leaders genuinely feared that "America would invade the Soviet Union and we would go to war."[57]

This was the world Stalin was leaving to his heirs. He had doubted their ability to handle such crises on their own, warning them that "the imperialists would wring their necks like chickens."[58] But his lieutenants were proving to be more adept than he had anticipated. With Malenkov's offer the Kremlin was looking to shift the onus for tensions in Europe and Asia onto the United States. Eisenhower now regretted his earlier hesitation, admitting to his aides that "it was too bad that he had not made his speech before Malenkov."[59]

The next day the president met with his aide Emmet Hughes. Hughes showed Eisenhower a draft of the speech he had written for him on US–Soviet relations, the speech that had been put off just days before. While Eisenhower liked what he read, he expressed his frustration to Hughes over how best to proceed. "I'm tired," he told Hughes, "and I think everyone is tired, of indictments of the Soviet regime. . . . What matters is this—what have WE got to offer the world? What are WE ready to do? If we cannot say that—A, B, C, D, E, F, G, H— just like that—these are things we propose—then we really have nothing to say. Malenkov isn't going to be impressed by speeches."

Eisenhower was looking for specific proposals to offer the Kremlin. "Let us come out, straight, no double-talk, no slick sophisticated propaganda devices—and say: this is what we'll do—we'll withdraw our armies from there if you'll withdraw yours. . . . We want to talk to the Russian people—if their government will give us so much unjammed time, we would do our best to give them facilities to state their side of the case." The president wanted to emphasize to the Kremlin how much each side could gain from a halt to the arms race. A jet plane "costs three quarters of a million dollars . . . more money than a man earning $10,000 every year is going to make in his lifetime." It would be better for the two countries to choose disarmament and invest the enormous sums they were otherwise wasting on weapons to produce "butter, bread, clothes, hospitals, schools, the good and necessary things of decent living."

While Hughes was in full agreement, he reminded Eisenhower that the State Department would oppose any suggestion of American troop withdrawals from Europe. Hearing this, Eisenhower could barely contain his anger. "If these very sophisticated gentlemen in the State Department, Mr. Dulles and all his advisers, really don't mean they can talk about peace seriously, then I'm in the wrong pew. I surely don't know why I'm wasting my time with them. Because if it's war we should be talking about—I know the people to discuss that with, and it's not the State Department. Now we either cut out all this fooling around and make a serious bid for peace—or we forget the whole thing."[60] But if Eisenhower wanted to push for "a serious bid for peace," as he suggested to Hughes, what was he prepared to offer Moscow?

Three days later Eisenhower responded to Malenkov at the outset of a press conference. "As you know, there has been an expression of an intent to seek peace, from the Kremlin. I can only say that that is just as welcome as it is sincere. There is a very direct relationship between the satisfaction of such a thing and the sincerity in which it is meant. They will never be met less than halfway . . . because the purpose of this administration will forever be to seek peace by every honorable and decent means, and we will do anything that will be promising towards that direction."[61] But such a vague pronouncement did not include a specific change in policy. Eisenhower continued to hesitate.

Behind the scenes, he was growing impatient with his advisers. As James Reston wrote, "There has been a lot of high-level brooding going on here about the significance of Stalin's death."[62] Eisenhower recognized that Malenkov's statements were "startling departures from the ways of his predecessor."[63] He talked of wanting to test "whether the Soviets were really changing their outlook, and whether some kind of modus vivendi might not at long last prove possible."[64] With Stalin out of the way, his instincts told him that "the new leadership in Russia, no matter how strong its links with the Stalin era, was not completely bound to blind obedience to the ways of a dead man."[65] His closest advisers, though, were themselves divided. Unlike Eisenhower, Foster Dulles dismissed Malenkov's rhetoric as a verbal sleight of hand. "We have evaluated these speeches," Foster Dulles told a press conference on March 20, "but we do not receive any great comfort."[66] His views prevailed.

While the administration continued to hesitate, the Kremlin rolled out a "peace offensive" of its own. Its many parts—a host of gestures and substantial policy changes, all reversing positions associated with Stalin—stunned Western statesmen. For the *New York Times* they constituted "a Soviet diplomatic offensive of broad scope and great speed. . . . Diplomatic moves in big and little issues [came] so rapidly that it [was] difficult for embassies in Moscow to keep track of them."[67]

The most immediate concession came over Korea when, on March 19, the Kremlin signaled its desire for serious negotiations to the Chinese. By that time, twenty months of futile negotiations had passed. Although the US, China, and both North and South Korea had all been looking for a way to end the conflict, it was Stalin's stalling and willingness to prolong the bloody stalemate that had gotten in the way. Ultimately, the Korean War would cause the deaths of 35,000 Americans, millions of Koreans on both sides, and hundreds of thousands of Chinese. By agreeing to exchange sick and wounded prisoners and releasing British and French civilians who had been captured and interned in North Korea—including two French diplomats, a newsman, and several nuns, along with an Irish priest—the communist side made humanitarian gestures that could not be ignored. The Chinese also suggested the return of all prisoners who wished to be repatriated and dropped their insistence on forcible repatriation. By resuming peace talks at Panmunjom, the Kremlin and its allies changed the course of the conflict, leading to an armistice agreement—essentially a military truce—on July 27, which persists to this day.[68]

Other changes soon followed that March and April. Within weeks after Stalin's death the Soviet delegation grew more cooperative at the United Nations. It stopped prolonging the process of replacing Trygve Lie as secretary general and accepted the appointment of the Swedish diplomat Dag Hammarskjöld. Hammarskjöld was from a neutral country, but everyone understood he was essentially a Western statesman; Moscow dropped its objections, thereby permitting the transition to go forward.

In a divided Germany Stalin had found ways to impede travel and commerce. With his death, Soviet military personnel opened checkpoints on the roads to West Berlin and stopped imposing unwarranted delays on heavy trucks. In August 1952, Stalin had closed locks on the Mittelland Canal "for repairs." This was the principal inland waterway that runs between western and eastern Germany, connecting numerous cities to other countries all the way to the Baltic Sea. His heirs opened the locks in another gesture of good faith. The Kremlin also decided to provide substantial funds to churches in East Germany so they could repair wartime damage. And the Soviet guard at Spandau prison in Berlin—where the four powers held the convicted German war criminals Rudolf Hess and Albert Speer—was instructed to greet his American counterpart by taking off his glove before shaking hands, a superficial but altogether human reversal of a Stalinist-era habit. Of greater importance, Soviet officials apologized to the British government for a recent fatal air collision over East Germany, and then arranged for the United States and France to join Soviet and British officers to discuss air-corridor safety.

The Kremlin was also looking for ways to appeal to Winston Churchill and the British public. It ordered the lowering of flags to half-mast in East Berlin on the day of Queen Mary's funeral in London; the grandmother of the young Queen Elizabeth, and consort of the late King George V, she had died on March 24. Three months later a Soviet warship participated in a naval review in honor of the Queen's coronation. The cruiser *Sverdlov* was the first Soviet warship to visit Britain since the war. Members of the crew were able to enjoy the tourist sites of London, including Windsor Castle, the House of Commons, and Karl Marx's grave. That spring Soviet officials also pardoned a British sailor named George Edward Robinson who had been detained following a drunken argument in Arkhangelsk; he was released as part of the broad amnesty decree. Other Soviet sailors enjoyed a rare pleasure: for the first time since World War II a group of eighteen from a ship that docked at Rouen came to Paris and mingled with the Easter tourists. In Moscow, the Kremlin informed American and British officials that their embassies, which had been ordered to move from their prime locations near Red Square, could now remain. The British decided to keep their embassy where it was, but the Americans, needing more space, moved theirs anyway.

Western reporters in Moscow also noted several other unexpected changes. The Kremlin issued visas to a group of seven American newspaper and radio executives, allowing them to tour the Soviet Union, a gesture the *New York Times* said "made history."[69] The group was led by James Wick, a prominent conservative journalist who had long sought to visit the Soviet Union. The resident foreign correspondents marveled at how well the Wick group was treated; with little interference they were allowed to take photographs and interview ordinary citizens. Thomas Whitney of the Associated Press saw for himself "how burdensome restrictions . . . could be lifted in order to make a good impression." The visitors were permitted to file dispatches directly by telephone from their hotel rooms with little if any censorship. Whitney organized a farewell party for them on their final evening in Moscow and invited American diplomats and officials of the Soviet Press Department to join them at a restaurant. He was astonished when several Soviet officials, along with their wives, joined the gathering in a relaxed and friendly manner.[70]

These gestures and changes in policy were matched by an invitation from the Soviet ambassador in Washington, Georgi Zarubin, to

Charles Bohlen to meet with him on the eve of his departure for Moscow. Zarubin was friendly and emphasized how all ambassadors should work to improve bilateral relations. Noting positive steps over the question of the Korean War, he expressed the hope for progress in other areas as well.

Time found these changes "bewildering, welcome, sinister."[71] The *New York Times* saw things differently, noting in an editorial on April 2 that "an unmistakably softer wind has begun to blow out of Moscow and the various communist moves are beginning to fall into a pattern which, if completed and validated, holds out the promise of at least a temporary easing of international tensions."[72] Six days later—and four days after the Kremlin's public disavowal of the Doctors' Plot—CIA director Allen Dulles spoke before a meeting of the National Security Council. He described in some detail the changes coming out of Moscow. It was true "that the CIA had originally believed that after Stalin's death [his heirs] would play a very cautious game [and] ... would faithfully adhere to Stalin's policies for a very considerable time." But now Dulles acknowledged that "neither of these estimates had actually proved to be true." In what must have been a startling report for everyone in the room, he confirmed that the new Soviet leaders were adopting "quite shattering departures ... from the policies of the Stalin regime," including audacious domestic reforms and major departures in foreign policy that had to be recognized as not only "significant" but "astonishing."[73] (A month earlier Walt Rostow had advised the State Department that "As in the case of Lenin's death, the regime is likely to use the device of invoking Stalin's name in justification for all its major acts."[74] The opposite was, in fact, taking place. The new Soviet leaders were taking one step after another and each was repudiating some aspect of Stalinist policy.) In conclusion, Dulles conceded that this new set of policies "had come much earlier and was being pursued much more systematically than the CIA had expected."[75] A State Department official also acknowledged that "there have been more Soviet gestures toward the West than at any other similar period."[76] These developments bewildered Dulles. Like his brother, the secretary of state, he refused to see these changes as an opportunity to improve relations with Moscow, advising the president that there was "no ground for the belief that there [will] be any change in the basic hostility of the Soviet Union to the free world."[77] Soviet moves so startled American leaders that they reinforced their assumptions about Kremlin politics rather than causing them to review their assumptions in light of these unforeseen developments.

Watching from Moscow, Harrison Salisbury recalled a famous passage from Bernard Pares' classic history of Russia. A century before, the conservative and deeply repressive Tsar Nicholas I had died on March 2, 1855, "and with him fell in ruins the system of which his personality was everywhere regarded as the incarnation.... The new sovereign, Aleksandr II, had had his political training under the oppressive and reactionary regime of his father, to whom he was greatly attached and entirely loyal," as Pares wrote. But Aleksandr II soon embarked on a program of serious reform. The initial changes were relatively modest; he gave permission for travel abroad and relaxed restrictions on university life that Nicholas I had imposed. He soon relaxed political censorship, as well. "Alexander's first liberal measures were greeted with the greatest enthusiasm, but the public, which had not recovered from the pressure of the police regime under Nicholas, waited more or less passively for benefits to be thrown to it."[78] It was not until 1861 that Aleksandr declared the emancipation of the serfs, a dramatic break with this longstanding and shameful Russian tradition. For his series of reforms, Russians often remember Aleksandr II as the "Tsar-liberator." But there was no expectation that he, on succeeding his reactionary father, would initiate such extraordinary changes. For Salisbury, the lesson was clear. "If one asks how men who loyally served Dictator Stalin can put into effect a series of liberal policies, I can only point to the parallel of Alexander," he wrote that July. But American policymakers preferred to ignore the lessons of Russian history, the ebb and flow of repression and reform that Pares so noted. "There seems to be a persistent tendency on the part of some of the single-track American commentators to relate all the easing of restrictions inside Russia to a 'peace offensive,'" Salisbury wrote. "I think this is short-sighted. These are dramatic changes put into effect for domestic reasons by people who give every appearance of believing in what they are doing."[79] It would be up to Eisenhower to sort out what direction to take his administration.

* * *

In light of the Soviet "peace offensive," President Eisenhower saw the need to appear flexible and forthcoming. "The past speaks for itself," he told Hughes. "I am interested in the future. Both their government and ours have new men in them. The slate is clean. Now let us begin talking to each other."[80] But the White House required another month of intense drafting and debate as Eisenhower and his advisers grappled with the text of a major speech about Soviet–American relations, the speech that had been initially proposed for the day after Stalin's funeral. They were equally divided over the setting of the president's address: before Congress or the United Nations General Assembly, the Pan-American Union, or even a fireside chat similar to how Franklin Roosevelt had soothed American nerves during the Depression. The drawn-out process tried the patience of Eisenhower's advisers. As C. D. Jackson wrote to him on April 2, "we have given a virtual monopoly to the Soviets over the minds of people all over the world—and in that month, they have moved with vigor and disarming plausibility."[81] Still, the administration was not ready.

Emmet Hughes was principally responsible for drafting the speech. He was in regular contact with the State Department so that Foster Dulles could review the text. Foster Dulles was especially worried that Eisenhower's words might prove to be too conciliatory, leaving the president obliged to meet with Malenkov should the Kremlin respond with an invitation of its own; the Secretary of State wanted to make sure that the speech would not lead to direct negotiations. Eisenhower, for example, was willing to meet "halfway" any tangible proposals in "any congress or conference or meeting" with the Soviets. But Foster Dulles had the words removed. Under pressure from the secretary of state, Hughes took out the president's idea that each side grant the other unjammed radio time; it savored "too much of a publicity stunt." Hughes also cut Eisenhower's "renewed offer to travel to meet Soviet leaders." As he explained to the president, no doubt with the encouragement of Foster Dulles, the offer crossed the line "between *firm* and *conciliatory*" and might "suggest an over-anxiety far from our intentions."[82] Foster Dulles, moreover, insisted that the speech refer to ongoing disputes, like the signing of the Austrian State Treaty where, under Stalin, negotiations had dragged on without result, and the release of surviving German prisoners of war who were still held in Soviet camps. He wanted Eisenhower to require the Kremlin to permit "genuine political self-determination for the captive nations of Eastern Europe," as Townsend Hoopes concluded in his biography of Foster Dulles. "This last point," for Hoopes, "went to the roots of the emotional Soviet concern for its own safety," as Foster Dulles surely understood, and so it was "safe to say that his move to include it was another effort to foreclose any possibility of serious negotiation with the post-Stalin government."[83] Foster Dulles was determined to prevent any move by the president that could be taken as a lack of resolve. As he declared at a meeting of the National Security Council on March 25, he continued to look for "ways and means of ending the peril represented by the Soviet Union. This . . . could be done by inducing the disintegration of Soviet power. This power is already overextended. . . . If we keep our pressures on, psychological and otherwise, we may either force a collapse of the Kremlin regime or else transform the Soviet orbit from a union of satellites dedicated to aggression, into a coalition for defense only."[84] Foster Dulles was in no mood to relent.

While the Soviet "peace offensive" continued, it was not until the middle of April, six weeks after Stalin's death, that Eisenhower was ready to address both the American people and the Soviet leadership. This was his famous speech—The Chance for Peace—which he delivered to a meeting of the American Society of Newspaper Editors in Washington on April 16. Three factors governed Eisenhower's approach. He wanted to regain the initiative, "to say what we've got to say so that every person on earth can understand it."[85] He wanted to challenge the Kremlin while reassuring European allies that American policies would neither provoke war nor increase the continent's vulnerability to communist subversion. Finally, he wanted to be careful not to ruffle the feathers of right-wing Republicans, most notably Senator McCarthy, who would be alert to any hint of "appeasement" with the Kremlin.

For many of Eisenhower's admirers this speech remains among his most politically significant, "certainly one of the highlights of his presidency," according to Sherman Adams.[86] Coming eighty-nine days after his inauguration, it was his "first formal address to the American people," as the president himself emphasized. Even today Eisenhower's heartfelt plea for the benefits of mutual disarmament remains among his most memorable statements. "Every gun that is made, every warship launched, every rocket fired," Eisenhower declared, "signifies, in the final sense, a theft from those who hunger and are not fed, those who are cold and are not clothed." For Eisenhower, "this was not a way of life at all. . . . Under a cloud of war, it was humanity hanging from a cross of iron." He advocated a reduction "in the burden of armaments," offered to negotiate over the size of military forces, and urged the promotion of atomic energy "for peaceful purposes only," while ensuring "the prohibition of atomic weapons." He challenged the Kremlin to reap the benefits of additional funding for peaceful purposes, including "a new kind of war, . . . a total war, not upon any human enemy, but upon the brute forces of poverty and need." And if it would not agree on a reduction in armaments, "where then is the concrete evidence of the Soviet Union's concern for peace?" As for Soviet foreign relations, "The world knows that an era ended with the death of Joseph Stalin. . . . The Soviet system shaped by Stalin and his predecessors was born of one world war. It survived with stubborn and often amazing courage a second world war. It has lived to threaten a third." Speaking bluntly, Eisenhower said that "it was the amassing of Soviet power" that was causing tension and fear in the world. It was Soviet moves that had "alerted free nations to a new danger of aggression" and compelled them "in self-defense" to rearm and unite. For Eisenhower it was now ironic that "the Soviet Union itself has shared and suffered the very fears it has fostered in the rest of the world." Knowing that the new Soviet leadership was embarking on its own peace offensive, Eisenhower challenged it to match its rhetoric with deeds. "Is it prepared to allow other nations, including those in Eastern Europe, the free choice of their own form of government?" This was a point he repeated more than once. As Eisenhower made clear, he was seeking to "end the present unnatural division of Europe."[87]

The American press responded with deep enthusiasm. *Newsweek* said that it "lifted hearts in the entire free world."[88] For the *New York Times*, the speech was "magnificent and deeply moving"; it congratulated the president for "[seizing] the peace initiative from the Soviets and [putting] their peaceful words to the test."[89] It was Eisenhower's soaring rhetoric that captivated most people—Sherman Adams credited Hughes with "elevating the President's language"[90]—earning Eisenhower praise from observers who had not been inclined to applaud him, including liberal-minded news outlets. For the *New York Post* it was "America's voice at its best,"[91] while the *New Yorker* columnist Richard Rovere, who often criticized the president, called the speech "an immense triumph. It firmly established [Eisenhower's] leadership in America and re-established America's leadership in the world."[92]

Sensing an opportunity, the White House organized an across-the-board diplomatic and propaganda effort to distribute the speech on both sides of the Iron Curtain. As *Newsweek* summarized its plans, "The Voice of America broadcast it to 46 countries. Radio Free Europe, which customarily broadcasts only in the satellite tongues, added Russian to its programming to reach Soviet residents and troops in its satellite states. US diplomatic missions in 70 countries were instructed to deliver copies of the address to foreign offices. . . . In Belgrade . . . thousands of Yugoslavs lined up to get them during the first day after the speech was given."[93] Similar coverage blanketed a host of other countries. In Germany, the speech was distributed to 921 newspapers and magazines. Three million copies were printed for distribution throughout Europe and Latin America. In New Delhi, over 100,000 pamphlets were handed out in eight different languages.[94]

The response to Eisenhower's speech thrilled the White House. According to Sherman Adams, "people behind the Iron Curtain prayed and wept as they listened to it, and Winston Churchill sent a personal message in praise of it to Molotov."[95] But aside from trumpeting the president's rhetoric there was little if any thought over how to follow up. The day after the president's speech, both a White House staff meeting and a cabinet meeting were held. They both frustrated Hughes, for one, as neither discussed what to do next. Eisenhower was in Georgia for much needed rest, leaving

Vice President Nixon to preside over the cabinet meeting. There was no mention of the speech or of US–Soviet relations in general. Under Nixon's guidance, the entire discussion revolved around tariff policies, the mid-term elections of 1954, and the need for Republicans in Congress to support the president's programs. The meeting left Hughes sorely disappointed, as reflected in his diary notes for the day: "I suppose a lot of people thought we spent this day in the White House talking about the peace of the world."[96] But as for addressing the arms race or the division of Germany, there was little appetite.

The following day Foster Dulles had the stage to himself. Reluctant to soften American policy in any fashion, he spoke to the same group of newspaper editors in Washington but adopted more aggressive rhetoric than the president had. Where Eisenhower had appeared generous-minded, Foster Dulles was harsh. Where Eisenhower had reached out, Foster Dulles threatened. "All will know," he told the journalists, "and I am confident that the Soviet leaders know best of all, that what we plan is not greater weakness but greater strength. The productivity of the free world is so prodigious, its inventiveness so phenomenal, that a military aggressor that attacked our free world partnership would be doomed to sure defeat." The US planned to beef up support for the defeated Chinese nationalists who had retreated to Formosa and to tighten a naval blockade of communist China. It was ready to increase "military and financial assistance" so the French could "suppress the Communist-inspired civil war" in Indochina (what Americans came to know simply as Vietnam). As for the satellite countries of Eastern Europe, Foster Dulles made clear "to the captive people that we do not accept their captivity as a permanent fact of history. If they thought otherwise and became hopeless, we would unwittingly have become partners to the forging of a hostile power so vast that it would encompass our destruction."

But Foster Dulles could not entirely ignore recent moves out of Moscow. "They initiated what presents to you and to me one of the most perplexing problems of our times," he said. "The Kremlin launched what is commonly called a 'peace offensive.' Whatever it is that the Kremlin has launched—and no one can be sure just yet what it is—it is not a peace *offensive*. It is a peace *defensive*." Their startling signals were not enough to signify a new, more positive direction and could not be trusted; for Foster Dulles, perhaps for Eisenhower as well, the changes coming out of the Kremlin were insincere, a kind of cosmetic window dressing. "We are not dancing to any Russian tune," he declared. The US would not let its guard down or allow superficial Soviet gestures to compromise Western unity. Given their history, Foster Dulles had little faith in the motives that guided the new Soviet leaders or what the future was likely to bring between them and the United States. "That must always remain obscure so long as vast power is possessed by men who accept no guidance from the moral law," he concluded.[97]

Taken together, the speeches by Eisenhower and Foster Dulles embodied the ambivalence of the administration. The president did not offer any substantial concessions to the Kremlin. Calling on Moscow to agree to a peaceful settlement in Korea, to sign the Austrian State Treaty, to allow free elections and the reunification of Germany along with full independence for the countries of Eastern Europe, he was not offering the hand of reconciliation. He was asking Moscow to capitulate, to accept Western terms for a peaceful settlement of their differences and Western terms for a new, post-Cold War arrangement for all of Europe. While his eloquent plea for mutual disarmament caught the world's attention and earned him much good will, he did not invite Kremlin leaders to join him at the negotiating table. As the scholar Blanche Wiesen Cook described it, the speech was "the opening gun of the post-Stalin phase of the Cold War."[98] And Eisenhower then allowed his secretary of state to deliver a speech whose tone and overall message contradicted his own. As close an observer as Walt Rostow commented that it "appeared to undercut the spirit, if not the letter, of what Eisenhower had said" two days before.[99] The veteran Soviet diplomat Oleg Troyanovsky felt the same way; to him Foster Dulles' speech sounded "as if [he] were correcting the president,"[100] as if he reserved for himself what he could not get Eisenhower to say on his own. Were Eisenhower and Foster Dulles working together, anxious to score a diplomatic victory in the eyes of the world but not commit the United States to an ambitious and uncertain negotiation with an adversary whose ultimate intentions remained obscure? In the weeks that followed, after all, there was no substantial diplomatic follow-up, no quiet diplomacy to build on the President's speech.

The president and his secretary of state did not operate independently of each other. "[Foster Dulles] always cleared everything with the President first," Richard Goold-Adams, an early biographer of Foster Dulles, wrote about them. "No major speech, no major move, no major contact with a foreign statesman was made without the White House knowing about it first."[101] German Chancellor Konrad Adenauer saw this for himself. He was in Washington that April for his first visit to the United States. "American foreign policy was definitely that of President Eisenhower and Mr. Dulles' role was simply to execute it."[102] Taken together, their speeches were meant to seize a propaganda advantage, to place the onus for the arms race on the Kremlin, increase the psychological pressure on an untested Kremlin leadership, and remind the world that it was Soviet intransigence keeping Europe divided. Neither Eisenhower nor Foster Dulles was interested in face-to-face negotiations with Malenkov or with any other Soviet leader. As Eisenhower later admitted, he had delivered his speech "with little hope [it] could evoke any immediate response in the Kremlin."[103]

The Kremlin, nonetheless, surprised Washington. The following week both *Pravda* and *Izvestia* carried a full translation of Eisenhower's speech, including the president's criticism of Stalin for the division of Europe, the needless arms race, and the Cold War in general. As Bohlen reported from Moscow, its appearance "without deletions or any attempt to soften the vigor of the comment on Soviet policies are in themselves of great importance and in my experience unparalleled in the Soviet Union since the institution of Stalinist dictatorship."[104] The Soviet public was being given an unprecedented and unfiltered opportunity to read a Western statesman's views of how the Kremlin was regarded abroad. Moscow was inviting its citizens to read Eisenhower's address and make up their own mind about his intentions. *Pravda* then followed with a thoughtful response of its own. Long, detailed, and respectful, the editorial challenged the president to outline specific actions he would advance in Germany and in Asia where tensions remained high. Yes, Eisenhower was blaming the Kremlin for the breakdown in the wartime coalition, but he failed to concede that there were actions taken by the Western powers and the United States in particular that contributed to tensions in post-war Europe.

As for Foster Dulles, *Pravda* did not hold back. The speech by the secretary of state was "belligerent," a word it invoked several times about various parts of his remarks. But in spite of such rebukes, the editorial concluded on a positive and constructive note: that "the Soviet side [is ready] for a serious, businesslike discussion of problems both by direct negotiations and, when necessary, within the framework of the UN. . . . As for the USSR, there are no grounds for doubting its readiness to assume a proportionate share in settling controversial international issues." In the context of the Cold War, the public give-and-take between Washington and the Kremlin was as startling as the "peace offensive" itself. But it would require both sides to move this unexpected dialogue to the level of actual negotiations.[105]

Both Bohlen and Kennan, among others, recognized the unprecedented tone of the Moscow editorial. For Kennan, as he wrote to

Allen Dulles, the new Kremlin leaders "are definitely interested in pursuing with us the effort to solve some of the present international difficulties." But the US should proceed with care, not expect negotiations to unfold in public. "Put out your feelers: we will respond," was how Kennan understood their offer.[106] Bohlen's note was also cautiously positive. "A great deal of thought and care [had] gone into preparation" of the Kremlin's response, he reported from Moscow. They were now "[tossing] the ball back to the United States" and hoping to continue a dialogue through diplomatic channels. Bohlen concluded with a recommendation that "US official comment continues to follow present line inaugurated by President's speech." But the US failed to follow up with the kind of creative diplomacy that the moment required.

Working in Moscow, Charles Bohlen saw for himself how the tone of propaganda coming out of the Kremlin was dramatically changing. While Stalin was still alive in November 1952, the ubiquitous parade slogans marking the anniversary of the Revolution were the usual denunciations of "war mongers," "imperialist aggressors," and "foreign usurpers." For May Day in 1953, though, "there were expressions of confidence in the ability to resolve all differences between nations," a theme consistent with Malenkov's declarations in March and a stark departure from Stalinist-style rhetoric.[107]

Writing in *Pravda*, Ilya Ehrenburg adopted a similar message. In a May Day article entitled "Hope," the legendary propagandist heralded the renewal of negotiations over Korea. "Everyone understands," he wrote, "that the time for monologues has passed, that now is the time for dialogue. Negotiations are not simply talks. Negotiations presume good faith from all the participants, a desire not only to talk but to reach an agreement." And he went further. "If a truce is possible in a hot war that is tearing Korea apart, so everyone understands that a truce is possible in a cold war that is ravaging all peoples, a truce that the world should support."[108] Coming from

Ehrenburg, the article was an unmistakable signal that the Kremlin would consider broader negotiations with the United States.

The "peace offensive" also continued. Already in April, with the disavowal of the Doctors' Plot, Israel took the initiative to renew diplomatic relations even though it had been the Kremlin that had broken them off. Relations were restored in July, which the Soviet press respectfully and prominently reported.[109] The Kremlin moved as well to lessen post-war tensions with Turkey, a NATO country with a long border with the Soviet Union. In 1945, Stalin had made claims on several northern Turkish provinces and looked to gain control of the Dardanelles. But the new Kremlin leaders publicly withdrew these demands. And in early June, Molotov started the process of renewing relations with Yugoslavia, letting it be known that Moscow wanted to send an ambassador to Belgrade. There was another, more personal issue that had also bedeviled Soviet–American relations. Hundreds of Russian women had married Westerners attached to various embassies in Moscow; others had married American correspondents. After the war the Kremlin made it illegal for Soviet citizens to marry foreigners, making it easier for officials to deny visas to Russian women who wanted to accompany their husbands out of the country. By June, though, such restrictions were withdrawn; two prominent Americans, Eddy Gilmore of the Associated Press and US embassy official Robert Tucker, began the process of leaving for America with their wives.[110]

These continuing gestures, though, did not move either Eisenhower or Foster Dulles. The secretary of state remained convinced that nothing could be gained through a face-to-face meeting of Soviet and American leaders. It was Winston Churchill who continued to press for a summit. As long as his health held up, Churchill was unrelenting. With his sense of history he saw the need to rise to the occasion, to put aside long-held assumptions over what talks with the Kremlin could achieve. On May 11, Churchill spoke in the House of Commons during the first debate on foreign affairs since Stalin's death. Here again, Churchill, hoping to encourage Eisenhower, called for a summit "on the highest level." Anticipating objections from the Americans, he declared that "It would, I think, be a mistake to assume that nothing can be settled with the Soviet Union unless or until everything is settled."[111] Churchill's speech went far beyond his call for a summit. Impressed by domestic reforms coming from the Kremlin along with the "peace offensive" in foreign affairs—what he termed "the supreme event"—he did not want "to impede any spontaneous and healthy evolution which might be taking place there." He then set forth a broad set of guarantees that took into account the Kremlin's compelling security needs. Unlike any other Western statesman before him, he publicly recognized why Soviet leaders insisted on a friendly Poland. "I do not believe that the immense problem of reconciling the security of Russia with the freedom and safety of Western Europe is insoluble," he declared. "Russia has a right to feel assured that as far as human arrangements can run the terrible events of the Hitler invasion will never be repeated, and that Poland will remain a friendly Power and a buffer, though not, I trust, a puppet State."[112] Envisioning a united and neutral Germany, Churchill even offered to make Great Britain the guarantor of peace on the continent, an audacious and thoroughly unrealistic promise that belied his country's diminished power. But coming in 1953, just two months after Stalin's death, Churchill was challenging both sides of the East–West conflict to put aside the status quo, to reject the division of Germany and the broader division of Europe as a stable, satisfactory, and inevitable arrangement. By calling for negotiations "on the highest level . . . without long delay" he was insisting that Western and Soviet leaders could dramatically reduce tensions if they would be willing to meet with each other to settle their differences.[113]

In London, *The Times* was effusive in its praise for the prime minister. The speech "was magnificent in its broad survey and penetrating in its analysis," "the fruit of deep reflection and long experience."[114] The *New York Times* responded positively, as well. "When Sir Winston Churchill speaks on foreign affairs we hear what is probably the most qualified and is certainly one of the wisest voices on the subject in the free world." It recognized that he "was speaking for all of Europe" with his call for a summit, reflecting "a consensus in Europe that a meeting should be tried."[115] But in a news article the same day the newspaper recognized that "the British, like the French, appeared to be more eager for formal talks with the Russian leaders, even at the risk of failure, than was Washington."[116] It was no surprise that the White House and the State Department offered Churchill little support. Publicly, Eisenhower was respectful but hardly encouraging, insisting that he "first wanted ... some concrete evidence of good faith from Moscow."[117] The State Department referred reporters to the president's speech in April with its call for dramatic changes in Soviet policies. James Reston also cited official concern about the ongoing discussions over Korea and Austria, where lower-level discussions had still not yielded satisfactory results. Furthermore, the US was uncertain who could legitimately represent Moscow at the "highest level." Would it be Malenkov or Beria, or perhaps Foreign Minister Molotov? "Nobody in the United States Government pretends to know."[118] In Congress, Senate Majority Leader William F. Knowland compared Churchill's speech to Neville Chamberlain's appeasement of Hitler at Munich in 1938, a shocking objection given Churchill's ringing opposition to Chamberlain's negotiations with the Nazis.

For the famous American reporter Edward R. Murrow, the tepid response in Washington underscored American "hatred and hysteria." He remained "worried ... that our intransigence causes our allies in Europe to come to believe that we do not really want to ease the tension ... [that we are] determined to follow a path where the Russians must make all the concessions while we make none."[119] Murrow, as he often did, was not afraid to challenge Washington's official line and wonder about its motives out loud.

Churchill's speech also troubled Chancellor Adenauer. Determined to safeguard the sovereign independence of West Germany and oversee its integration into an American-led military alliance, Adenauer did not want to sacrifice West Germany's freedom as "the price of a fresh understanding with the Soviets."[120] A united Germany, which was disarmed and at least officially neutral, would not be able to join NATO or any other Western defense coalition. Among the allies, only the French government responded enthusiastically, hoping to be included in any anticipated Big Four summit.

Although the Kremlin had reservations about Churchill's speech, it publicly expressed some appreciation, particularly for stating that the freedom and independence of Western Europe could be reconciled with recognition of Soviet security needs, and applauding his call for "a top-level conference." *Pravda* also saw some advantage to highlighting divisions among the Western allies, noting how "Churchill, unlike certain other statesmen of the West, does not tie his proposal for a conference to any preliminary obligations for one or the other side." This was a direct reference to Eisenhower's "Chance for Peace" speech in April in which the president had laid out demands before the Kremlin.[121]

Behind the scenes, however, Kremlin leaders raised troubling questions of their own. Churchill had never been their favorite Western leader. He had championed Allied intervention in the Russian Civil War, hoping to dislodge the new Soviet government in coalition with its many enemies, foreign and domestic. His "Iron Curtain" speech in Fulton, Missouri on March 5, 1946 (seven years to the day before Stalin's death) signaled greater Western resolve in the face of growing Soviet domination of Eastern and Central Europe. But now it was Churchill, more than any other Western leader, who was calling for negotiations. Given Malenkov's appeal for talks within ten days after

Stalin's death and other explicit endorsements of negotiations, like Ehrenburg's May Day column in *Pravda*, it is important to recognize that Kremlin leaders were not in total agreement over the question of talks with their Western counterparts. In his memoirs Nikita Khrushchev belittled the idea of a summit so soon after Stalin's death. Suspicious of the British leader, he claimed that Churchill wanted a meeting "before the corpse was cold," hoping to "wring some concessions out of Stalin's successors before we had our feet firmly on the ground."[122] The Kremlin also understood that Great Britain was playing a secondary role in the Western alliance; that in spite of his prestige, Churchill was not in a position to mediate between East and West, and that without the approval of the United States Churchill's initiatives—even an Anglo–Soviet summit—would not lead anywhere significant. Internal tensions inside the Kremlin were also at play. Khrushchev had misgivings over Malenkov's suitability to lead a Soviet delegation to any summit. "After Stalin's death [Malenkov] was completely without initiative and completely unpredictable," Khrushchev claimed. "He was unstable to the point of being dangerous because he was so susceptible to the pressure and influence of others."[123] Molotov, too, having regained his position as foreign minister, was not about to allow Malenkov to outshine him in an arena where he had already represented Soviet interests to Western governments. Molotov and Khrushchev were well aware of Malenkov's insecurity and could not forget how he had ordered the doctoring of a prominent photograph within days after Stalin's death as if he alone, alongside Stalin, had welcomed Mao to Moscow in February 1950. That had been a clumsy maneuver to overshadow his "comrades-in-arms." It would not be repeated.

Western officials, though, could not dismiss Churchill's appeal altogether. A week later, the American, British, and French governments announced they would hold a summit of their heads of state in Bermuda on June 17 to coordinate their policies with regard to the Kremlin. Speculation soon followed that a high-level conference including the Soviet Union would soon take place, which Eisenhower felt compelled to deny at a news conference on May 28.[124] Moscow, as might be expected, raised concerns about the proposed Bermuda meeting, fearing its true agenda would be to "[counterpose] one state against another on principles of ideology and social political system." It preferred Churchill's call for a four-power summit with heads of state.[125] But then political difficulties in France disrupted plans for the meeting in Bermuda, forcing it to be rescheduled.

Churchill remained unyielding. On June 2, he sent a personal note to Molotov in which he assured the Soviet foreign minister of his hope that the forthcoming Bermuda conference would result "in bridges being built, not barriers, between East and West."[126] According to the diary notes of Soviet ambassador in London, Yakov Malik, Churchill told him on June 3 that he wanted to arrange secret talks with Malenkov much in the way he had enjoyed similar talks with Stalin. Once he had the chance to confer with Eisenhower, whom he was hoping to see in Bermuda at the end of June, he intended to convince the president to agree to a four-way summit meeting. Ever confident and ambitious, Churchill saw the opportunity "to improve international relations and create an atmosphere of greater confidence for at least three to five years."[127] But Molotov remained suspicious of Churchill's peaceful intentions and doubtful of his ability to persuade the United States to soften its sharp anti-communist stance. He would not support an Anglo-Soviet summit between Churchill and Malenkov. Churchill's health had also been faltering. On June 23 he suffered a stroke, which was covered up for many months; due to Churchill's "fatigue," the meeting in Bermuda was indefinitely postponed and did not take place until the following December.[128] By then, Churchill was no longer in a position to influence world affairs with the authority he had once commanded.

* * *

A yawning divide continued to separate East and West. There remains a feeling that Washington was caught unprepared for the concessions and reforms, both substantial and symbolic, that flowed from the Kremlin. There was almost an instinctual desire to dismiss these signals as a stratagem to undermine Western resolve, "a ruse designed to cause the free world to 'let down its guard,'" a belief Townsend Hoopes ascribed to Foster Dulles.[129] American officials could not bring themselves to recognize that Soviet leaders were seeking to free themselves from Stalin's legacy within the framework of their ideological assumptions. They did not want a war. They wanted to negotiate an end to the fighting in Korea and were discussing an accommodation over Germany; these were the two most urgent flashpoints between the two powers. Domestically, the new regime released over a million prisoners from the Gulag and publicly disavowed the Doctors' Plot, which was the culmination of several years of both a covert and openly aggressive campaign against the country's Jews. None of this was an exercise in subtle propaganda.

But Stalin's heirs faced a reluctant American leadership. Writing about those months, Oleg Troyanovsky described the frustration in Moscow that the Western powers "did not seem to appreciate moderation and refused to acknowledge the obvious truth that constructive steps by one party required a similar response from the other side." He remained convinced that "US policymakers did not show any signs of encouragement to those sections of the Soviet political spectrum that stood for better relations with the West."[130] Adam Ulam also sensed a missed opportunity. For him, "The wartime experiences left the American statesmen with an almost superstitious fear about negotiating directly with the Russians," as if Stalin had gotten so much the better of both Roosevelt and Truman that no subsequent American president would dare face a Kremlin leader again.[131]

Foster Dulles, in particular, worried that Kremlin peace-feelers constituted a calculated strategy to dilute the fear of Soviet aggression which was the basis of the Western alliance. (For A. J. Liebling, Foster Dulles was facing "a new terror": if the Kremlin relaxed pressure on the West, it would "de-frighten Europeans."[132]) In his memoirs Bohlen wrote that Foster Dulles "seemed to have a built-in fear of any personal association with Soviet officials. I do not know that he felt that the influence would be corrupting, but he believed that if Americans were seen in friendly conversation with Russians, the will to resist Communism would be weakened throughout the world."[133] For Foster Dulles, Soviet concessions were a moral challenge to resist rather than an opportunity to explore. How else can we understand his apocalyptic warning to Eisenhower on May 8 when he insisted that "the existing threat posed by the Soviets to the Western World is the most terrible and fundamental in the latter's 1000 years of domination. This threat differs in quality from the threat of Napoleon or Hitler. It is like the invasion by Islam in the tenth century. Now the clear issue is: can western civilization survive? . . . The present course we are following is a fatal one for us and the free world."[134] Perhaps Foster Dulles sincerely believed his own rhetoric, what the Cold War historian John Lewis Gaddis called his "penchant for overstatement."[135] Or perhaps, sensing how Eisenhower remained torn between his ingrained opposition to a summit and his desire to take advantage of a unique moment in history, Foster Dulles believed that his job was to remind the president that Stalin's heirs had inherited a ruthless dictatorship that they were not about to dismantle.[136]

CHAPTER SEVEN

THE END OF THE BEGINNING

Oleg Troyanovsky joined the Soviet Foreign Ministry staff a month after Stalin's death. As a ranking assistant to Molotov he saw for himself how multiple foreign crises confronted the new Kremlin leaders:

> There was a war going on in Korea and another in Indochina; the two superpowers were facing each other with daggers drawn; the arms race was steadily gaining momentum; the German problem hung like a dark cloud over Europe; there was no settlement of the Austrian problem in sight; the Soviet Union had no diplomatic relations with either West Germany or Japan; and thousands of prisoners of war were still in camps in Russia; the Soviet Union was at loggerheads with Tito's Yugoslavia for reasons that remained obscure to ordinary mortals; Turkey had turned to the West because of Soviet territorial and other demands; the situation in some East European countries was becoming more and more disturbing.[1]

At least in Korea serious negotiations got underway in April to resolve the fighting. This left the division of Germany and the potential for unrest in other satellite states as the most urgent foreign policy challenge facing the Kremlin. With the Red Army ensuring control throughout Eastern Europe, Stalin had imposed harsh one-party rule along with rapid industrialization and the forced collectivization of agriculture. Not surprisingly, these policies proved to be highly unpopular among the occupied populations. During the final months of Stalin's life, even as he reinforced political control of these regimes with trials of former party leaders, Soviet officials were receiving intelligence briefings from Czechoslovakia, Hungary, and Romania warning of "gross inadequacies," "misguided policies," and "extremely detrimental conditions and disruptions" in the economy. Under Stalin, the Kremlin chose to ignore such reports, but his heirs understood the need to address them.[2]

Unrest in Bulgaria and Czechoslovakia, where workers protested the economic if not political arrangements imposed by the Kremlin, spurred their anxiety. In Bulgaria demonstrations in early May were confined to two cities each about ninety miles south of the capital, Sofia: Plovdiv and Khaskovo. That spring, labor conditions led to lack of work for many people in the tobacco industry. The official union arranged lists of who would continue to work and who would not, a process that angered the workers. According to an internal party report, "After looking for work at different places and not finding anything, people became absolutely desperate and that was what led to their fury."[3] Hundreds declared a strike and engaged in unruly demonstrations. As far as historians can document, this was the first example of popular resistance after the death of Stalin.

The immediate cause of the unrest was a rise in production norms, a frequent tactic by party officials to increase worker output without a similar increase in pay. Bulgaria's leader at the time was Vulko Chervenkov, who styled his rule after Stalin, assuming dictatorial powers as both premier of the government and secretary general of the Communist Party. As the strike persisted, Chervenkov was compelled to dispatch one of his party rivals, Anton Yugov, to mediate talks with the disaffected workers. Yugov had once worked in a tobacco factory in Plovdiv and his rapport with the workers helped to defuse tensions. They accepted his promises that the party would rescind the increased quotas and address other grievances. According to the *Manchester Guardian*, Yugov "was cheered and carried shoulder-high during a fresh wave of demonstrations."[4] There is no evidence that the workers had other, more political demands.

Events in Czechoslovakia troubled the Kremlin even more. As in Bulgaria, it was harsher economic measures that set things off. For over a year there had been rumors that a monetary reform would significantly reduce the value of the Czechoslovak koruna. But the regime promised otherwise, assuring workers that their savings were protected. So when the 1953 Currency Reform Act went into effect at the beginning of June, people were shocked and angry, none more so than thousands of workers at the Skoda automobile plant in the western Bohemian city of Pilsen. (Americans were familiar with the city because the US Army under General George Patton had liberated Pilsen in early May 1945.) Unconvinced by the explanations of party agitators, who were sent in to explain the new law and appease the workers, about 3,000 left the plant and headed for City Hall, which was two miles away, to see what, if anything, the mayor could tell them. Once in the streets, they were quickly joined by young people who broadened the workers' economic grievances to include outright political demands. For the first time since the imposition of Stalinist rule, demonstrators in the streets of an Eastern European city demanded the end of Soviet domination.

Angry and frustrated, they stormed and ransacked City Hall. "Party posters, propaganda material, busts and pictures were torn from the walls and trampled underfoot. ... Busts of Stalin and Gottwald [the late Czechoslovak leader] came flying out of the windows." A similar riot unfolded at a nearby court building where angry demonstrators destroyed files and office equipment. According to one participant, "the crowd tore down the red stars from two buses which had been parked [on] a side street and destroyed the flower bed depicting the Soviet star which had replaced the US Army Memorial." People displayed Czechoslovak and American flags in their windows, alongside pictures of Edvard Beneš and of Jan Masaryk, two revered non-communist Czechoslovak leaders. Aside from the ransacking of City Hall and the court building the only other violence was directed at members of the secret police—if they could be identified—and anyone foolish enough to still be wearing a party emblem on their coat. Local authorities were incapable of quelling the rebellion. It was only brought under control on the second day when security units from Prague reached the city. They imposed a curfew and martial law and arrested about 2,000 people. In complete control of the media, the regime succeeded in suppressing news about the riots and the nature of the demonstrators' anger. There was little coverage in the West.[5]

This turmoil compelled Soviet leaders to take unprecedented action. The question of Germany remained at the heart of their concerns. With the close of World War II, the Soviet Union, America, Great Britain, and France had taken control of specific sectors of the country. As Cold War tensions emerged, Berlin, which had also been divided into sectors, became a point of superpower confrontation with heavily armed Western and Soviet forces facing each other. By 1949, Germany was officially divided into separate countries: the much larger Federal Republic of Germany, or West Germany, and the German Democratic Republic (GDR), or East Germany. (The population of West Germany was around 51 million; for East Germany, it was closer to 18 million.) But the idea of German reunification did not disappear. From our perspective today, with the fall of the Berlin Wall in November 1989 and the reunification of Germany the following October, it seems hard to believe that Stalin or his successors ever seriously considered supporting German reunification. But Stalin was wary of a two-state policy, knowing that an independent and prosperous West Germany would eventually become a key part of an economic and military alliance with the Western democracies: to prevent West German rearmament became a preeminent goal of Soviet foreign policy. With this in mind Stalin offered a plan for German reunification in the spring of 1952 with an understanding that Germany would not rearm and that Soviet troops would remain in the country to guarantee the peace. Sensing the overwhelming advantages Stalin was seeking for the Kremlin, the West rejected his offer.

Stalin's heirs looked for an alternative. They knew his extreme policies had created the potential for unrest in East Germany, where a refugee crisis was undermining Moscow's confidence in the local communist leadership. In the initial four months of 1953 nearly 120,000 people fled across the border into West Berlin. But this did not deter Walter Ulbricht—deputy prime minister and head of the ruling Socialist Unity Party (SED)—from pushing through an onerous set of labor quotas requiring workers to produce ten per cent more for the same wages. Such a hardline plan exacerbated the crisis, compelling the Kremlin to try to avoid a looming disaster.

Just ten days after Stalin's funeral, the Kremlin rejected a proposal from East German officials to tighten controls at the border between East and West Berlin. Molotov called the idea "politically unacceptable and grossly simplistic," understanding that it "would evoke animosity and discontent among the Berlin population vis-à-vis the GDR government and the Soviet authorities in Germany." Two months later, Beria reported to the Presidium that "The increasing number of flights to the West [from the GDR] can be explained . . . by the fear among small and medium entrepreneurs about the abolition of private property and the confiscation of their possessions, by the desire of some young people to evade service in the GDR armed forces, and by the severe difficulties that the GDR is experiencing with the supply of food products and consumer goods for the population." It was a realistic assessment, based on candid and well-informed intelligence sources. But what were Soviet leaders willing to do about it? What could they do about it?

As refugees continued to stream into West Berlin, the stability of the East German regime grew increasingly fragile. The Kremlin grew more and more frustrated with Walter Ulbricht, who was determined to build up his own, Stalinist-inspired, cult; Ulbricht, for example, was planning an elaborate celebration of his sixtieth birthday at the end of June. Faced with this dilemma, the Presidium held a special session to review their policies on May 27, when they agreed on the need for serious changes throughout the satellite states, including East Germany. Soviet officials decided to force Ulbricht out and shift the country's policies in a more liberal direction.

What is striking is that Kremlin leaders had no illusions about the situation they faced in the wake of Stalin's death. The disturbances that had already taken place in Bulgaria and Czechoslovakia portended growing political instability throughout Eastern Europe. Stalin's rush to impose "socialist construction," including the inevitable rounds of harsh political repression, needed to be reversed. Three months after his death they were ready to insist on across-the-board economic and political reforms: a combination of more collective leadership, less repression, a greater emphasis on light industry, more tolerance for religious practice, and an end to forced collectivization. On purely pragmatic grounds, men like Molotov, Beria, Malenkov, Bulganin, and Khrushchev all agreed on the urgency for these reforms and the need to press communist subordinates to implement them.

In the initial weeks of June, they summoned the leaders of East Germany, Hungary, and Albania to Moscow. And they planned on holding similar top-secret meetings in July with leaders from

Czechoslovakia, Romania, Poland, and Bulgaria. In this setting, it is astonishing to hear the voices of Kremlin leaders speaking in plain language. Away from the limelight they were candid and discerning, with little evidence of ideological cant as they grappled with how to avoid severe disorders in the Eastern Bloc.

What they told the Hungarian communist leader, Mátyás Rákosi, applied to all of the satraps: "The Soviet Union bears joint responsibility for the type of regime that now exists in Hungary. If the CPSU [Communist Party of the Soviet Union] provided incorrect advice in the past, we recognize that, and we are taking steps to fix it. . . . But the key thing is that we must jointly devise measures to correct [the Hungarian authorities' own] mistakes."[6] And what were those mistakes? Soviet leaders chided them for the scale of their repressive policies. Beria, of all people, asked, "Could it be acceptable that in Hungary—a country of 9,500,000 inhabitants—persecutions were initiated against 1,500,000?" He acknowledged that even Stalin made the mistake of "[giving] instructions for the questioning of those arrested." Rákosi should not make the same mistake. "It is not right that Comrade Rákosi gives directions regarding who must be arrested; he says who should be beaten. A person that's beaten will give the kind of confession that the interrogating agents want, will admit that he is an English or American spy or whatever we want. But it will never be possible to know the truth this way. This way, innocent people might be sentenced. There is law, and everyone has to respect it. How investigations should be conducted, who should be arrested, and how they should be interrogated must be left to the investigating organs."

Molotov shared Beria's concerns, referring to "a virtual wave of oppression against the population. . . . They punish for everything, and punish insignificant acts arbitrarily." Yes, it was true, Molotov acknowledged, that "The tendency for bossiness that plagued Comrade Rákosi . . . originated in the Soviet Union." Beria continued the theme. "It is not right that [Rákosi] does everything. It was not even right for Comrade Stalin to be everyone in one person." For Beria, relations between the Kremlin and the satellite states needed to be reformed. "It was not the proper kind of relationship, and this led to negative consequences," he told Rákosi. "Celebratory meetings and applause constituted the relationship. In the future we will create a new kind of relationship; a more responsible and serious relationship."[7]

In all three instances—in East Germany, Hungary, and Albania—the party leaders of these satellite states came away chastened, pledging to implement the new, more liberal-minded policies outlined by the Kremlin. In Hungary, Mátyás Rákosi stepped down as prime minister, allowing the Moscow-backed party official Imre Nagy to replace him. (Imre Nagy went on to head the reform movement in Hungary in 1956, leading to the violent intervention by Soviet forces and Nagy's own execution in June 1958 on charges of treason.) In Albania, Enver Hoxha, who earlier in 1953 held virtually every significant position in the party and government—from prime minister, foreign and defense minister to internal affairs minister all at once—agreed to give up his responsibilities as defense minister and foreign minister.

But such intervention was too late.

* * *

On June 11, East German newspapers carried word of a New Course. Dictated by Moscow, communist officials were now acknowledging their "grave mistakes" and agreeing to "abolish forced collectivization, shift emphasis from heavy industry to consumer production, safeguard private enterprise, encourage free political debate and participation, restore 'bourgeois' instructors and students to the schools from which they had been expelled, guarantee freedom of religion,

[and] rehabilitate the victims of political trials." As the Harvard scholar Mark Kramer observed, "This sudden announcement, after a year of unrelenting austerity and oppression, came as a thunderbolt in East Germany." It was an admission of failure, a display of self-criticism, and a set of promises that were all unprecedented in the communist world, as startling as the Kremlin's disavowal of the Doctors' Plot two months earlier.[8]

Several substantial and symbolic changes soon followed. The regime announced the release of over 5,000 prisoners. They had been held or were awaiting trial for various property crimes, but if they faced no more than three years in jail they could now be set free. (Political prisoners were apparently not included.) And a pastoral letter from the German Evangelical Church Council was read from pulpits, "thanking the Government for having made peace with the Church."[9] Only weeks before, communist officials had severed telephone circuits between the two parts of Berlin, but now they ceased uprooting the telephone cables, reducing their efforts to isolate the people of East Berlin from their Western counterparts.

But the SED failed to enforce a consistent line, either within party circles or in the propaganda directed to the country at large. One party official ordered that references to the "construction of socialism" be removed from all party slogans and posters, a repudiation of Ulbricht's policies. But two days later *Neues Deutschland*, the country's leading communist newspaper, published an article in which it praised labor brigades who were said to have "voluntarily increased their own work norms by as much as 20–40%." Under communism, this kind of article would be part of a campaign to increase pressure on all workers to follow such an inspiring example of selfless labor.[10]

The authorities now appeared to vacillate, infuriating workers and leaving them with a sense that the regime could not make up its mind. This became an opportunity to press their case all the harder.

Strike threats and slowdowns grew more severe, with workers connected to the regime's showcase project along East Berlin's Stalinallee (Stalin Boulevard) taking the lead. Even while wartime ruins lay everywhere throughout East Berlin the SED was rebuilding along Stalinallee, creating luxury apartments and high-end stores that only party leaders would be able to afford. It was here that ordinary workers began a revolt that galvanized world attention. Within days angry and violent demonstrators called for an end to the Soviet occupation in cities throughout the country.

Despite the Kremlin's close monitoring of events, the riots that engulfed the GDR in mid-June surprised Soviet leaders. On June 15, when a group of workers tried to approach Premier Otto Grotewohl with their demands, his office turned them away; officials did not want to encourage such a misguided appeal by treating it seriously. Their indifference backfired.

The next day hundreds of workers took to the streets, hoisting banners and commandeering sound trucks and bicycles to spread word of their actions. Their numbers soon swelled into the thousands as they marched down Stalin Boulevard and other central areas; within hours there was unrest at every building site. By coincidence the SED Politburo was holding its weekly session that day with a focus on how to implement the New Course and its political consequences. Rattled by the unexpected defiance, it still required several hours of debate before a vulnerable and chastened Ulbricht agreed to withdraw the quotas. Officials issued a long and carefully worded communiqué admitting that "the administrative raising of norms was an error, since such a step should be taken only on the basis of conviction and volition." It was now up to the workers to "unite around the party . . . and to unmask the hostile provocateurs who seek to bring discord and confusion to the ranks of the working class."[11] But the workers in whose name the regime purported to rule were not about to toe the line.

The demonstrators' slogans grew increasingly political, including an appeal for free elections. Confident and defiant, they remained in the streets late into the night: "on countless street-corners crowds of a dozen to several hundred listened while the dissidents and those loyal to the Government argued it out," according to the *New York Times*.[12] With the regime unwilling to negotiate, individual workers called for a general strike in the center of East Berlin for the next day. Although the American-run radio station RIAS (Radio in the American Sector), which was very popular in East Berlin,[13] briefly mentioned this appeal, even this modest "reference was withdrawn from all subsequent news bulletins at the request of the American authorities who insisted that nothing capable of provoking strikes or demonstrations in the GDR should be included in RIAS programs," Arnulf Baring wrote in his detailed account of the uprising.[14] Western officials preferred to adopt an attitude of cautious reserve. At least on June 16, it was the workers themselves, using a commandeered sound truck, who spread the word about a demonstration for the next day.

That June 17, tens of thousands took over major avenues and public squares. Six weeks earlier, on May Day, half a million supposedly loyal workers had paraded through Marx-Engels-Platz, East Berlin's Red Square, enthusiastically greeting government leaders and the Russian commander, General Vassily Chuikov. Now the crowds voiced explicitly political goals, calling for free, all-German elections and the release of fellow protestors who had already been detained. They attacked symbols of communist power, including posters and statues depicting the SED and Soviet leaders. When a crowd of 25,000 converged on the House of Ministries (the seat of government) their presence threatened control of the regime's headquarters and required the intervention of Soviet troops, equipped with tanks and armored vehicles, to secure the building. Martial law was declared, while a military barricade was erected to cut off East Berlin from the Western sectors of the city. But that did not prevent fighting from breaking out in several places where Red Army units and GDR police confronted demonstrators.

News of dramatic encounters reached the West. A famous photograph of young men hurling rocks at Soviet tanks flashed around the world. The East German deputy premier Otto Nuschke, who was the head of the Christian Democratic Union, a puppet party that had been compelled to join the communist government, was trapped by an angry crowd of demonstrators who pulled him from his limousine, then shoved him into the American sector where he was taken into custody for questioning. Near the border between the Soviet and Western sectors of the city, a crowd tore up boundary markers, ripped a red flag from a border control shack, then burned the flag and the shack to the cheers of onlookers. As thousands surged through the streets, shouting at police and troops, Soviet soldiers "drove trucks zigzagging wildly up and down Unter den Linden in front of the massive new Soviet embassy" intending to keep rioters away from the building. They would leap off the trucks "firing bursts from their machine pistols into the air." Another phalanx of soldiers advanced on the crowds with fixed bayonets. Blocks away, demonstrators climbed atop the Brandenburg Gate and tore away a red flag that had flown above the monument to mark the Soviet capture of the city in 1945. In its place two young men hoisted the black, red, and gold flag of the German Republic.[15]

Faced with hostile demonstrators, Soviet troops directed machine gun fire into crowds of unarmed people. The Soviet commandant in East Berlin ordered a Red Army firing squad to execute a West Berliner named Willi Göttling, an unemployed painter who had left home on the morning of June 17 to collect unemployment insurance. He had been traveling on the subway from West Berlin directly under the demonstrations when he was picked up. His wife claimed he was not affiliated with any political party; she had no idea how he could have been involved in the riots. But the Soviets carried out a summary execution, accusing the poor man of acting "on the order of a foreign intelligence agency" and being "one of the active organizers of provocations and riots in Soviet sector of Berlin."[16] He was dead before any appeal could be lodged or the true circumstances surrounding his presence in East Berlin clarified. Göttling was only one of many casualties. Five others were summarily executed, while at least 120 demonstrators were killed in the streets and 200 seriously wounded. No Soviet troops were killed or seriously wounded, while only seventeen East German officials, most of them from various security services, were killed and 166 wounded. In the days that followed, raiding squads of police and Communist Party functionaries broke into workers' apartments in East Berlin and in other cities looking for those responsible for strikes and riots; well over 3,000 people were arrested.[17]

RIAS reported on the demonstrations, helping to inspire further strikes away from the capital. One of the crucial aspects of the crisis was how quickly the demonstrations spread throughout the GDR. Over half a million people are now believed to have joined the protests, their demonstrations reaching 560 cities, including virtually all industrial centers. Workers took over local radio stations, post offices, and city halls. They beat up party members. In Magdeburg, a strike closed the Ernst Thälmann heavy machine tool plant where 13,000 workers were reportedly confronting East German police and trying to storm the Halberstädter Strasse jail with the hope of freeing political prisoners. Other strikes shut down shipyards in the Baltic ports of Rostock and Warnemënde, a silk factory in Rathenow, the famous Zeiss optical plant in Jena, and a factory in Leipzig which made buses and trucks for the Red Army. Production stopped at steel plants in Fürstenberg-Oder, Calbe, Brandenburg, and Hennigsdorf. There were reports of an angry mob at Rathenow lynching the local head of the secret police, while other policemen were killed in Magdeburg. Other strikes and disorders were also reported from Chemnitz, Halle, Dresden, and Erfurt. It seemed as if the entire industrial labor force of East Germany was not only on strike but was making clear, in both symbolic and substantial ways, that it wanted a change in the political arrangements of the country.

Western leaders, nonetheless, recognized the need for caution. They advised the mayor of West Berlin not to allow public meetings to be held without the authority of allied military leaders and ordered solidarity rallies to take place away from the boundary with East Berlin. They also limited public statements, wanting to avoid encouraging protests that inevitably could result in further bloodshed. Allied forces were not going to invade East Berlin to restore order or expel the Red Army. The West was deeply sympathetic, but powerless to intervene. As Ernst Reuter, the mayor of West Berlin, made clear, "The dreadful part of our situation is that we in West Berlin want to help but cannot. You can imagine what would happen if my West Berlin police marched into East Berlin. The Western Allies also cannot do anything."[18] But such restraint often frustrated ordinary citizens who wanted to help their fellow Germans in the Soviet sector. Crowds ransacked two separate offices of the SED in the American sector. Party officials had "to flee through the back door" while the crowd threw "furniture, propaganda publications, and pictures of Stalin and Communist East German leaders" into the street where it was all burned.[19] Throughout the week, residents of East Berlin tried to enter the Western sectors to escape the violence, including well over a hundred members of the People's Police seeking to desert with their families.

Faced with unprecedented disorder, communist officials knew where to place the blame, at least publicly. Premier Grotewohl pointed to "Fascist and other reactionary elements in West Berlin," even formerly active Nazis.[20] East German radio asserted that uniformed American officers "had directed the demonstrators from radio cars in West Berlin."[21] Soviet newspapers accused Eisenhower of "unceremonious meddling"[22] and also claimed that CIA director Allen Dulles had directed the Berlin rioting from a post inside the city itself, an accusation he publicly laughed off. *Pravda* referred to "foreign hirelings," a suitably vague allegation.[23] Tass blamed the US, British, and French commandants in Berlin for instigating the riots. Most of the unrest subsided by June 20, no doubt prompted by the intervention of 25,000 heavily armed Soviet troops. Communist officials regained sufficient confidence that they organized a "loyalty" parade on June 26, sending compliant workers down the same route in East Berlin where tens of thousands had rioted only days before.[24]

Walter Ulbricht survived the crisis, stunning Western governments. On June 19, the *New York Times* aired the conventional expectation about the fate of East German officials. Citing unnamed "observers" who were probably US government officials, the article claimed that the "uprising demonstrated conclusively the fragility of [communist] authority and power." All this left "the East German communist leaders ... in jeopardy. Soviet authorities may seek to transform yesterday's uprising to their advantage by denouncing the East German Communist leaders as saboteurs, oppressors and traitors, and telling people they (the Soviet officials) have stepped in to rectify abuses of power." But the opposite, in fact, occurred.[25]

Ulbricht not only remained in power but succeeded in cashiering other officials who had questioned his leadership. Ironically, even as Soviet leaders understood that it was his hardline policies that had provoked the riots, they were reluctant to hold him publicly responsible. They were caught between their earlier criticism of Ulbricht and the realistic assumption that their push for reform had helped to destabilize the country. On June 24, the Kremlin's leading officials filed a long, detailed report on the riots from a Soviet perspective. While the memorandum included the claim that "the events of June 17 [were] a great international provocation, prepared earlier by the three Western powers and their accomplices from the circles of West German monopolistic capital," the bulk of the long report described a full array of mistakes by leaders of the SED, beginning with the drive for the "accelerated construction of socialism" in the summer of 1952. This misguided and unrealistic policy objective had led to the weakening of food production and light industry, and a broad series of austerity measures that further impoverished the population. The report even referred to a shipyard worker whose cow had died but who was still required to deliver milk to the district council! In the face of such unrelenting stupidity and failure, the report made clear that a series of "unhealthy developments ... were the basis of the disturbances and agitations that broke out in the GDR 17–19 June." It concluded by recommending a series of dramatic measures, including the curtailment of reparation payments from East Germany to Poland and the Soviet Union, a broader provision of food and other material goods to raise the standard of living to match life in West Germany, and the removal of Ulbricht from his government post as deputy prime minister and abolition of his position as general secretary of the SED.[26] But the Soviet Presidium rejected this course of action, leaving Ulbricht in place. Soviet and German communist officials remained committed to the New Course, assuring workers that there was some merit to their actions—the SED conceded that dissident workers "believe they have been deserted by the party and government"—and offered specific concessions to mollify them: "increased wages, lower work norms, more shoes and clothing, better housing and more schools, theaters and kindergartens."[27] While these measures involved material aspects of life, there were no promises to address the political monopoly by the SED, to reduce the Kremlin's ultimate control of security and order, or to relax the censorship that dominated political and cultural life in the country. East Germany remained a Soviet-style dictatorship. Ulbricht emerged as the ultimate victor of the crisis. He held onto power as head of the SED, assuming the presidency of East Germany in 1960 as well, a position he enjoyed at his death in 1973. The regime lasted another sixteen years until the Berlin Wall collapsed, leading to the long overdue reunification of the country under democratic rule.

In an irony of history the controversial case of Julius and Ethel Rosenberg, who had been convicted of treason and conspiracy to commit espionage for passing information about the design of America's atomic bomb to the Kremlin, reached its conclusion while riots were unfolding in German cities: they were executed on June 19. They had both proclaimed their innocence, while communist parties around the world adopted them as martyrs to American injustice. With their executions, the communist press tried to use their deaths to overshadow the violence of Soviet tanks in East Berlin. Albert Camus, for one, objected to this cynical maneuver. Speaking at a protest rally in Paris on June 30, he refused to accept any moral equivalence between the two episodes. "But if I don't believe it is possible for the Berlin mutiny to allow us to forget the Rosenbergs, it seems to me still more horrid that men who claim to be of the left can attempt to hide the German victims in the shadow of the Rosenbergs."[28] For Camus, the uprising in East Berlin was the most significant event since the liberation of France in 1944. He joined others in demanding that an international trade union panel of inquiry be allowed into East Germany, an appeal that was summarily rejected.

* * *

It was Lavrenti Beria, not Ulbricht, who grew more vulnerable. In the aftermath of the riots, the *New York Times*, citing "diplomatic sources," expected both Beria and Molotov to face the most "significant repercussions": Molotov because "in his post he has at least nominal control of Soviet policy in Germany," and Beria because "his subordinates . . . failed to spot and uproot . . . an extensive underground anti-Communist movement."[29] Molotov, though, survived the crisis unscathed. Beria was not so fortunate.

Throughout that spring Khrushchev had been looking for a way to remove Beria. His designs against him originated while they all attended to the dying Stalin. In his memoirs Khrushchev recounted how he had alerted Bulganin that they would have to move against Beria at some point soon. Khrushchev was certain that Beria would regain control of the state security agencies and that, he told Bulganin, "will be the beginning of the end for us. He'll take that post for the purpose of destroying us.... If we don't do something and do it right away, it will mean disaster for the Party. This issue involves more than just us personally, although of course we don't want to let Beria stab us in the back. If Beria has his way, he could turn back the clock to 1937–38—and he could do worse, too." Writing for posterity, Khrushchev insisted that his motives for opposing Beria embodied at least some moral principle and were not based solely on his instinct for self-preservation. He had survived Stalin and now he had to outlive Beria.[30]

As editor of *Pravda*, Dmitrii Shepilov enjoyed a close-up view of how the new leaders were sizing each other up. He recognized that Khrushchev and Beria were the two most ambitious rivals to survive Stalin's death. "Both thirsted for power," he wrote.

> Both knew that after Stalin's death the machinery of one-man rule was not scrapped and consigned to the annals of history. It was preserved in toto; one only had to master it and start it up again. Like two beasts of prey, they eyed each other, sniffed each other, circled each other, each trying to guess if the other would make the first leap to crush the opponent and sever his jugular with his teeth. Khrushchev knew full well that of all the top party leaders, Beria was his only serious opponent, the only serious obstacle to his unchecked ambitions. He also knew that he was dangerous.[31]

By consolidating control of the security services, Beria was seizing an enormous amount of power. He controlled security for the Kremlin, the border troops, the secret police and its armed divisions, while supervising the personal security of the party and government leadership. According to Shepilov, Beria was "in charge of the entire governmental communications network and knew how to use it for his own purposes."[32] Stalin had also put Beria in charge of the atomic bomb project. He had supervised the country's leading scientists and engineers, assigned untold thousands of prisoners to build the necessary facilities, and took credit for the first successful Soviet atomic bomb test in August 1949. By the time of Stalin's death, the country was on the verge of testing a thermonuclear weapon—a hydrogen bomb—a project that Beria continued to supervise. With so much power and authority at Beria's disposal, Khrushchev had to move quietly to ensure that Beria not be aware of any maneuvering against him. Otherwise, the conspirators could easily fall victim to Beria's revenge.[33] By June, Khrushchev gained a majority within the Presidium to remove Beria, including the key support of Malenkov. But this was not enough. They needed the assistance of military officers to take Beria into custody and keep him securely from secret police units that could look for ways to rescue their chief. With Bulganin's help, they approached General Kirill Moskalenko, the commander of the Moscow Air Defense Region, and Marshal Georgy Zhukov, the deputy minister of defense, who both agreed to cooperate. Many military leaders hated Beria, knowing how thousands of high-ranking officers had been summarily killed in the 1930s on trumped-up charges. Their support would prove crucial to the success of the conspiracy.

The plot came together in the Kremlin on the morning of June 26. Bulganin, as minister of defense, arranged for a small group of lightly armed, senior military officers to gain entry to the Kremlin which was being guarded by troops under Beria's command. Marshal

Zhukov met them in Bulganin's office where they learned about their assignment from Bulganin and Khrushchev: to arrest Beria once they received a signal to interrupt a meeting of the Presidium. They were then brought to a waiting area which was connected by three separate doors to the conference room inside Malenkov's office.

As chairman of the CPSU Presidium, Malenkov opened the meeting with the startling announcement that the agenda would focus on Beria's activities. In Malenkov's eyes, Beria had "wanted to place the MVD (Ministry of Internal Affairs) above the party and the government … to pursue [his] criminal aims. … The MVD organs occupy a place in the state apparatus that offers immense opportunities for the abuse of power." Beria, moreover, had flagrantly violated the principles of "collective leadership" with his attempts to set one Presidium member against another, while during the recent bilateral talks with leaders from Hungary and East Germany Beria has behaved in a rude manner. Mark Kramer has examined a great many documentary sources about this meeting and concluded that Malenkov's initial accusations "were notably vague, feeble, or unfounded," as if Malenkov and the others knew they had to be rid of Beria but could not bring themselves to charge him with his genuine crimes.

As punishment for his transgressions, Malenkov then suggested that Beria be removed from several positions of high authority, including from his roles as minister of state security, deputy prime minister, and head of the nuclear weapons project. And still unwilling to call for Beria's arrest, he proposed that Beria be appointed minister of the oil industry, an important role within the broader leadership of the country but far removed from the levers of coercive power.

Having framed the initial accusations, Malenkov called on other Presidium members to air their criticisms of Beria. Several recalled how Beria had tried to promote himself at their expense, even during the time when Stalin was still alive and he could use his "privileged position" as head of state security to undercut other members of the leadership. Khrushchev, as might be expected, was the most outspoken. He outlined "specific charges with personal invective and obscenities."[34] ·

The meeting had gone on for over two hours when Malenkov pressed a button under the conference table, alerting Zhukov and Moskalenko to lead their men into the room. They entered by all three doors to pre-empt any possible escape. Beria was taken into custody at gunpoint. When they searched him, they found a scribbled note in a pocket on which he had written the word "alarm" several times in big red letters, evidently hoping to pass along a plea for help to his nearby men.[35] Beria was quickly led away to a secluded room where the group remained until evening when new guards would be on duty and it would be safer to bring him out of the Kremlin. To further hinder any escape attempt, they took away Beria's belt and cut off the buttons on his pants, making him use both hands to hold them up, a humiliating and effective means to prevent any surprise action. Under orders from Moskalenko, thirty heavily armed soldiers were brought to the Kremlin in special defense ministry limousines. Once they secured the Kremlin, Moskalenko put Beria into one of these vehicles and, surrounded by armed troops, he was taken to a cell in Lefortovo prison. In a sign of the anxious uncertainty that surrounded the operation, the troops were ordered to shoot Beria if he attempted to escape or if MVD men tried to intervene. Within days Beria was transferred under heavy guard and with other reinforcements deployed throughout Moscow—including "twelve armored personnel carriers, twenty T-34 main battle tanks, twenty-three self-propelled artillery systems, and forty-eight military support vehicles," according to US intelligence—to an underground, two-story, military bunker near the Moscow River.[36] Built underneath a small apple orchard, the facility was so secret that even Beria had not been aware of its existence.

It took Khrushchev and the others two weeks to begin a propaganda campaign against him. But first they sent a subtle signal to the public. The day after Beria's arrest the entire leadership attended the premiere of a new opera, *The Decembrists*, at the Bolshoi Theater; this was their first collective appearance since the days following Stalin's death. (Ironically, the story commemorated a failed coup attempt by disaffected, liberal-minded soldiers against Tsar Nicholas I in 1825.) But when *Pravda* reported on their attendance on June 28, listing each Presidium member by name, Beria's name was notably absent. Experienced readers understood that Beria was no longer in favor.

Another week passed before members of the Presidium explained Beria's arrest to a Central Committee plenum. The transcript of these secret discussions, which first became public in 1991, embodies the charade that came to surround the case against him. As Mark Kramer once observed, the meeting "was convened by Beria's rivals to reassure the Central Committee that Beria's arrest had been a matter of high principle, and not simply part of a power struggle."[37]

With Khrushchev presiding, Malenkov addressed the meeting first. He set the stage, decrying Beria's attempt to "dishonestly and— as it became more and more clear—with criminal intent—take advantage of our aspirations for unity, for harmonious operations in the collective leadership." Beria wanted to "place the MVD above the party and the government"; he went beyond their shared criticism of the East German leadership, preferring "to maintain a course for a bourgeois Germany"; he implemented the mass amnesty in March with "evil haste," needlessly releasing "recidivist-thieves."

Khrushchev weighed in next, accusing Beria of being a "great schemer," "a crafty person." He "was not a Communist" but rather "a careerist and an instigator." "Perhaps he was getting orders from foreign espionage agents." He is "someone alien to us, a man from the anti-Soviet camp." Molotov accused Beria of wanting to see

Germany "united as a bourgeois, peace-loving state," thereby relin-quishing the Soviet Union's advanced position in central Europe.[38]

As the plenum wore on, speakers continued to invoke ever more colorful abuse: Beria was now a "degenerate of degenerates," a "pigmy," a "bedbug," and a "chameleon" whose "program was—to create the type of state bourgeois order which would be useful to the Eisenhowers, Churchills, and Titos."[39] Among the political charges, the closest anyone came to the truth was when V. M. Andrianov from Leningrad painted Beria as a "Bonaparte, ready to climb to power over mountains of bodies and rivers of blood."[40] This was true and applied to all of them, though not in the way Andrianov intended. Having heard from the leadership, the Central Committee obedi-ently and unanimously endorsed the decision to bring Beria to trial.

We know now that the stenographic account that was published in 1991 was heavily doctored. Among other differences, Molotov originally acknowledged that Beria was urging a united Germany "which will be peace-loving and under the control of the four powers."[41] This was Molotov's own position at the time and hardly constituted the outright abandonment of the GDR to the nefarious intentions of the West. But now was not the time for candor. Now was the time to discredit Beria. The German crisis became a useful means for denouncing him and constituted the most outspoken language against him.

It was a coincidence of history that just as the Kremlin was suppressing the riots in East Germany and regaining control of its cities, Khrushchev's plan to arrest Beria was about to unfold. The timing was propitious. The unrest in East Germany made it easier to accuse Beria of wanting to relinquish Soviet hegemony, "to hand it over to the imperialists," a position it is hard to believe he ever fully advocated. In the wake of the turmoil, each of these men had good reason to distance himself from Beria and shift the blame onto him for any policy failures over the German question.

It is here that the subsequent denunciations of Lavrenti Beria by Khrushchev, Andrei Gromyko, and others make it difficult to reconstruct just how far Beria was willing to go for détente with the West. There was a consensus that Ulbricht's plan for headlong "socialist construction" had failed, contributing to economic collapse and the flight of refugees out of the country. The memoir literature, though, has several vivid accounts of how Beria disparaged the East German communist regime. Their consistency in substance and tone creates the suspicion that these accounts—coming from Andrei Gromyko, Vyacheslav Molotov, Dmitrii Shepilov, Nikita Khrushchev, and the longtime spy Pavel Sudoplatov, who worked closely with Beria— were meant to discredit a deposed, disgraced, and executed leader who would be arrested a month after the May 27 session.

While the Presidium was recognizing Ulbricht's disastrous approach, Molotov remembered Beria asking, "Why should socialism be built in the GDR? Let it just be a peaceful country. . . . The sort of country it will become is unimportant." According to Gromyko, Beria spoke dismissively about East Germany. "What does it amount to, this GDR?" he heard Beria tell the Presidium. "It's not even a real state. It's only kept in being by Soviet troops," a point that soon proved to be true. Shepilov provided the most vivid portrait of Beria's alleged attitude: "While his face twitched convulsively and his arms gesticulated wildly, Beria spoke of the new government that was being formed there in the most scathing terms. He berated it in every way. I could not stand this any longer and spoke up from my place at the end of the table. 'We must remember that the future of the new Germany is socialism.' Lurching forward as though he had been hit with a whip, Beria shouted, 'What socialism? What socialism? We must put an end to this irresponsible twaddle about socialism in Germany.'" Even Pavel Sudoplatov recalled in his controversial memoirs how Beria ordered him "to prepare top-secret intelligence probes to test the feasibility of unifying Germany. . . . This would mean concessions from us, but the issue could be resolved by compensating the Soviet Union, actually blackmail money for demoting the Ulbricht government from its central role to a peripheral one. East Germany ... would become an autonomous province in the new unified Germany." Khrushchev later claimed that Beria wanted "to hand over 18 million East Germans to American imperialist rule."[42] They were all maintaining, in other words, that Beria was willing to relinquish Soviet control of East Germany and allow a unified state to re-emerge in the center of Europe with only a pallid promise of political neutrality. And this only years after Nazi Germany, riding a wave of militarism, had plunged the continent into war and invaded the Soviet Union. If this were, in fact, Beria's position, there is no evidence that the other Presidium members were willing to go along.

The documentary record, though, does not support the claim that Beria's position on East Germany was significantly out of step with his colleagues. It was Molotov, in his role as foreign minister, who had control of Soviet foreign policy. He initiated discussions over the fate of the GDR. He edited the principal policy statements and guided the Presidium discussions over how to proceed. When Kremlin leaders met with East German party officials in June, they were all outspoken in their contempt for the nature of the East German state. After all, once the regime announced Beria's arrest to the public, it engaged in a systematic campaign of defamation that had little to do with his actual crimes. Arrested just days after Soviet tanks had crushed the riots in East Germany, it was easy to exaggerate whatever Beria might have said about Ulbricht's regime.

But after the plenum, the Kremlin still required several more days before *Pravda* broke the news of Beria's downfall on July 10. Such hesitation is easy to understand. On the eve of his arrest Beria had been serving as first deputy premier and minister of internal affairs, and was the second ranking member of the Presidium of the Central Committee of the Communist Party. After fifteen years in the highest circles of Soviet power, he had also received numerous prestigious awards, including Hero of Socialist Labor, five Orders of Lenin, the Order of Suvorov First Degree, and two Orders of the Red Banner. But now official denunciations reflected the content and tone of the rhetoric that had animated discussions at the plenum. As *Pravda* declared, Beria's "criminal anti-party and anti-state activity was deeply hidden and masked, then in the latest period, Beria, having become crude and rampant, began to disclose his genuine face—his face, the face of a malignant enemy of the Soviet people." His alleged crimes were varied and vivid. He tried "to place the Ministry of Internal Affairs over both the party and the government," to "damage the collective farms and create difficulties in producing supplies for the country," to "damage relations between various peoples of the Soviet Union," and to delay "liquidating violations of Soviet legality and strengthening the legal safeguards for Soviet citizens." Beria had "lost the appearance of a Communist," had undergone "a bourgeois regeneration" and had become an "agent of international imperialism."[43] To underscore his complete unmasking, Moscow radio engaged in a histrionic denunciation, calling him a traitor in nineteen languages.

It was all a deceitful evasion. The charges echoed the indictments from the show trials of the 1930s. Reaching into Stalin's bag of tricks—the only apparent recourse they had—his heirs invoked similar charges against Beria. But this time "history [was] being rewritten in a moment's time," the *New York Times* wrote. "It took a decade or more before Stalin's defeated enemies were transformed from great builders of the Soviet state to its supposed worst enemies. In Beria's case it required only the appearance of yesterday's *Pravda*." But the news out of Moscow left unanswered an intriguing question: would "Andrei Vyshinsky [preside] over another judicial phantasmagoria such as he created in the great trials of the Nineteen Thirties[?]"[44] That would require an open and abject confession from Beria and any accomplices the Kremlin would likely corral.

The announcement of Beria's removal both encouraged and confused official circles in the West. Commenting on the charge that Beria had been an agent of "foreign capital," an anonymous Washington official joked, "I wish we had known he was for sale. We would have paid plenty."[45] While government leaders understood there was a power struggle going on, they found it hard to discern its contours. Did his ousting presage "a period of cold civil war" as London's conservative-minded *Daily Telegraph* speculated?[46] Could it mean the imminent collapse of the regime itself, as at least some officials in Washington, DC, hoped for? For Allen Dulles, as he told a cabinet meeting, the arrest of Beria was "the greatest shock to USSR in a long time—almost as grave as Stalin's death."[47] Foster Dulles, according to Charles Bohlen, "was excited about the prospects of Beria's arrest's setting off a bloody struggle for power that might lead to the overthrow of the Soviet regime."[48] British officials "assumed . . . that there had been a struggle between one group that wanted to liberalize the Soviet regime and another that wished to continue the stringent Stalinist policy. But the commentators did not agree on which group was which."[49] On the streets of Moscow, though, aside from "great queues of people at newspaper kiosks . . . there was no sign that the news had aroused anything that might be described as panic or disorder in the ranks of Soviet citizens," Harrison Salisbury reported.[50]

Communist officials in China played along with their Soviet allies. Only four months earlier they had instructed "all party cadres" to study the orations at Stalin's funeral by Malenkov, Beria, and Molotov. Now Beria was joining former leaders like Trotsky, Bukharin, Zinoviev, and Kamenev among the disgraced traitors to the party. "Imperialist anti-Soviet elements have not been able to disguise their disappointment at the removal of Beria," the *People's Daily* asserted. "Now that their dreams have gone up in smoke they can do nothing but spread rumors of one kind of another." Presumably, this meant that the West was regretting the loss of a highly placed secret agent, just as Kremlin propaganda was suggesting.[51]

* * *

Beria was far from the only prisoner whose case awaited resolution. Hundreds of thousands of political prisoners remained behind barbed wire. The large-scale amnesty in March had not included them. Being left out only provoked greater defiance among the prisoners and led to disorders that spring and summer. With Stalin dead and Beria discredited they would not allow themselves to be forgotten.

Attacks on guards and informers, strikes, and escape attempts had occurred under Stalin, fueled by the impoverished, inhuman conditions and bolstered by the solidarity of the prisoners, particularly among the thousands from Ukraine and the Baltic republics. But none of these incidents reached the level of a mass uprising; conditions under the dictator were too extreme and unforgiving. After the amnesty of March 1953, however, prisoners in the special-regime camps grew angrier over their conditions. These camps had been organized in 1948 and given idyllic-sounding names, all the better to camouflage what made them so "special": Gorlag or "Mountain Camp," Rechlag or "River Camp," Dubrovlag or "Leafy Grove Camp," Ozerlag or "Lakeshore Camp," and Steplag or "Steppe Camp." With over 2 million prisoners in the Gulag, Stalin was looking for a way to organize the camp system into a more efficient part of the broader economy. Men and women were now more strictly separated. Political prisoners, who were considered more socially dangerous than a simple thief or murderer, were moved into special-regime camps, although the camp administrators found it useful to throw in at least some ordinary criminals who could be rewarded with cushy jobs in the kitchen or the camp stores in exchange for serving as informers or assaulting political prisoners if so instructed.

The security arrangements and punitive nature of the camps exceeded what the prisoners experienced in "ordinary" forced labor camps. For Aleksandr Solzhenitsyn, who was consigned to Ekibastuz, a part of the huge Steplag complex in Kazakhstan, in 1950, it had "an entrance but no exit, devouring only enemies and producing only industrial goods and corpses." (His novel *One Day in the Life of Ivan Denisovich* is set in Ekibastuz.) Solzhenitsyn's biographer, Michael Scammell, described what he found upon his arrival in Ekibastuz: security was "reinforced with double fences of barbed wire, between which Alsatians prowled leashed to a wire. A ploughed strip was created round the perimeter to reveal footprints if anyone attempted to escape, sharp-pointed stakes were set into the ground inclined towards the living compound at a forty-five-degree angle, the guards' weapons were updated and increased, and in some camps machine-guns were set up on the paths used by the prisoners to cover their movements from the living compound to the work compound, or from barrack hut to canteen."[52] Living under prison-like security, the inmates, except for working hours, were confined for the day in barracks with iron bars on the windows and then locked up for the night. Although permitted to receive letters and parcels once each month, they could only write home twice a year. Designated as "especially dangerous state criminals," this category of prisoners included tens of thousands who had joined armed resistance groups to fight against the Soviet regime during and after World War II—members of various Ukrainian and Baltic nationalist organizations, and soldiers in the Polish Home Army. Conditions in the Gulag had not broken them. They remained angry and defiant. Knowing of the March amnesty decree, they wanted a review of their cases and the right to benefit from the promises of change and reform (and rumors of change and reform) that were sweeping over the country. Most of all, they wanted to go home. That spring and summer, two episodes in the camps were particularly dramatic.

The first unfolded at a mining camp in Norilsk, a major forced labor point. Located in Siberia—Norilsk today is one of the most northern of Russian cities—the camp complex contained over 70,000 prisoners, many engaged in mining for copper and nickel. The uprising centered around Gorlag, a division within the Norilsk camp complex which contained several mines. According to different accounts, the transfer to Gorlag of 1,200 Ukrainian and Baltic inmates in the fall of 1952 led to the uprising. Their anger boiled over in May following the shooting of a prisoner. By the first week of June, a total of 16,379 were refusing to work.

The authorities hesitated over how to respond. The prisoners insisted on speaking with a representative of the Central Committee, understanding that local officials could not satisfy their demands for an outright amnesty. Under Stalin, violence was the only answer to such resistance. But in the spring of 1953, the Kremlin seemed willing to negotiate. A commission from Moscow, led by an interior ministry general, offered what seemed like a generous set of concessions: a nine-hour work day, visits from relatives, the ability to receive letters and money from home. But the prisoners dismissed the offer, wanting nothing less than the amnesty they had been denied. At that point, the Kremlin lost its patience. Troops descended on the striking camps, surrounded the inmates, then sorted out the ringleaders. When prisoners continued to resist—at one point 500 rushed the troops with rocks and clubs—the soldiers opened fire. Within days the uprising was over, leaving scores of prisoners dead.

Similar unrest broke out in Vorkuta, an enormous camp complex in the Komi region of Siberia just north of the Arctic Circle. With the discovery of large coal fields in 1930, the regime established a forced labor camp complex two years later to support major industrial mining. Within a few years, Vorkuta became the largest complex of Gulag camps in European Russia—there were over 50,000 inmates in July 1953—comprising many separate departments engaged in coal mining and forestry, with prison labor providing the timber necessary to build and maintain the mines.

Beria's arrest contributed to the turmoil. "Beria's fall was like a thunderclap," Solzhenitsyn recalled. "The officers and warders suddenly showed an uncertainty, a bewilderment even, of which the prisoners were keenly aware." The prisoners, particularly in Rechlag, a special-regime camp within Vorkuta, had managed to obtain radios and so were able to follow the news, not only about Beria but also about the large-scale demonstrations in East Germany and their suppression by Soviet troops. As Solzhenitsyn documented from his interviews with former prisoners, "the great excitement caused by Beria's removal coincided with the arrival of the mutineers trans-ported from Karaganda and Taishet (most were Western Ukrainians). Vorkuta was still servile and downtrodden and the newly arrived zeks astounded the locals with their intransigence and their audacity." Hoping to take advantage of a vulnerable moment within the Kremlin, the prisoners believed they could press for the amnesty to include them.

As at Gorlag, a number of the strike leaders at Rechlag hailed from Ukraine, Poland, and the Baltics. By the end of July, over 15,000 inmates refused to work, passively remaining behind the barbed wire perimeter of the camp. And as at Gorlag, the Kremlin sent high officials to investigate and carry out negotiations. But the prisoners wanted more than an improvement in their work and living conditions; they wanted a serious review of their cases by honest prosecutors and the right to benefit from the earlier amnesty decree. But the strike was not entirely peaceful. On July 26, inmates targeted one of the most hated parts of the camp, the maximum security compound where prisoners were punished with isolation in freezing, damp cells; they released several dozen, infuriating officials who now decided to intervene with force. Most of the prisoners relented, peacefully following orders to leave the camp in groups of a hundred.

Troops then sorted out the leaders. But in one camp alongside mine no. 29, hundreds of prisoners refused to comply and stormed the troops, only to be met with live gunfire. "There were three volleys,— with the machine gun fire in between." Scores, perhaps hundreds, were killed; the true figure may never be known. "The rest ran away. Guards with clubs and iron bars rushed after the zeks, beating them and driving them out of camp."[53]

The revolts that began in 1953 mushroomed into far more extensive and violent confrontations the following year. Solzhenitsyn was among the first to describe the prisoner revolt in Kengir, a subdivision of Steplag near the city of Dzhezkazgan, in the spring of 1954.[54] After forty days of open defiance, the regime crushed the strike with tanks and heavily armed soldiers. This confrontation, even though it ended with the death of nearly fifty inmates, compelled the regime to review more and more cases, to release broader categories of political prisoners, and permit their reintegration into Soviet society. By January 1, 1959, the total number of political prisoners convicted of counter-revolutionary crimes was reduced to 11,000, a harsh and unforgivable number for any society but a substantial move away from what Stalin had fashioned.

There should be no attempt to romanticize the changes his heirs initiated. It is true that after 1953 Soviet culture began to tolerate new and more diverse voices and greater openness to Western culture, including books, music, and works of art. The regime sought to improve the standard of living and guarantee a measure of personal security after decades of arbitrary and outright mass terror. But the Kremlin remained intolerant of "bourgeois liberties" and enforced its ideological presumptions with arrests, prisons, labor camps, psychiatric hospitals, internal exile, even deportation abroad. There would be no tolerance for any challenge to one-party rule, not within the Soviet Union or the broader empire. Still proud Bolsheviks, Khrushchev and his successors could condemn Stalin's worst crimes and yet preserve enough of the dictatorship to maintain their power and authority. Only after Mikhail Gorbachev decided, in the late 1980s, to stop arresting people for their non-violent activities or beliefs, release remaining political prisoners, and do away with censorship did the Soviet Union collapse altogether. That came in 1991. Without Stalin's brutal mechanisms of control the system of dictatorial rule which he had imposed could no longer be sustained.

EPILOGUE

After the initial public announcement of Beria's arrest in July, there was the usual round of tailor-made resolutions for workers to endorse, but these meetings soon petered out. The public heard that the investigation was proceeding and learned about the arrest of other secret police officials. As *Pravda* laconically reported, the Supreme Soviet, the country's nominal legislature, formally approved Beria's ousting on August 8 and ordered him brought to trial before the Supreme Court. But then the press grew silent; for several months there were no more rallies to denounce him, no further revelations of his crimes, no hysterical campaign calling for his execution. Perhaps Khrushchev and the others understood that Beria, more than they, carried the stigma of terror and repression and that if they pushed the limits of denunciation too far such a campaign would raise too many questions about their own collusion in the crimes for which he was *not* being charged. As Ehrenburg wrote of that time, "Millions of people still believed that Stalin had had no part in the crimes, but Beria was universally hated and was spoken of as a cruel and base creature corrupted by power."[1] Only a few months before, Beria had been among the triumvirs who stood by Stalin's casket and offered a eulogy. Now he was in disgrace—helpless, isolated, and under interrogation like his myriad victims.

Desperate to save himself, Beria dispatched several letters to his erstwhile comrades. He apologized for his "unacceptably rude and insolent behavior toward Khrushchev and Bulganin during discussions over the German question" and for his "tactless" conduct toward the Hungarian delegation during their recent meeting. He pleaded with them as if he were an unruly student apologizing to a teacher. He closed one letter with an offer to work anywhere they wished to send him and they would see that "within two or three years I will still be useful." Writing from an underground cell, he also asked for their understanding for his poor handwriting: the lighting was weak and he no longer had his pince-nez.[2] Beria repeated his groveling the next day, insisting that the Presidium appoint a commission to investigate the handling of his case, "otherwise it will be too late." He urged them to intervene and prevent their "innocent old friend from being destroyed."[3] Their only response was to take away his access to paper and pencils.

The Presidium still had to deal with the repercussions of his arrest. Vsevolod Merkulov was a longtime security official who had known and worked with Beria in Georgia and in Moscow for thirty years. Under duress, Merkulov sent Khrushchev a long letter in which he outlined the history of his work with Beria for the purpose of helping to explain how such a veteran party leader could become a traitor. As Merkulov observed, "It does not happen that such things occur suddenly in one day. Evidently, some kind of prolonged internal process took place." But all Merkulov could say was that Beria had always schemed to advance his career, that he had cheated at chess, flattered those above him and abused his subordinates, that "he did not love Comrade Stalin as a leader, a friend, or a teacher, but in reality even waited for his death (in the final years, of course) in order to deploy his own criminal activity." In the days following Stalin's demise, when Beria summoned Merkulov to his office and asked him to go over the draft of his eulogy, Beria was "happy, joking, and smiling."[4]

Other letters were not so useful for the party. A small group of Chechen-Ingush individuals wrote to Khrushchev from their place of exile in Kazakhstan. As survivors of the mass deportations in 1944, they knew Beria as "a heartless cannibal and barbarian. He exiled us employing the most severe methods." The letter went on to describe how whole families had been crammed into cattle cars and how the bodies of young children were tossed from the trains at stops along the way. There were only positive references to Stalin.[5] Their letter held Beria solely responsible. But the regime never referred to the deportations, either behind closed doors or in any list of his transgressions. For Khrushchev, whose authority was steadily increasing, and the others, such a letter, which spelled out an actual atrocity and not an imagined crime, must have been an awkward inconvenience.

Another letter reached Malenkov from an exiled prisoner in Kazakhstan. Yevgeny Gnedin had once been a prominent press officer in the Ministry of Foreign Affairs. But he was arrested after the dismissal of Maxim Litvinov as foreign minister in the spring of 1939 and accused of espionage. In his letter Gnedin described how he had been beaten "with rubber clubs" in front of Beria in Beria's own office by Bogdan Kobulov, who now was himself under arrest. They had wanted Gnedin to admit to various crimes in order "to deceive the party and the government." But he insisted on his innocence and paid for his courage with years of prison, labor camp, and exile. Gnedin's letter did not become part of the indictment against Beria and his accomplices. It touched on actual crimes that someone like Molotov, for example, who had succeeded Litvinov, would not want to see explored.[6]

A long draft of the indictment against Beria was drawn up in September. Almost a hundred pages long, it included a host of nefarious accusations: that his anti-Soviet activities originated during the Russian Civil War; that he unilaterally sought to negotiate with Hitler soon after the German invasion and agree to hand over large portions of Soviet territory in return for a negotiated peace; that in the summer of 1942 he was willing to hand over oil fields in the Caucasus to the invading Germans; that he plotted to seize power after Stalin's death.[7] There was no end to Beria's treachery.

The prosecutors took four months to complete their investigation before issuing an indictment on December 16. "Steeped in the dark rhetoric of Communist terror," as the *New York Times* observed, it repeated the earlier denunciations and found it useful to add a few more. Beria and his accomplices "carried out terrorist murders of persons from whom they feared exposure"—namely other party and police officials—and sought "to weaken the defensive capacity of the Soviet Union." If the initial charges echoed the language of the 1930s, these additional charges seemed similar to the Doctors' Plot without the layer of antisemitic invective.[8]

A closed-door trial began on December 18. Presided over by the famous World War II commander Ivan Konev, a marshal of the Soviet Union, along with other high-ranking party and military officials, it lasted for six days. As far as we know, this was the only trial where a Red Army marshal presided over a civilian court; the proceedings, in fact, unfolded "in the office of a member of the Moscow Military District."[9] Khrushchev had relied on the military to detain Beria so it may well have been necessary to sustain its involvement in order to ensure Beria's fate. The court confirmed the charges and supposedly heard the defendants—Beria, along with Stepan Mamulov, Vsevolod Merkulov, Vladimir Dekanozov, Bogdan Kobulov, Sergei Goglidze and Pavel Meshik—the so-called "Beria men" who were most closely associated with his crimes—admit their guilt. This was not an open show trial and the full transcript has never been released. According to Dmitri Volkogonov, Malenkov, Khrushchev, Molotov, Voroshilov, Bulganin, Kaganovich, Mikoyan, Shvernik and some others sat in the Kremlin and listened to it on a specially installed link."[10] As in the 1930s, mass rallies took place throughout the country, "from sailors at sea and from miners in Siberia," all demanding the death penalty.[11] Duly convicted, Beria and the others were shot on December 23, within hours after the trial concluded.

His guard, Hizhnyak Gurevich, accompanied him to his execution. He tied his hands to an iron ring where five officers were waiting. "At one point he went pale and his left cheek began to tremble." It was Major General Pavel Batitski who first shot Beria in the back of his head. Six others then fired from point-blank range. Gurevich wrapped the body in a tarpaulin before taking it to a crematorium where he pushed it into the flames.

Reporting to the State Department, Ambassador Charles Bohlen understood the implications of how the case had been handled. "There is of course elementary justice in the fate of Beria and his [secret police] associates, but it would have been more fitting if retribution had been meted out by his victims rather than his accomplices."[12] The party had carried out a political exorcism, offering up Beria as a sacrificial lamb to atone for the sins it refused to acknowledge.

With his execution, the regime had the awkward task of turning Beria into a "non-person." The previous August, a party bureaucrat had reported from Georgia how "a massive number of monuments to Beria" remained in the country. His name adorned "the finest streets, city squares, parks, industrial plants, collective farms, and social-cultural institutions." In one district, there were no less than eighteen monuments to him. This past year in Batumi, "hundreds of thousands of rubles and hundreds of tons" of construction materials had been dedicated to honoring him. Now they would all have to be dismantled.[13] The latest edition of the *Great Soviet Encyclopedia* posed a more complicated challenge. Volume 5, which had appeared in 1950, contained a full-page photograph and a fawning entry on Beria. In January 1954, subscribers worldwide were sent instructions to remove the pages on Beria with a small knife or razor blade and replace it with a four-page insert carrying photographs and new information about the Bering Sea. (George Orwell could not have imagined a more efficient "memory hole" in *Nineteen Eighty-Four*.) George Kennan and others had long argued that a struggle for power among Stalin's heirs would expose the fragility of his regime. But Beria's downfall confirmed their ability to work together and preserve the prerogatives of authority that they had inherited.

* * *

Beria's removal, coming after months of unexpected reforms in Moscow, left Eisenhower's aide Emmet Hughes with a feeling of deep frustration. He had watched Eisenhower and Foster Dulles stumble over how to respond to Stalin's demise, and to appeals for a summit. That summer Hughes confided to his diary that "We have been confronted with matchless opportunity in Stalin's death, the uneasy triumvirate, the Germans' revolt, now Beria's fall—and the sober truth is that we have no idea what to do with these opportunities." His concerns were falling on deaf ears.[14]

Hughes, in fact, long bemoaned how Eisenhower "conferred all his trust, and much of his power, upon a Secretary of State unique in modern American diplomacy for his distrust of compromise and conciliation."[15] Writing about the events of that spring, Townsend Hoopes observed that "Stalin did Dulles a philosophical and practical disservice by dying, but Dulles retaliated by continuing to act as though the death had not occurred."[16] He failed to grasp that Stalin's death utterly changed the political landscape. The Soviet Union had not simply turned into a dictatorship without the dictator, but a dictatorship without that *particular* dictator. He could only think in terms of the world that Stalin had created and was now leaving behind. Years later Walt Rostow voiced regret over Eisenhower's lack of resolve, for his failure "to come directly to grips with the new Soviet leadership and assess what could or could not be wrung from the new situation."[17] Charles Bohlen, as well, regretted that he did not push Eisenhower harder to sit down with Malenkov. "Looking back, I believe I was remiss at the time of Stalin's death in not recommending that Eisenhower take up Churchill's call for a 'meeting at the summit.' . . . Dulles batted down the idea. . . . But I think I made a mistake in not taking the initiative and recommending such a meeting."[18] Opinion polls in America and Great Britain reflected a similar outlook; overwhelming majorities in both countries favored a summit meeting between Eisenhower and Malenkov. But a combination of Eisenhower's natural caution and Foster Dulles' belligerent moralism ensured that whatever opportunities may have been staring them in the face—to significantly reduce tensions? To relax the arms race? To reunite Germany? To end the Cold War?— were not going to be pursued. Eisenhower refused "to find out exactly what the new leaders in the Kremlin had in mind," the Cold War historian Klaus Larres concluded, leaving a heavy weight of suspicion and hostility over Washington and Moscow.[19]

In any case the window of opportunity was probably narrow, extending from the time of Eisenhower's speech on April 16 to the outbreak of riots in East Germany on June 17. Even with the best of intentions in Washington and Moscow, those two months could not have provided an adequate amount of time for either side to grow less wary of the other and successfully enter into the kind of open-ended negotiations that Winston Churchill kept advocating. The riots in East Germany shook the Kremlin's confidence, reinforcing its determination not to allow popular discontent to challenge its hegemony in the satellite states. Regardless of its moves toward more relaxed control in the spring of 1953, the Red Army intervention in East Germany—much like the more dramatic episodes of revolt in Hungary in 1956 and then Czechoslovakia in 1968 which would require outright invasions to put down—made clear that the Kremlin would use force to sustain its control. Once the Kremlin suppressed the turmoil in East Germany it buried any possibility of a peaceful reunification of Germany or negotiating a broader relaxation of tension at that time. Then in August the Soviet Union exploded a hydrogen bomb, startling the West with its advances in research and technology so soon after World War II and bringing the country closer to strategic parity with the United States. Eisenhower and Khrushchev did not meet until the four-way Geneva summit in July 1955 and did not hold a full-scale US–Soviet summit until Khrushchev's visit to the United States in September 1959. While the Cold War dragged on across another four decades, each side armed itself with increasingly destructive weapons of mass destruction, intensifying the political rivalry that divided Europe.

NOTES

Introduction

1. Abram Tertz (Andrei Sinyavsky), *Goodnight!* (New York: Penguin, 1989), 227.

Chapter 1: The Death of Stalin

1. The government statement and medical bulletin can both be found in *New York Times*, March 4, 1953, 3.
2. Konstantin Simonov, *Glazami cheloveka moego pokoleniia* (Through the Eyes of a Man of My Generation) (Moscow: Novosti, 1988), 254–55.
3. Ilya Ehrenburg, *Lyudi, gody, zhizn* (People, Years, Life), vol. III (Moscow: Sovietskii pisatel, 1990), 229.
4. US Ambassador George Kennan, who reached Moscow in May, 1952, was also aware of such rumors. "There are evidences that he is stimulating research on extension of human life and I believe he puts this ahead of anything else." George F. Kennan papers, MC076, Box 233, Folder 1, from his diary of 1953, 13. Seeley G. Mudd Manuscript Library, Princeton University.
5. These newspaper accounts are discussed in Yoram Gorlizki and Oleg Khlevniuk, *Cold Peace: Stalin and the Soviet Ruling Circle, 1945–1953* (Oxford: Oxford University Press, 2004), 177 n. 3.
6. Ibid., 177 n. 8.
7. Cited in ibid., 54.
8. *Nezavisimaia gazeta* (Independent Newspaper), March 4, 1993, 5.
9. See Sheila Fitzpatrick, *On Stalin's Team: The Years of Living Dangerously in Soviet Politics* (Princeton: Princeton University Press, 2015), 197; she was able to calculate his time away from Moscow by examining a log of visits to his Kremlin office.
10. US Embassy in Warsaw to Secretary of State, January 9, 1952. (Unless otherwise noted, State Department material references are available in a microfilm project of University Publications of America, Inc. entitled *Confidential US State Department Central Files: The Soviet Union, Internal Affairs 1950–1954 and Foreign Affairs 1950–1954*, edited by Paul Kesaris. The microfilm was examined at Harvard's Lamont Library under the reference code Film A 575.1 (1950–1954).)
11. US Embassy in Ankara to Secretary of State, February 1, 1952.
12. US Embassy in Moscow to Secretary of State, February 1, 1952.

13. Harrison E. Salisbury, *Moscow Journal: The End of Stalin* (Chicago: University of Chicago Press, 1962), 244–45.
14. *Foreign Relations of the United States, 1952–1954*, 138th Meeting of the National Security Council, March 25, 1953 (Washington: US Government Printing Office, 1984), vol. VIII: Eastern Europe; Soviet Union; Eastern Mediterranean (hereafter *FRUS*, VIII), 963.
15. Salisbury, *Moscow Journal*, 245.
16. US Embassy in Moscow to Secretary of State, June 20, 1952, in *FRUS*, VIII, 1014–15.
17. George Kennan, *Memoirs*, vol. II (Boston: Little, Brown, 1972), 132.
18. US Embassy in Moscow to Secretary of State, August 25, 1952, in *FRUS*, VIII, 1044.
19. Svetlana Alliluyeva, *Twenty Letters to a Friend* (New York: Harper & Row, 1967), 206.
20. Salisbury, *Moscow Journal*, 324.
21. Kitchlew had been a leader alongside Mahatma Gandhi in India's independence movement. A Muslim, he had opposed partition into separate Muslim and Hindu countries. He grew closer to India's communist party and was a leader of both the Indian- and the Soviet-sponsored World Peace Council, the factors that led to his receiving the Stalin Peace Prize. The Kremlin valued his friendship; on March 10, *Pravda* featured a photograph of Kitchlew in the Hall of Columns paying his respects to Stalin, an honor mostly reserved for communist leaders.
22. Salisbury, *Moscow Journal*, 327.
23. When word of Stalin's illness was announced on March 4, the American chargé Jacob Beam recalled Stalin's meeting with Menon and Kitchlew just weeks before. Since they had reported that Stalin appeared to be in good health, Beam shared his belief with the State Department that the stroke was "unexpected and quite possibly unprepared for." He then went on to speculate that "Embassy does not consider it feasible that any of Stalin's long-rumored doubles, even if they actually exist, could have taken his place and concealed his death for substantial time." See *FRUS*, VIII, 1084.
24. Alliluyeva, *Twenty Letters*, 208.
25. Nikita Khrushchev, *Khrushchev Remembers* (Boston: Little, Brown, 1970), 299.
26. Ibid., 316. These late-night dinners did not always go so well. In his memoirs, Khrushchev recalled how these could be "interminable, agonizing dinners": ibid., 301. The dissident Yugoslav writer Milovan Djilas had attended such gatherings during and after the war as a representative of Tito's regime and saw for himself how they could upset Stalin's companions. "It all rather resembled a patriarchal family with a crotchety head whose foibles always made his kinfolk somewhat apprehensive"; see Milovan Djilas, *Conversations with Stalin* (Harmondsworth: Penguin, 1969), 64.
27. A. T. Rybin, "Ryadom s I. V. Stalinym" (Side by Side with I. V. Stalin), *Sotsiologicheskie issledovaniya* (Sociological Researches), May–June 1988, 84–94.
28. Nadezhda Mandelstam, *Hope Against Hope* (New York: Atheneum, 1979), 383.
29. Khrushchev, *Khrushchev Remembers* (1970), 319.
30. Ibid., 317.
31. *Nezavisimaia gazeta*, March 4, 1993, 5.
32. Aleksandr Myasnikov, *Ya lechil Stalina* (I treated Stalin) (Moscow: Eksmo, 2011), 295. Myasnikov was among a group of doctors involved with the journal *Klinicheskaia meditsina* (Clinical Medicine). His name remained on the masthead throughout 1952 and into 1953; he was not arrested in connection with the Doctors' Plot.
33. Yakov Rapoport, *The Doctors' Plot of 1953* (Cambridge: Harvard University Press, 1991), 151–52.
34. Alliluyeva, *Twenty Letters*, 6–7.
35. Khrushchev, *Khrushchev Remembers* (1970), 318.
36. Alliluyeva, *Twenty Letters*, 7. Once Beria was arrested and then executed, Khrushchev had every reason to denigrate his reputation. Svetlana Alliluyeva also had reasons to denounce Beria, but there is less reason to believe that her account of what happened at the dacha was compromised by such feelings. Khrushchev's memoirs were not released before Svetlana Alliluyeva wrote her own book.

37. Ibid., 212.
38. Ibid., 214.
39. Eddy Gilmore, *Me and My Russian Wife* (Garden City, New York: Doubleday, 1954), 290.
40. *New York Times*, March 4, 1953, 1.
41. Salisbury, *Moscow Journal*, 336.
42. Sherman Adams, *Firsthand Report: The Story of the Eisenhower Administration* (New York: Harper and Brothers, 1961), 96.
43. Adams, *Firsthand Report*, 96.
44. Memorandum of Discussion at the 135th Meeting of the National Security Council, Washington, March 4, 1953, in *FRUS*, VIII, 1091–93.
45. *New York Times*, March 5, 1953, 10.
46. Dwight David Eisenhower, *Mandate for Change 1953–1956: The White House Years, A Personal Account* (Garden City, New York: Doubleday, 1963), 143.
47. *New York Times*, March 5, 1953, 11. According to Eisenhower, Dulles opposed issuing the statement, believing it "might be read as an appeal to the Soviet people in mourning to rise up against their rulers"; see Eisenhower, *Mandate for Change*, 144.
48. Kumara Padmanabha Sivasankara Menon, *The Flying Troika* (London: Oxford University Press, 1963), 36 and xiii. A *fortochka* is a small, hinged window pane used for ventilation.
49. *Newsweek*, March 16, 1953, 23.
50. US Embassy in Brussels to Secretary of State, March 4, 1953.
51. US Embassy in Bonn to Secretary of State, March 4, 1953.
52. Secretary of State Dulles to American Embassy in Moscow, March 4, 1953.
53. US Consulate in Munich to Secretary of State, March 5, 1953.
54. *New York Times*, March 6, 1953, 1.
55. Senator Styles Bridges of New Hampshire claimed that the "withdrawal of Bohlen's name had been urged on 'top' Eisenhower aides. 'We had an election and the Acheson–Truman policies were repudiated.'" But Ohio's Robert Taft defused the controversy. He did not believe that the Moscow posting was important enough for a big fight between Republican senators and a new Republican administration. "Our Russian ambassador can't do anything. He is in a box at Moscow. All he can do is observe and report. He will not influence policy materially"; see *Time*, March 23, 1953, 26.
56. In his memoir, *Multiple Exposure*, Beam wrote that "By virtually expelling Kennan by forbidding his return to Moscow, the Soviets had to forfeit their own ambassador in Washington and faced a suspension of diplomatic activity of their own making. . . . I was instructed simply to observe, report, and above all, to avoid incidents." Jacob Beam, *Multiple Exposure: An American Ambassador's Unique Perspective on East–West Issues* (New York: Norton, 1978), 29.
57. US Embassy in Moscow to Secretary of State, March 5, 1953.
58. Secretary of State Dulles to "Certain American Diplomatic Officers" at US embassies in Moscow, Prague, Warsaw, Budapest, and Bucharest, March 4, 1953.
59. US Diplomatic Office in Berlin to Secretary of State, March 5, 1953.
60. US Embassy in Belgrade to State Department, March 5, 1953.
61. *New York Times*, March 5, 1953, 10.
62. *Time*, March 23, 1953, 62.
63. *New York Times*, March 6, 1953, 1.
64. *New Yorker*, "The Wayward Press: Death on the One Hand," March 28, 1953, 105.
65. *New York Times*, March 6, 1953, 12. Eisenhower had visited the Ohrdruf concentration camp on April 12, 1945, accompanied by Generals George Patton and Omar Bradley. Located near Weimar, it was the first camp to be reached by American forces, on April 4.
66. *New York Times*, March 6, 1953, 12.
67. Cited in Steven A. Barnes, *Death and Redemption: The Gulag and the Shaping of Soviet Society* (Princeton: Princeton University Press, 2011), 201.

68. Gilmore, *Me and My Russian Wife*, 286–87.
69. Myasnikov, *Ya lechil Stalina*, 299.
70. *Nezavisimaia gazeta*, March 4, 1993, 5.
71. *New York Times*, March 6, 1953, 14.
72. Simonov, *Glazami cheloveka*, 257–59.
73. Alliluyeva, *Twenty Letters*, 10.
74. Khrushchev, *Khrushchev Remembers* (1970), 320.
75. Myasnikov, *Ya lechil Stalina*, 300.
76. Alliluyeva, *Twenty Letters*, 8.
77. Khrushchev, *Khrushchev Remembers* (1970), 322, 324.
78. Alliluyeva, *Twenty Letters*, 8–14. Within days Beria ordered the dacha closed, collected all of the furnishings and Stalin's belongings, and dismissed the staff. Two of the bodyguards committed suicide; see *Twenty Letters*, 23.

Chapter 2: A New Purge

1. See G. D. Embree, *The Soviet Union Between the 19th and 20th Party Congresses 1952–1956* (The Hague: Springer Netherlands, 1959), 5, for details on how the essay was distributed.
2. Adam Ulam, *Stalin* (New York: Viking, 1973), 729–31.
3. The full text of Stalin's statement about the economy can be found in Leo Gruliow (ed.), *Current Soviet Policies: The Documentary Record of the Nineteenth Party Congress and the Reorganization after Stalin's Death* (New York: Praeger, 1953), 1–20.
4. *New York Times*, October 3, 1952, 7.
5. Auguste Lecœur, *Le Partisan* (Paris: Flammarion, 1963), 261–62.
6. Dmitrii Shepilov, *The Kremlin's Scholar: A Memoir of Soviet Politics Under Khrushchev* (New Haven: Yale University Press, 2007), 228.
7. Gruliow, *Current Soviet Policies*, 117.
8. Ibid., 120.
9. Ibid., 214.
10. Shepilov, *The Kremlin's Scholar*, 229.
11. Ibid., 228.
12. Ibid., 235–36.
13. *Memoirs of Nikita Khrushchev*, vol. 2, *Reformer [1945–1964]*, ed. Sergei Khrushchev (University Park, Pennsylvania: Pennsylvania State University Press, 2004), 108.
14. Ibid., 89.
15. Shepilov, *The Kremlin's Scholar*, 234.
16. Cited in Gorlizki and Khlevniuk, *Cold Peace*, 149.
17. Shepilov, *The Kremlin's Scholar*, 232.
18. Simonov, *Glazami cheloveka*, 240–41.
19. Shepilov, *The Kremlin's Scholar*, 234.
20. Gorlizki and Khlevniuk, *Cold Peace*, 136.
21. Vladislav M. Zubok, *A Failed Empire: The Soviet Union in the Cold War From Stalin to Gorbachev* (Chapel Hill: University of North Carolina Press, 2009), 74.
22. Shepilov, *The Kremlin's Scholar*, 234.
23. Sergei Khrushchev, *Nikita Khrushchev: Reformator* (Reformer) (Moscow: Vremya, 2010), 86.
24. Nikita Khrushchev, *Memoirs*, vol. 2, *Reformer*, 106.
25. Anastas Ivanovich Mikoyan, *Tak bylo: razmyshleniya o minuvshem* (How It Was: Reflections About the Past) (Moscow: Vagrius, 1999), 580.
26. *The Anti-Stalin Campaign and International Communism: A Selection of Documents*, ed. Russian Institute, Columbia University (New York, 1956), 84.
27. Gennadi Kostyrchenko, *Out of the Red Shadows: Anti-Semitism in Stalin's Russia* (Amherst, New York: Prometheus Books, 1995), 120.

28. Cited in Oleg Khlevniuk, *Master of the House: Stalin and his Inner Circle* (New Haven: Yale University Press, 2009), xiii–xiv.
29. Felix Chuev, *Sto sorok besed s Molotovym* (One Hundred Forty Conversations with Molotov) (Moscow: Terra, 1991), 473.
30. Mikoyan, *Tak bylo*, 573.
31. Shepilov, *The Kremlin's Scholar*, 235.
32. N. G. Kuznetsov, *Neva*, no. 5 (Leningrad, 1965), 161.
33. Khlevniuk, *Master of the House*, 214.
34. *New York Times*, October 17, 1952, 19.
35. *L'Humanité*, September 17, 1952, 1.
36. Ernest Hemingway, *For Whom the Bell Tolls* (New York: Scribner's, 1940), 417. Hemingway's portrait of André Marty was a significant reason why the novel was banned in the Soviet Union. Ehrenburg read the novel in a Russian translation in July 1941; it was being prepared for publication but ultimately not permitted to appear. In his memoirs, Ehrenburg wrote about his distaste for Marty and included quotations from the novel although *For Whom the Bell Tolls* itself did not see publication in the Soviet Union until 1968, the year after Ehrenburg's death.
37. Ehrenburg, *Lyudi, gody, zhizn*, vol. II (Moscow, 1990), 136.
38. *New York Times*, October 5, 1952, 17.

Chapter 3: Stalin's Paranoia and the Jews

1. Cited in Joshua Rubenstein and Vladimir Naumov (eds), *Stalin's Secret Pogrom: The Postwar Inquisition of the Jewish Anti-Fascist Committee* (New Haven: Yale University Press, 2001), xiii. Komarov remained in prison and was executed in December 1954.
2. The Slansky trial had an additional, unique feature. Three of the defendants survived; two of them wrote memoirs as did three of the wives of those who were condemned. Two Israelis who were also arrested in Prague—Mordechai Oren and Shimon Orenstein—and forced to give damaging testimony were convicted at subsequent trials and sent off to prison for many years. But they gained their release following Stalin's death, returned to Israel, and wrote memoirs of their own. Taken all together, these memoirs provide an unusually detailed and vivid account of how the case unfolded, including the torture of the defendants. The memoir of Artur London, in particular, which was first published in French in 1968 under the title *L'Aveu* (The Confession; it was published in English under the title *On Trial*), was made into a famous movie by Costa-Gavras, in 1970, starring Yves Montand and Simone Signoret. Exposing the full horror of the Slansky case also became a priority for the reform-minded Czechoslovak communist leadership of 1968. But their review of the relevant archival materials came to a halt after the Warsaw Pact invasion that August which ended the Prague Spring and any hope of reform for years to come.
3. Meir Cotic, *The Prague Trial: The First Anti-Zionist Show Trial in the Communist Bloc* (New York: Cornwall Books, 1987), 144.
4. *The Times*, January 14, 1953, 7.
5. *Pravda Ukrainy* and *Radyanska Ukraina*, November 29, 1952, 1, as translated in *The Current Digest of the Soviet Press*, January 3, 1953, vol. IV, no. 47, 16. The article was entitled "A Band of Wreckers."
6. Cited in Salisbury, *Moscow Journal*, 308.
7. *New York Times*, December 23, 1952, 7.
8. Salisbury, *Moscow Journal*, 308.
9. Shimon Redlich (ed.), *War, Holocaust and Stalinism: A Documented Study of the Jewish Anti-Fascist Committee in the USSR* (Luxembourg: Harwood Academic Publishers, 1995), 464.
10. Cited in Benjamin Pinkus (ed.), *The Soviet Government and the Jews 1948–1967* (Cambridge: Cambridge University Press, 1984), 183–85.

11. *The Correspondence of Boris Pasternak and Olga Freidenberg 1910–1954*, compiled and edited with an introduction by Elliott Mossman; trans. Elliott Mossman and Margaret Wettlin (New York: Harcourt Brace Jovanovich, 1982), 295.

12. An abridged, English translation of the transcript of this secret trial can be found in Rubenstein and Naumov, *Stalin's Secret Pogrom*.

13. Khrushchev made these claims in his "Secret Speech" to the Twentieth Party Congress on February 25, 1956. The text can be found in *The Anti-Stalin Campaign and International Communism*, 64.

14. See Jonathan Brent and Vladimir P. Naumov, *Stalin's Last Crime: The Plot Against the Jewish Doctors, 1948–1953* (New York: HarperCollins, 2003), 212–13, 232–33.

15. V. Malyshev, "Dnevnik narkoma" (Diary of a People's Commissar), *Istochnik* (Source), no. 5, 1997, 140–41.

16. *Documents on Israeli–Soviet Relations 1941–1953, Part II: May 1949–1953* (London: Frank Cass, 2000), 849. Eban's coded telegram was dated January 5, 1953.

17. Ibid., 846. P. I. Ershov's coded telegram was dated December 8, 1952.

18. Ibid., 849.

19. Ibid., note 2, 849, where Ben-Gurion responded to Eban on January 9, 1953.

20. Salisbury, *Moscow Journal*, 312.

21. Roy Medvedev, *Let History Judge: The Origins and Consequences of Stalinism* (New York: Knopf, 1971), 494.

22. See Mordekhai Oren, *Prisonnier politique à Prague (1951–1956)* (Paris: Julliard, 1960), 315.

23. The full text of the Tass communiqué and the front-page editorial about the Doctors' Plot in the January 13, 1953, edition of *Pravda* can be found in the *Current Digest of the Soviet Press*, January 31, 1953, vol. IV, no. 51, 3–4.

24. Salisbury, *Moscow Journal*, 297.

25. *New Yorker*, "Apparatchik," March 21, 1953, 28.

26. *Documents on Israeli–Soviet Relations*, 851. W. Eytan's coded telegram was dated January 14, 1953.

27. Ibid., 855–58.

28. *Le Figaro*, January 17–18, 1953, as cited in Raymond Aron, *La Guerre Froide* (The Cold War) (juin 1947 à mai 1955) (Paris: Fallois, 1990), 950.

29. *The Times*, January 14, 1953, 7.

30. *New York Times*, January 14, 1953, 30.

31. Ibid., January 18, 1953, E1.

32. Cited in Yehoshua A. Gilboa, *The Black Years of Soviet Jewry 1939–1953* (Boston: Little, Brown, 1971), 301.

33. Ibid., 305–6. Harrison Salisbury kept a running description of such articles in *Moscow Journal*, 314–24.

34. Cited in Gilboa, *Black Years of Soviet Jewry*, 302.

35. Rapoport, *The Doctors' Plot of 1953*, 84. The *New York Times* carried a front-page interview with him on May 13, 1988.

36. Ehrenburg, *Lyudi, gody, zhizn*, vol. III, 227.

37. See the volume *Sovietskie evrei pishut Ilye Erenburgy 1943–1966* (Soviet Jews Write to Ilya Ehrenburg) edited by Mordechai Altshuler, Yitshak Arad, and Shmuel Krakowski (Jerusalem: The Centre for Research and Documentation of East-European Jewry, The Hebrew University of Jerusalem and Yad Vashem, 1993).

38. *L'Humanité*, January 27, 1953, 3.

39. *New York Times*, February 18, 1953, 12. In July 1942, 13,000 French Jews were driven to the Vélodrome d'Hiver—the Paris indoor cycling stadium—where they were kept for several days before being taken to Auschwitz. It is not known if the PCF chose this particular site for the rally in defense of the Rosenbergs because of its tragic role in French Jewish history; the Vel' d'Hiv roundup, as it was called, had occurred less than ten years earlier.

40. Cited in David Fanning, *Mieczyław Weinberg: In Search of Freedom* (Hofheim: Wolke Verlag, 2010), 83.
41. See Robert R. Reilly, "Light in the Darkness: The Music of Mieczyslaw Vainberg," *Crisis*, vol. 18, no. 2, February, 2000, 52–53; Shostakovich and Weinberg together burned the letter to Beria at a dinner party following Weinberg's release. Weinberg's fate reflects the tragedy of so many Jews of his generation. Born in Warsaw in 1919, he escaped Poland after the German invasion in September 1939. His parents and sister were not so fortunate; they were trapped and later killed in a Nazi death camp. Weinberg resumed his musical studies in Minsk but after the German invasion of Soviet territory in June 1941, he was evacuated to Tashkent where he met Natalya Vovsi-Mikhoels. They were married in 1942.
42. *Pravda*, February 14, 1953, 4.
43. These incidents are described in: "Otkliki na notu sovietsogo pravitelstva o prekrash-chenii diplomaticheskikh otnoshenii s pravitelstvom Izraelya" (Reactions to the note of the Soviet government about the breaking of diplomatic relations with the government of Israel), *Istochnik* no. 3, 1999, 108; and "The Party and Popular Reaction to the 'Doctors' Plot' (Dnepropetrovsk Province, Ukraine)," introduction by Mordechai Altshuler and Tat'iana Chentsova, *Jews in Eastern Europe*, Fall 1993, 49–65. In her memoir, Ludmilla Alexeyeva recounts a similar episode from the time of the anti-cosmopolitan campaign in the spring of 1949. Komsomol officials in her school were quick to emphasize that they were exposing "cosmopolitanism" rather than hard-working people of "Jewish nationality." But as the harsh propaganda against cosmopoli-tanism continued, at least some students thought it was acceptable to denounce "kikes" out loud and express the urge to "strangle them all." In this case, at least, the offending student "was officially reprimanded for antisemitism." See Ludmilla Alexeyeva and Paul Goldberg, *The Thaw Generation: Coming of Age in the Post-Stalin Era* (Boston: Little, Brown, 1990), 44.
44. David Shrayer-Petrov, *Okhota na ryzhego dyavola* (Hunting for the Red-Haired Devil) (Moscow: Agraf, 2010), 7.
45. G. V. Kostyrchenko (ed.), *Gosudartsvennyi antisemitizma v SSSR ot nachala do kulmi-natsii 1938–1953* (Official Anti-semitism in the USSR from the Beginning to its Culmination) (Moscow: Materik, 2005), 344. Malenkov himself was not above acts of Jew-baiting. One former *Izvestia* reporter remembered how Malenkov had behaved during a meeting of industrial managers. "In a sudden burst of anger [Malenkov inter-rupted] an explanation of why nail production had fallen off to announce that the leader in charge of production was a Jew and shout at him, 'If these nails were for Stalin's coffin, you'd have them soon enough!' Malenkov thereupon gave the leader three days in which to bring production up to schedule. When the leader failed to do so, he was arrested, and disappeared." See *New Yorker*, "Apparatchik," March 21, 1953, 27–28.
46. *Newsweek*, January 26, 1953, 50.
47. Brent and Naumov, *Stalin's Last Crime*, 294–95.
48. Ibid., 182.
49. Ibid., 298.
50. This was the famous phrase *zu versuchen im Sinne des Führers ihm entgegenzuarbeiten*.
51. In 1944, when Solomon Mikhoels and other members of the Jewish Anti-Fascist Committee approached the regime with the idea of settling displaced Jewish survivors of the Nazi massacres in the Crimea, they understood that the Volga Germans had already been deported from their ancestral lands, while the Crimean Tatars had been deported from theirs, leaving parts of the peninsula available for others to populate; see Rubenstein and Naumov, *Stalin's Secret Pogrom*, 258.
52. *The Times*, January 14, 1953, 6.
53. Roy Medvedev, *Let History Judge*, 494.
54. Mikhail Heller and Aleksandr Nekrich, *Utopia in Power: The History of the Soviet Union from 1917 to the Present* (New York: Summit, 1986), 503–4.

55. Anton Antonov-Ovseenko, *The Time of Stalin: Portrait of a Tyranny* (New York: Harper & Row, 1981), 291.
56. Aleksandr I. Solzhenitsyn, *The Gulag Archipelago 1918–1956: An Experiment in Literary Investigation*, vol. I (New York: Harper & Row, 1973), 92.
57. In his memoirs, the physicist and heralded dissident Andrei Sakharov also described the plan to deport the Jews in the final weeks of Stalin's life; he too referred to Chesnokov who was said to be preparing a lead article for *Pravda* about how the Russian people would rescue the Jews. This is just another example of how widespread the belief in this rumor had become; see Andrei Sakharov, *Memoirs* (New York: Knopf, 1990), 162.
58. I met with Alya Savich several times in Moscow in the 1980s. She and her husband, the journalist Ovady Savich, were particularly close friends of Ehrenburg. She related to me that a policeman once told her that he and several of his colleagues had been asked to compile a list of Jews in their Moscow district.
59. Aleksandr N. Yakovlev, *A Century of Violence in Soviet Russia* (New Haven: Yale University Press, 2002), 209–10.
60. *The Times*, April 16, 1956, 8. Adam Ulam, too, was suitably cautious when he referred to the threat of deportations in his biography of Stalin. "It is possible that had [Stalin] lived a few more years, the Jews would have been subjected to wholesale deportation as the kulaks had been between 1930 and 1934." See Ulam, *Stalin*, 685.
61. In 1992, Kaganovich denied that any such discussions ever took place. See Felix Chuev (ed.), *Tak govoril Kaganovich: ispoved' stalinskogo apostola* (So Spoke Kaganovich: The Confession of a Stalinist Apostle) (Moscow: Otechestvo, 1992), 173–77.
62. Andrei Vyshinsky, not Molotov, was foreign minister at that time.
63. According to another variation of this story, it was Kaganovich who tore up his party membership card and threw it in Stalin's face; see Roy A. Medvedev, *On Stalin and Stalinism* (Oxford: Oxford University Press, 1979), 158.
64. *New York Times*, June 8, 1957, 8.
65. *The Times*, September 8, 1959, 11.
66. Anton Antonov-Ovseenko later claimed that it was Malenkov who challenged Stalin about deporting the Jews, a highly unlikely version given Malenkov's absolute servility to his master; see Antonov-Ovseenko, *The Time of Stalin*, 290.
67. The one-time Polish communist official Stefan Staszewski claimed that on March 20, 1956, Khrushchev told a group of high-level government and party members in Warsaw how Stalin, near the close of 1952, had ordered the Presidium to "organize groups of armed men" for the purpose of killing Jews; see *"Them": Stalin's Polish Puppets* by Teresa Toranska (New York: Harper & Row, 1987), 171. In the same interview, Staszewski related how Khrushchev discussed the case against the Jewish Anti-Fascist Committee, how members of the committee, including Ilya Ehrenburg, had visited Stalin to petition for the Crimea to become a place for Jews to settle now that the Tatars had been exiled, leaving the Crimea "deserted." But no such meeting with Stalin ever took place. Members of the committee did see Molotov. As for Ehrenburg, he was never in favor of any kind of special settlement for Soviet Jews. He vigorously opposed the idea of petitioning for Jewish settlement in the Crimea and had long been an opponent of Birobidjan as a special district for Jewish autonomy.
68. For a comprehensive review of how two Russian-based scholars have explored this episode, see two articles in the Russian-Jewish journal *Lekhaim* (To Life) by Gennadi Kostyrchenko, the first in September 2002 about how the belief in such a plan to deport the Jews originated in a broader impulse to believe many myths about the Soviet period, and the second in February 2004 about a film by Arkady Vaksberg which made claims about a plan to deport the Jews; also Boris Frezinsky, "Ilya Erenburg v gody stalinskogo gosantisemitizma—polemika s g. Kostyrchenko" (Ilya Ehrenburg During the Years of Stalin's Official Anti-semitism—An Argument with Mr. Kostyrchenko), *Pisateli i sovietskie vozhdi* (Writers and Soviet Power) (Moscow: Ellis lak, 2008), 544–88.

Versions of the "collective letter to Pravda" are cited in these articles. David Brandenberger also reviewed much of this literature in his essay-review of *Stalin's Last Crime* by Brent and Naumov, in *Kritika: Explorations in Russian and Eurasian History*, vol. 6, no. 1, Winter 2005 (New Series), 187–204.

69. Kaganovich refused to sign, explaining to Stalin that he was not a Jewish cultural worker but a member of the Presidium; it was beneath his dignity to add his signature as if he were just another Jewish writer or composer. But if it were necessary, he offered to sign the letter as a member of the Presidium. See Chuev (ed.), *Tak govoril Kaganovich*, 173–77.

70. I interviewed Vasily Grossman's friend Semyon Lipkin in April 1982, and Margarita Aliger in May 1988, during separate trips to Moscow for my biography of Ilya Ehrenburg.

71. Ehrenburg, *Lyudi, gody, zhizn*, vol. III, 228.

72. Ehrenburg and his wife, Lyubov Kozintsev, together described what happened to their friend, the Moscow artist Boris Birger. Birger wrote the story down and passed along this unpublished manuscript to the St. Petersburg scholar Boris Frezinsky, who is the foremost student of Ehrenburg's life and career. I also interviewed Birger in Moscow in May 1984. It is worth noting that Birger had been connected to the emerging human rights movement in Moscow in the late 1960s. He signed appeals on behalf of political prisoners, which led to his expulsion from the party and demotion within the Artists' Union. He became a close friend of Academician Andrei Sakharov and his wife, Elena Bonner. When I visited him in May 1984, Bonner had just been detained in Gorki— where Sakharov had been confined since January 1980—and prevented from returning to Moscow. She would soon be indicted and convicted of "anti-Soviet slander." Birger was expecting to meet her at a Moscow train station; when I saw him, he showed me a telegram from her with her expected arrival time: a trip she never made.

73. Veniamin Kaverin, *Epilog* (Moscow: Moskovskii rabochii, 1989), 316–20 for his description of this incident.

74. Ehrenburg's letter to Stalin was found in the archive at Stalin's dacha several months after the dictator's death. It was reprinted in the Moscow journal *Istochnik* in January 1997, 141–46, with the full archival references; this article also contains the text of the collective letter that he ultimately signed.

75. Solzhenitsyn, *The Gulag Archipelago*, vol. I, 92.

76. See Gennadi Kostyrchenko, *Tainaia politika Khrushcheva: vlast, intelligentsia, evreyskii vopros* (The Secret Politics of Khrushchev: Power, the Intelligentsia, the Jewish Question) (Moscow: Mezhdunarodnye otnosheniia, 2012), 15. The Order of Lenin was reinstated by a decree of the Presidium on April 30, 1953; see Kostyrchenko (ed.), *Gosudartsvennyi antisemitizma*, 119.

77. Ibid., 257.

78. Ibid., 254.

79. This incident is discussed in Orlando Figes, *The Whisperers: Private Life in Stalin's Russia* (New York: Metropolitan, 2007), 519–20.

80. Kostyrchenko (ed.), *Gosudartsvennyi antisemitizma*, 345–46.

Chapter 4: The Kremlin Moves On

1. *Pravda*, March 7, 1953, 2.

2. Vera Kopylova, "Upravlial gosudarstvom, v sushchnosti bol'noi chelovek" (A sick man was heading the government), *Moskovskii komsomolets*, no. 85, April 21, 2011. This article is based on the notes of Dr. Myasnikov. See also Myasnikov, *Ya lechil Stalina*, 304.

3. Copies of the original photograph and the doctored photograph can be found in the *Current Digest of the Soviet Press*, March 28, 1953, vol. V, no. 7, 11.

4. *New York Times*, March 7, 1953, 1.

5. In the weeks following Stalin's death, *Time* enjoyed mocking Malenkov. In its eyes, he was "gross and flaccid in appearance," or "pale and pasty as the cream buns he loves"; see *Time*, March 16, 1953, 29 and 31.

6. The *New York Times* was mistakenly asserting that Stalin was married to Kaganovich's sister, Roza; *Time* magazine carried the same misinformation on March 16, 1953, 30. On November 22, 1953, the *New York Times*, on page 3, compounded this mistake with the baseless claim that Kaganovich's son was married to Stalin's daughter.
7. Lenin had died at his estate outside of Moscow. His body arrived in Moscow by train, with crowds waiting at every station along the way. It was then carried for five miles from the capital's Paveletsky Station to the center of Moscow. Over the next four days, nearly a million people streamed through the Hall of Columns to view Lenin's body, with crowds remaining in nearby streets through the night, huddling around bonfires in the bitter cold.
8. *New York Times*, March 6, 1953, 8.
9. *New York Times*, March 7, 1953, 1.
10. Gilmore, *Me and My Russian Wife*, 290.
11. Salisbury, *Moscow Journal*, 341–42.
12. Resis, A. (ed.), *Molotov Remembers: Inside Kremlin Politics. Conversations with Felix Chuev* (Chicago: I. R. Dee, 1993), 210.
13. Salisbury, *Moscow Journal*, 343–44.
14. Ehrenburg, *Lyudi, gody, zhizn*, vol. III, 229.
15. Salisbury, *Moscow Journal*, 344.
16. *Pravda*, March 9, 1953, 1.
17. Salisbury, *Moscow Journal*, 344.
18. Yevgeny Yevtushenko, *A Precocious Autobiography* (New York: Dutton, 1963), 84–87. The crush of the crowds that accompanied Stalin's death and funeral is often compared to what happened during the coronation of Tsar Nicholas II in May 1896; following the ceremony over 1,300 people were trampled to death in the rush for refreshments and souvenirs on Khodynka Field in Moscow.
19. Abram Tertz (Andrei Sinyavsky), *Goodnight!*, 251.
20. My interview with Sergei Nikitich Khrushchev, Cranston, Rhode Island, on December 20, 2012; see also his account of the funeral in *Nikita Khrushchev: Reformator* (Reformer), 95–102.
21. Shepilov, *The Kremlin's Scholar*, 31.
22. Tertz, *Goodnight!*, 252.
23. Among the many examples of misreporting in the Western press at that time, *Newsweek* wrote: "It can be flatly stated that the Moscow news reports about the long lines of mourners passing Stalin's body as it lay in state were false. The turnout of mourners was by no means impressive"; *Newsweek*, March 23, 1953, 17.
24. Online interview with Gennady Rozhdestvenskii to mark the fiftieth anniversary of Prokofiev's death, *Rossiiskaia gazeta* (Russian Newspaper), March 6, 2003, accessed on August 19, 2012.
25. *Time* magazine mistakenly reported that "thousands filed into Composers Hall, where his body lay in state"; see *Time*, March 16, 1953, 57.
26. In her memoirs, the soprano Galina Vishnevskaya remembered Khrennikov as "a clever, scheming courtier. He had sold his soul to the devil, had paid dearly for it with his own creative sterility, and had exhausted himself in impotent rage and professional jealousy." See Vishnevskaya, *Galina: A Russian Story* (San Diego, 1984), 219.
27. Cited in Simon Morrison, *The People's Artist: Prokofiev's Soviet Years* (Oxford: Oxford University Press, 2009), 387.
28. Rostislav Dubinsky, "The Night Stalin Died," *New York Times Magazine*, March 5, 1989, 42–45. The article was adapted from his memoir *Stormy Applause: Making Music in a Workers' State*. Dubinsky was the founder of the legendary Borodin Quartet.
29. *New York Times*, March 6, 1953, 22.
30. Ibid., 9.
31. Ibid., 10.
32. Ibid., 9.

33. *The Times*, March 6, 1953, 7.
34. David Dallin and Boris Nicolaevsky, *Forced Labor in Soviet Russia* (New Haven: Yale University Press, 1955), ix.
35. *Le Monde*, March 5, 1953, 1, 3.
36. *New York Times*, March 7, 1953, 5.
37. *Pravda*, March 10, 1953, 5.
38. *New York Times*, March 7, 1953, 5.
39. *New Yorker*, April 21, 1953, 61.
40. From an article in the London-based *Daily Mail* as cited in *Time*, March 30, 1953, 26. On the Picasso controversy, see *New York Times* editorial, March 20, 1953, 12.
41. *Pravda*, March 10, 1953, 6. See *New York Times*, March 10, 1953, 10, for coverage of the work stoppage.
42. Three years later, after Khrushchev's "secret speech" in which he sharply criticized Stalin's "cult of personality," Hoxha repudiated Stalin, accusing him of "open and shameful deviation from the Leninist principle of collective leadership"; see *The Economist*, June 16, 1956, 1110, for coverage of events in Tirana in 1953 and 1956.
43. American legation in Bucharest to Secretary of State, March 13, 1953.
44. US Embassy in Bucharest to Secretary of State, March 8, 1953.
45. American legation in Bucharest to Secretary of State, March 13, 1953.
46. State Department to various US embassies on reactions in Eastern Europe, March 13, 1953; see also telegram from US Embassy in Warsaw to Secretary of State, March 6, 1953.
47. American legation in Bucharest to Secretary of State, March 13, 1953.
48. See US Embassy in Budapest to Secretary of State, March 7, 1953; and US Embassy in Ankara to Secretary of State, March 9, 1953.
49. *New York Times*, March 7, 1953, 6; the reference for the misprint in the East German newspaper can be found in *New York Times*, March 9, 1953, 4.
50. Alexander Pantsov, with Steven I. Levine, *Mao: The Real Story* (New York: Simon & Schuster, 2012), 400; and *New York Times*, March 9, 1953, 1.
51. Pantsov, *Mao*, 400.
52. *Time*, March 16, 1953, 44.
53. *The Times* (London), March 7, 1953, 5.
54. *Time*, March 16, 1953, 44.
55. Ibid.
56. Ibid., and *Documents on Israeli–Soviet Relations*, 889.
57. *The Times* (London), March 11, 1953, 7.
58. *Time*, March 16, 1953, 44.

Chapter 5: The Surprise of Reform

1. *Time*, March 16, 1953, 33.
2. Secretary of State to Jacob Beam at US Embassy in Moscow, March 7, 1953.
3. Simonov, *Glazami cheloveka*, 270.
4. The eulogies by Malenkov, Beria, and Molotov can be found in the *Current Digest of the Soviet Press*, March 28, 1953, vol. V, no. 7, 8–10.
5. Salisbury, *Moscow Journal*, 347.
6. *Istochnik* 2, 2001, 46–49, for a report to Khrushchev on March 11, 1953, about the process of embalming Stalin's corpse. His body was removed from the Mausoleum in October 1961 following further revelations about his crimes at the Twenty-Second Party Congress. The imposing granite Mausoleum was covered in plywood for several weeks while workers made the necessary adjustments. Stalin was buried next to the Kremlin Wall with a bust on a pedestal standing on a cement slab. As of this writing Lenin's mummy remains alone in the Mausoleum in spite of occasional public appeals for a proper burial.

7. Alexeyeva, *The Thaw Generation*, 4.
8. Vishnevskaya, *Galina: A Russian Story*, 99.
9. Juliane Fürst, *Stalin's Last Generation: Soviet Post-War Youth and the Emergence of Mature Socialism* (Oxford: Oxford University Press, 2010), 121.
10. Alexander Solzhenitsyn, *Cancer Ward* (New York: Bantam, 1969), 311.
11. Yevtushenko, *A Precocious Autobiography*, 84.
12. Aleksandr Nekrich, *Forsake Fear: Memoirs of a Historian* (Boston: Unwin Hyman, 1991), 74–75.
13. Tamm was awarded the Nobel Prize in Physics in 1958 for his work on electromagnetic radiation.
14. Sakharov, *Memoirs*, 163–64.
15. Yevtushenko, *A Precocious Autobiography*, 84.
16. Michael Scammell, *Solzhenitsyn: A Biography* (New York: Norton, 1984), 317.
17. Eugeniya Ginzburg, *Within the Whirlwind* (New York: Harcourt Brace Jovanovich, 1981), 358.
18. Interview with Tatiana Yankelevich, the daughter of Elena Bonner, Brookline, Massachusetts, April 5, 2013.
19. From the resolution of the assistant prosecutor of the Department for Special Cases of the Krasnoyarsk region on the case of B. A. Basov, June 4, 1953. GARF (State Archive of the Russian Federation), collection (*f.*) R-8131, inventory (*op.*) 31, file (*d.*) 38248, pages (*ll.*) 5–6.
20. Nikolai Bobol, "Who Stalin dragged after him," *Novaya gazeta.ru* (The New Newspaper), accessed online May 28, 2012, 2–4 for a description of these cases.
21. Vladimir Kozlov, Sheila Fitzpatrick, and Sergei Mironenko (eds), *Sedition: Everyday Resistance in the Soviet Union under Khrushchev and Brezhnev* (New Haven: Yale University Press, 2011), 67–68.
22. Tertz (Andrei Sinyavsky), *Goodnight!*, 238.
23. *The Times* (London), "New Structure of Soviet Leadership," March 9, 1953, 9.
24. In his memoirs George Kennan reported how Khrushchev, at least in the summer of 1952, was regarded as the "least influential member of the Politburo"; see Kennan, *Memoirs 1950–1963*, vol. II, 152. Eisenhower had a similar impression. He thought of Khrushchev as "a little-known official"; see *Mandate for Change*, 144.
25. *The Times* (London), March 9, 1953, 9.
26. *Time*, March 23, 1953, 29. Stalin's portrait had appeared ten times on the cover of *Time*.
27. Jan Plamper has traced the further evolution of Stalin's appearance (or rather disappearance) in the pages of *Pravda*. "Shortly after Stalin's death began the silent phase of de-Stalinization," he writes in *The Stalin Cult: A Study in the Alchemy of Power* (New Haven: Yale University Press, 2012), 84. "The tectonic, if underground, shift was lost on no one. No even partially discerning *Pravda* reader could have missed it. During the entire remainder of 1953, Stalin appeared in pictures a mere five times: once in a poster on the May Day demonstration, once (on 30 July) in the well-worn photograph with Lenin in Gorky on the occasion of the fiftieth anniversary of the Bolshevik Party's founding, three times on posters in the background at the Day of the October Revolution celebrations (twice with Lenin, once by himself)." There was no mention of his birthday on December 21, while on March 5, 1954, on the first anniversary of his death, a full portrait of Stalin dressed in a simple, dark army uniform returned to *Pravda*'s front page. It was all his heirs cared to do. I am indebted to Professor Plamper for his research and insights into how Stalin's death was covered in *Pravda*.
28. *Literaturnaia gazeta*, March 19, 1953, 1; see also *New York Times*, March 20, 1953, 6.
29. Simonov, *Glazami cheloveka*, 284–86.
30. William Taubman, *Khrushchev: The Man and His Era* (New York: Norton, 2003), 245.
31. Noble had been born in the United States but spent the war in Dresden with his parents where they survived as enemy aliens. He was arrested when the Red Army liberated the city.

32. John Noble, *I Was a Slave in Russia: An American Tells his Story* (Broadview, Illinois: Cicero Bible Press, 1962), 141. The 1,200 killings seem like a wild exaggeration, an inflated figure in line with camp lore.

33. Miriam Dobson, *Khrushchev's Cold Summer: Returnees, Crime, and the Fate of Reform After Stalin* (Ithaca: Cornell University Press, 2009), 39–43; some of this material is also drawn from Gaël Moullec and Nicolas Werth (eds), *Rapports secrets soviétiques: La Société russe dans les documents confidentiels, 1921–1991* (Paris: Gallimard, 1994), 409–16.

34. See Kostyrchenko, *Out of the Red Shadows*, 300–301.

35. Oleg V. Khlevniuk, *Stalin: New Biography of a Dictator* (New Haven: Yale University Press, 2015), 311.

36. *Khrushchev Remembers: The Last Testament* (Boston: Little, Brown, 1974), 79. It is worth noting that Khrushchev used the word "thaw" which Ilya Ehrenburg had introduced into the country's vocabulary in 1954 over the objections of the regime and its cultural bureaucrats.

37. See *Pravda*, April 4, 1953, 2.

38. The articles can be found in the *Current Digest of the Soviet Press*, April 18, 1953, vol. V, no. 10, 3, and April 25, 1953, vol. V, no. 11, 3–4.

39. Ehrenburg, *Lyudi, gody, zhizn*, vol. III, 243.

40. *Newsweek*, April 6, 1953, 44.

41. Cited in *New York Times*, April 5, 1953, 12. But the French communist press was caught flat-footed, surprised by the unexpected turn-around in Moscow. Just as the doctors were being released, its journal *La Nouvelle Critique* denounced the very same doctors for their "perverted science" and "monstrous acts"; see Dr. Louis Le Guillant, "Les médicins criminels ou la science pervertie," *La Nouvelle Critique*, no. 44, March 1953, 32–66. Publication of the issue, which also covered the death of Stalin, had been delayed and contributed to the poor timing of the PCF's attack on the wrongfully imprisoned doctors. The *New York Times* made note of the article on April 5, 1953, 9.

42. *New York Times*, April 5, 1953, E10.

43. *FRUS*, VIII, 1140. His cable was dated April 4, 1953.

44. *New York Times*, April 5, 1953, 1, 4.

45. About the fate of Etinger, see Brent and Naumov, *Stalin's Last Crime*, 111–12; Rapoport, *The Doctors' Plot of 1953*, 80.

46. Bohlen, *Witness to History* (New York: Norton, 1973), 347.

47. The report from the editors of *Pravda* can be found in Harvard's Widener Library, A1046, reel 002, *delo* 5.

48. *Pravda*, April 17, 1953, 2.

49. Ibid., April 16, 1953, 2.

50. Ibid., May 11, 1953, 2.

Chapter 6: A Chance for Peace?

1. Kennan was referring to the violent purges that marked Stalin's consolidation of control, including his defeat of Leon Trotsky and other once-prestigious and powerful party leaders.

2. The quotations are from Kennan's famous "Long Telegram" dated February 22, 1946. They can be found in his *Memoirs*, vol. I, 558.

3. *FRUS*, VIII, 1080.

4. Psychological Strategy Board, Washington, DC, *Program of Psychological Preparation for Stalin's Passing From Power*, November 1, 1952. This is a three-page paper.

5. Cited in Christopher J. Tudda, "'Reenacting the Story of Tantalus': Eisenhower, Dulles, and the Failed Rhetoric of Liberation," *Journal of Cold War Studies*, vol. 7, no. 4, Fall 2005, 9; Foster Dulles wrote this part of the Republican platform.

6. *Life*, May 19, 1952, 146.

7. Ibid., 154.

8. *New York Times*, December 25, 1952, 1.
9. Cited in Blanche Wiesen Cook, *The Declassified Eisenhower: A Divided Legacy* (Garden City, New York: Doubleday, 1981), 178.
10. Salisbury, *Moscow Journal*, 309.
11. Eisenhower, *Mandate for Change*, 143.
12. Adams, *Firsthand Report*, 96.
13. Steven Fish, "After Stalin's Death: The Anglo-American Debate Over a New Cold War," *Diplomatic History 10* (no. 4, 1986), 336.
14. Richard Goold-Adams, *John Foster Dulles, A Reappraisal* (New York: Appleton-Century, Crofts, 1962), 79.
15. *Newsweek*, February 9, 1953, 17.
16. Cited in Klaus Larres, *Churchill's Cold War: The Politics of Personal Diplomacy* (New Haven: Yale University Press, 2002), 186.
17. *Newsweek*, March 9, 1953, 27.
18. Within days after Eisenhower's inauguration, Foster Dulles traveled to Western Europe with the primary purpose of encouraging America's allies to ratify the European Defense Community.
19. Vojtech Mastny, "The Elusive Détente: Stalin's Successors and the West," in Klaus Larres and Kenneth Osgood (eds), *The Cold War After Stalin's Death: A Missed Opportunity for Peace?* (Lanham, Maryland: Rowman & Littlefield, 2006), 6.
20. See Harry Rositzke, *The CIA's Secret Operations* (New York: Reader's Digest, 1977), 168–72.
21. Leonard Mosley, *Dulles: A Biography of Eleanor, Allen, and John Foster Dulles and Their Family Network* (New York: The Dial Press, 1978), 331.
22. *FRUS*, VIII, 1091–93.
23. *Newsweek*, March 16, 1953, 19.
24. Larres, *Churchill's Cold War*, 197.
25. *FRUS*, VIII, 1090.
26. Ibid., 1084, dispatched on March 4, 1953.
27. Klaus Larres, "Eisenhower and the First Forty Days after Stalin's Death: The Incompatibilty of *Détente* and Political Warfare," *Diplomacy & Statecraft*, vol. 6, no. 2 (July 1995), 431.
28. Bohlen, *Witness to History*, 336.
29. Cited in Melvyn P. Leffler, *For the Soul of Mankind: The United States, the Soviet Union, and the Cold War* (New York: Hill & Wang, 2007), 101.
30. Bedell Smith's testimony can be found in the United States Congressional Record, Executive Session of the Senate Foreign Relations Committee, Historical Series, vol. V, 83rd Congress, First Session, 1953, 247–65; this quotation is from 248–49.
31. *The Times*, March 14, 1953, 6. As for Kennan, neither Eisenhower nor Dulles sought his counsel. Eisenhower was dismissive of Kennan, thinking of him as "too academic," as he told Hamilton Fish Armstrong, the editor of *Foreign Affairs*. "He could rationalize a lamb chop out of a baked potato"; see papers of Hamilton Fish Armstrong, Box 102, a memorandum in his Notebooks dated December 23, 1952, 3, Seeley G. Mudd Manuscript Library, Princeton University. Foster Dulles was equally cold. By not offering Kennan a new posting he was planning to end his diplomatic career by default. (According to State Department regulations, Kennan would face mandatory retirement within three months of not receiving a new position.) When Kennan visited Washington on March 10, he saw Charles Bohlen and C. D. Jackson, but neither Eisenhower nor Foster Dulles was interested in talking with him. Kennan was aware of the new administration's indifference to his experience or his views. As he wrote in his diary on March 13, 1953, "the Pres and JFD were apparently not interested either in discussing with me my future as that of the Moscow position, nor were they interested in my views about the Soviet Union or US–Soviet relations. . . . I could not help but view this as a very serious and disturbing situation"; see George F. Kennan papers,

MC076, Box 233, Folder 1, File no. 1-F, 2, Seeley G. Mudd Manuscript Library, Princeton University. Months passed before an intervention by Emmet Hughes in June 1953 prevailed upon Eisenhower to send Kennan a generous letter in recognition of his illustrious career.

32. See Herbert S. Parmet, *Eisenhower and the American Crusades* (New Brunswick: Transaction, 1999), 237.

33. Here again, Foster Dulles parted ways with the president. Once opposition began to develop in the Senate, Foster Dulles asked Bohlen if he intended to back out of the nomination. He then insisted they ride in separate cars to Capitol Hill for Bohlen's testimony so as to avoid being photographed together; see Bohlen, *Witness to History*, 324.

34. Bedell Smith's testimony, United States Congressional Record, 253 and 260. Regardless of his testimony before the Senate Foreign Relations Committee in 1953, Bedell Smith had predicted a different and altogether accurate outcome in his memoir which had appeared in 1949: that Molotov, Malenkov, and Beria would control the succession and that "no struggle is likely to occur that is in any way commensurate with the battle of giants which took place after Lenin's death." See Walter Bedell Smith, *My Three Years in Moscow* (New York: J. P. Lippincott, 1949), 95.

35. Emmet John Hughes, *The Ordeal of Power: A Political Memoir of the Eisenhower Years* (New York: Atheneum, 1963), 101; and his diary note for Friday, March 6, in Hughes Papers, MC073, Box 1, folder 5, Seeley G. Mudd Manuscript Library, Princeton University. A. J. Liebling picked up on the administration's confusion. "A formidable old man had died and nobody knew what to expect as a consequence"; see *New Yorker*, March 28, 1953, 105.

36. *New York Times*, March 6, 1953, 13.

37. Richard L. Bissell, Jr., papers, Walt and Eugene Rostow Series, Box 2 (A09–01) (hereafter "Rostow series"), Book III, 2, Dwight D. Eisenhower Presidential Library, Abilene, Kansas.

38. Rostow series, III, 103.

39. Hughes, *The Ordeal of Power*, 100–101.

40. See *FRUS*, VIII, 1075–77. Charles Edward Wilson, who had been CEO of General Electric, should not be confused with Charles Erwin Wilson, who served as secretary of defense under Eisenhower and later as CEO of General Motors. It is worth noting that he had initially made the same proposal to President Truman.

41. The draft memorandum by Harold Stassen, which was addressed to members of the Psychological Strategy Board on March 10, 1953, can be found in the Jackson, C. D.: Records, 1953–54, Box 1, Pre-Acc, in the folder marked "PSB Plans for Psychological Exploitation of Stalin's Death" at the Dwight D. Eisenhower Presidential Library.

42. Rostow series, III, 1.

43. *FRUS*, VIII, 1117.

44. Rostow series, III, 2.

45. Ibid., III, 3

46. Ibid., III, 5.

47. *FRUS*, VIII, 1122.

48. Rostow series, III, 17.

49. Cited in Larres, *Churchill's Cold War*, 133.

50. Their messages on March 11 can be found in Peter G. Boyle (ed.), *The Churchill–Eisenhower Correspondence, 1953–1955* (Chapel Hill: University of North Carolina Press, 1990), 31–32.

51. Frank Roberts, *Dealing with Dictators: The Destruction and Revival of Europe, 1930–1970* (London: Weidenfeld & Nicolson, 1991), 165.

52. *New York Times*, March 11, 1953, 1. I am indebted to Richard Stebbins, *The United States in World Affairs 1953* (New York: Council on Foreign Relations and Harper & Row, 1955), 114–16, for his account of these incidents.

53. Ibid., March 13, 1953, 26.

54. *The Times*, March 13, 1953, 8; March 14, 1953, 6, 7.
55. *Current Digest of the Soviet Press*, April 4, 1953, vol. 5, no. 8, 1953, 5. Beria is reported to have said something similar, remarking to his son that it was necessary "to end the confrontation with the outside world" in order to make life better for the Soviet people; see Sergo Beria, *Beria, My Father: Inside Stalin's Kremlin* (London: Gerald Duckworth & Co., 2001), 253.
56. Cited in Marc Trachtenberg, *A Constructed Peace: The Making of the European Settlement, 1945–1963* (Princeton: Princeton University Press, 1999), 95.
57. Nikita Khrushchev, *Khrushchev Remembers: The Glasnost Tapes* (Boston: Little Brown, 1990), 100–101.
58. Nikita Khrushchev, *Khrushchev Remembers* (1970), 392.
59. Rostow series, III, 62.
60. Hughes, *The Ordeal of Power*, 103–105. See also Deborah Welch Larson, *Anatomy of Mistrust: US Soviet Relations During the Cold War* (Ithaca: Cornell University Press, 1997), 43–44.
61. Cited in W. W. Rostow, *Europe After Stalin: Eisenhower's Three Decisions of March 11, 1953* (Austin: University of Texas Press, 1982), 47.
62. *New York Times*, March 20, 1953, 3. General Andrew Goodpaster, who worked closely with Eisenhower as his White House staff secretary and defense liaison starting in early 1954, recalled years later that he had heard "the administration did a great deal of floundering around trying to see what the significance of [Stalin's death] might be in terms of US interests and US actions"; in William B. Pickett (ed.), *George F. Kennan and the Origins of Eisenhower's New Look: An Oral History of Project Solarium* (Princeton Institute for International and Regional Studies, no. 1, 2004), 37.
63. Eisenhower, *Mandate for Change*, 148.
64. Cited in Leffler, *For the Soul of Mankind*, 105, from a meeting of the National Security Council on April 8, 1953.
65. Eisenhower, *Mandate for Change*, 144.
66. Cited in Townsend Hoopes, *The Devil and John Foster Dulles* (Boston: Atlantic Monthly Press, 1973), 171.
67. *New York Times*, April 3, 1953, 3.
68. There were moments that spring when the Eisenhower administration grew so frustrated and anxious over the course of the continuing war that it seriously considered using nuclear weapons against communist forces; see John Lewis Gaddis, *The Long Peace: Inquiries Into the History of the Cold War* (New York: Oxford University Press, 1987), 124–29.
69. *New York Times*, April 3, 1953, 5.
70. Thomas Whitney, *Russia in My Life* (New York: Reynal, 1962), 283. Weeks later Wick found himself objecting to Soviet press reports claiming that he and his group had endorsed the Soviet "peace offensive," convinced of the Kremlin's will to find a "peaceful solution of all conflicts." Soviet officials found their reports to be positive and were happy to trumpet their approval. Wick did not want to seem gullible and so denounced their praise "as so many lies . . . in so few words"; *New York Times*, April 18, 1953, 22.
71. *Time*, April 13, 1953, 28.
72. *New York Times*, April 2, 1953, 26.
73. Cited in Mark Kramer, "International Politics in the Early Post-Stalin Era: A Lost Opportunity, a Turning Point, or More of the Same?" in Larres and Osgood (eds), *The Cold War After Stalin's Death*, xiv.
74. Undated memorandum from Walt Rostow from early March 1953, 4, in C. D. Jackson, Records, 1953–54, Box 6, Pre-Acc, Rostow, Walter W. (4), Dwight D. Eisenhower Presidential Library.
75. Cited in Kramer, "International Politics in the Early Post-Stalin Era," xiv.
76. *FRUS*, VIII, 1138.
77. Cited in Kramer, "International Politics in the Early Post-Stalin Era," xv.

78. Bernard Pares, *A History of Russia* (New York, Knopf, 1944), 340–46.
79. Salisbury, *Moscow Journal*, 388.
80. Hughes, *The Ordeal of Power*, 104.
81. Cited in Leffler, *For the Soul of Mankind*, 103.
82. Cited in Cook, *The Declassified Eisenhower*, 179; from Hughes note to Eisenhower dated March 27, 1953.
83. Hoopes, *The Devil and John Foster Dulles*, 172. See also Larson, *Anatomy of Mistrust*, 47.
84. *Foreign Relations of the United States 1952–1954*, vol. II: National Security Affairs, Part 1, 267.
85. Hughes, *The Ordeal of Power*, 104.
86. Adams, *Firsthand Report*, 97.
87. The full text of Eisenhower's speech can be found in Rostow, *Europe After Stalin*, 113–22.
88. *Newsweek*, April 27, 1953, 27.
89. *New York Times*, April 17, 1953, 24.
90. Adams, *Firsthand Report*, 97.
91. *New York Post*, April 17, 1953, 43.
92. *New Yorker*, May 2, 1953, 116.
93. *Newsweek*, April 27, 1953, 28.
94. Information cited in Cook, *The Declassified Eisenhower*, 180–81.
95. Adams, *Firsthand Report*, 97.
96. Hughes, *The Ordeal of Power*, 118.
97. The full text of Dulles' speech can be found in Rostow, *Europe After Stalin*, 122–31.
98. Cook, *The Declassified Eisenhower*, 172.
99. Rostow series, III, 93.
100. Oleg Troyanovsky, "The Making of Soviet Foreign Policy," in William Taubman, Sergei Khrushchev, and Abbot Gleason (eds), *Nikita Khrushchev* (New Haven: Yale University Press, 2000), 211.
101. Goold-Adams, *John Foster Dulles*, 61. Walt Rostow, who was a close observer of these events, could only assume that Foster Dulles showed Eisenhower the text of his speech, "although the relevant speech file in Dulles' papers does not indicate that such clearance took place"; see Rostow, *Europe After Stalin*, 80, and 192 n. 45.
102. Cited in Larres, "Eisenhower and the First Forty Days after Stalin's Death," 457.
103. Eisenhower, *Mandate for Change*, 148.
104. Rostow, *Europe After Stalin*, 162–64 for the full text of Bohlen's response.
105. The full text of the Soviet commentary on Eisenhower's speech can be found in Rostow, *Europe After Stalin*, 150–62.
106. Kennan letter to Allen Dulles on April 25, 1953 in C. D. Jackson, Records 1953–54, Box 4, Folder: Kennan, Dwight D. Eisenhower Presidential Library.
107. Bohlen, *Witness to History*, 371.
108. *Pravda*, May 1, 1953, 4.
109. See *New York Times*, April 5, 1953, 1, about Israeli approaches to the Kremlin after the disavowal of the Doctors' Plot. See also articles that appeared in both *Pravda* and *Izvestia* on July 21, 1953, in *Current Digest of the Soviet Press*, August 15, 1953, vol. V, no. 27, 13–14.
110. Gilmore wrote about the experience in *Me and My Russian Wife*; Robert Tucker went on to become a widely respected professor of history and political science at Princeton and a biographer of Stalin.
111. Cited in Larres, *Churchill's Cold War*, 226.
112. Ibid., 223. I am indebted to Klaus Larres for his account of Churchill's speech and its political ramifications.
113. *The Times* (London), May 12, 1953, 3.
114. Ibid., 6.
115. *New York Times*, May 12, 1953, 26.
116. Ibid., 11.

117. Ibid., May 15, 1953, 1.
118. Ibid., May 12, 1953, 1. Two years later, in February 1955, when Khrushchev replaced Malenkov as Soviet premier, Eisenhower explained to his press secretary, James Hagerty, why he had resisted calls to meet with Malenkov in 1953. "It took an awful long time to get the British to realize that with the trouble going on inside of Russia, it would not be to the advantage of the free world for Churchill and myself and whoever the Frenchman would be to sit down publicly with any given leader of Russia. If we did that, it would serve notice, not only throughout the world but also within Russia, that we were recognizing Malenkov or Bulganin or whoever else it might be as the leader. That would give him a great advantage within Russia and would tend to minimize the struggles for power that are going on within Russia. We certainly don't want to do that and that's why I have never wanted to meet with the Russian leader—at least for the time being." Robert H. Ferrell (ed.), *The Diary of James C. Hagerty, Eisenhower in Mid-Course, 1954–1955* (Bloomington: Indiana University Press, 1983), 187–88.
119. Cited in *The Times* (London), May 13, 1953, 6.
120. Fish, "After Stalin's Death," 338.
121. A full translation of the *Pravda* article on May 24, 1953, can be found in *The Current Digest of the Soviet Press*, June 13, 1953, vol. 5, no. 18, 8–11.
122. Nikita Khrushchev, *Khrushchev Remembers: The Last Testament*, 362.
123. Nikita Khrushchev, *Khrushchev Remembers* (1970), 393.
124. *Public Papers of the Presidents of the United States, Dwight D. Eisenhower 1953* (Washington, DC: National Archives and Records Service, US Government Printing Office, 1960), 372.
125. *New York Times*, May 24, 1953, 1.
126. Cited in Uri Bar-Noi, "The Soviet Union and Churchill's appeals for high-level talks, 1953–54: New Evidence from the Russian archives," *Diplomacy & Statecraft*, vol. 9, no. 3 (November 1998), 115.
127. "Iz dnevnika Yakova Malika 30 iuniia 1953, zapis besedi s Premier-Ministrom Veliko-Britanii Cherchillem, 3 iuniia, 1953" (From the diary of Yakov Malik, June 30, 1953, a note about his conversation with British Prime Minister Churchill on June 3, 1953), *Istochnik* 2 (2003).
128. Churchill had in January 1953 visited New York, where he had a private meeting with Eisenhower before the inauguration. Their next meeting was in Bermuda in the first week of December.
129. Hoopes, *The Devil and John Foster Dulles*, 172.
130. Troyanovsky, "The Making of Soviet Foreign Policy," 214, 218.
131. Adam Ulam, *Expansion and Coexistence: The History of Soviet Foreign Policy, 1917–67* (New York: Praeger, 1968), 506.
132. *New Yorker*, March 28, 1953, 111.
133. Bohlen, *Witness to History*, 343–44.
134. Cited in Mark Kramer, "International Politics in the Early Post-Stalin Era," xxxi–xxxii, n. 20.
135. John Lewis Gaddis, *Strategies of Containment: A Critical Appraisal of Postwar American National Security Policy* (New York: Oxford University Press, 1982), 162.
136. A somewhat similar incident occurred at the height of Mikhail Gorbachev's reform efforts. Richard B. Cheney, who would later serve as vice-president under President George W. Bush, was the defense secretary under President George H. W. Bush. *Business Week* reported on April 9, 1990, that "While the rest of the Administration has embraced Soviet President Mikhail Gorbachev and his reforms, Cheney has become increasingly isolated in his insistence that the Soviet threat remains potent" (35). He was determined to oppose any relaxation in the US–Soviet military confrontation. Notwithstanding his views, the Soviet Union formally dissolved in December 1991.

Chapter 7: The End of the Beginning

1. Troyanovsky, "The Making of Soviet Foreign Policy," 209–10.
2. Mark Kramer, "The Early Post-Stalin Struggle and Upheavals in East-Central Europe," Part I, *Journal of Cold War Studies*, vol. 1, no. 1, Winter 1999, 6.
3. Christian F. Ostermann (ed.), *Uprising in East Germany 1953: The Cold War, the German Question, and the First Major Upheaval Behind the Iron Curtain* (Budapest: Central European University Press, 2001), 86–89. See also J. F. Brown, *Bulgaria Under Communist Rule* (New York: Praeger, 1970), 23–27.
4. *Manchester Guardian*, July 6, 1953, 1.
5. Otto Ulc, "Pilsen: The Unknown Revolt," *Problems of Communism*, vol. 14, no. 3 (May–June 1965), 47.
6. Cited in Kramer, "The Early Post-Stalin Struggle and Upheavals in East-Central Europe," Part I, 22, 23, 35.
7. "Transcript of Conversations between the Soviet Leadership and a Hungarian Workers' Party Delegation in Moscow, 13 and 16 June 1953," in Ostermann (ed.), *Uprising in East Germany*, 145–53.
8. See Kramer, "The Early Post-Stalin Struggle and Upheavals in East-Central Europe," Part I, 34.
9. *New York Times*, June 15, 1953, 5.
10. Victor Baras, "Beria's Fall and Ulbricht's Survival," *Soviet Studies*, vol. 27, no. 3 (July 1975), 386.
11. *New York Times*, June 17, 1953, 1.
12. Ibid.
13. By some estimates seventy per cent of the population listened to RIAS on a regular basis.
14. Arnulf Baring, *Uprising in East Germany: June 17, 1953* (Ithaca: Cornell University Press, 1972), 48–49.
15. *New York Times*, June 18, 1953, 1.
16. Ibid., June 19, 1953, 12.
17. For casualty figures, see Kramer, "The Early Post-Stalin Struggle and Upheavals in East-Central Europe," Part I, 54; and "Situation Report from Andrei Grechko and A. Tarasov to Nikolai Bulganin, 18 June, as of 8:00 a.m. Moscow Time (6:00 a.m. CET)," in Ostermann (ed.), *Uprising in East Germany*, 214–15, along with the editor's reference to updated research.
18. *New York Times*, June 18, 1953, 9.
19. Ibid., June 20, 1953, 4.
20. Ibid., June 18, 1953, 8.
21. Ibid., June 19, 1953, 12.
22. Ibid., June 20, 1953, 4.
23. Ibid., June 18, 1953, 8.
24. Ibid., June 27, 1953, 3.
25. Ibid., June 19, 1953, 12.
26. The full report can be found in "Document No. 60: Report from Vasilii Sokolovskii, Vladimir Semyonov, and Pavel Yudin—On the Events of 17–19 June 1953 in Berlin and the GDR and Certain Conclusions from These Events, 24 June 1953," in Ostermann (ed.), *Uprising in East Germany*, 257–85.
27. *New York Times*, June 23, 1953, 1.
28. Herbert R. Lottman, *Albert Camus: A Biography* (New York: George Braziller, 1980), 526.
29. *New York Times*, June 23, 1953, 8.
30. Khrushchev, *Khrushchev Remembers* (1970), 319.
31. Shepilov, *The Kremlin's Scholar*, 258.
32. Ibid., 263.

33. Khrushchev described how he conspired against Beria in *Khrushchev Remembers* (1970), 323–41.
34. Mark Kramer, "Political Succession and Political Violence in the USSR Following Stalin's Death," in Paul Hollander (ed.), *Political Violence: Belief, Behavior, and Legitimation* (New York: Palgrave Macmillan, 2008), 69–92. I am relying on this essay for my account of the meeting on June 26 and other dimensions to Beria's downfall and arrest.
35. See Amy Knight, *Beria: Stalin's First Lieutenant* (Princeton: Princeton University Press, 1996), 198; this book provides a vivid account of Beria's arrest.
36. Cited in Kramer, "Political Succession," 90.
37. Mark Kramer, "Declassified Materials from CPSU Central Committee Plenums: Sources, context, highlights," *Cahiers du Monde russe*, 40/1–2, janvier–juin 1999, 279.
38. For Malenkov's remarks, see "The Beria Affair," *Political Archives of Russia*, vol. 3, no. 2/3 (Commack, New York: Nova Science Publishers, 1992), 71–76. For Khrushchev's remarks, see ibid., 83. For Molotov's, see ibid., 85.
39. "The Beria Affair," 109–13, 156.
40. Ibid., 145.
41. Cited in Kramer, "Declassified Materials," 280.
42. Resis, *Molotov Remembers*, 334; Andrei Gromyko, *Memoirs* (New York: Doubleday, 1989), 317; Shepilov, *The Kremlin's Scholar*, 260; Pavel Sudoplatov and Anatoli Sudoplatov, with Jerrold L. and Leona P. Schecter, *Special Tasks: The Memoirs of an Unwanted Witness—A Soviet Spymaster* (Boston: Little, Brown, 1994), 363–64; "The Beria Affair," 82, for Khrushchev's denunciation of Beria.
43. *New York Times*, July 10, 1953, 1 and 5 for coverage of *Pravda's* article and a listing of Beria's other alleged crimes.
44. Ibid., July 11, 1953, 10.
45. Ibid., July 10, 1953, 1.
46. Cited in ibid., July 11, 1953, 4.
47. See Emmet John Hughes papers, MC073, Box 2, Folder 5, cabinet notes from early July; there is no written date. Seeley G. Mudd Manuscript Library, Princeton University.
48. Bohlen, *Witness to History*, 356.
49. The *New York Times* leading foreign affairs correspondent, C. L. Sulzberger, expressed similar confusion, remarking that "Probably no student of Soviet affairs has been certain in recent months which individual's name could be associated with what political view in the Soviet Union." Both quotations are from *New York Times*, July 11, 1953, 4 and 3.
50. Ibid., 1.
51. Ibid., July 13, 1953, 4.
52. Scammell, *Solzhenitsyn: A Biography*, 278.
53. Solzhenitsyn, *The Gulag Archipelago*, vol. III, 280–83.
54. See ibid., 285–331 for Solzhenitsyn's account of the Kengir revolt.

Epilogue

1. Ehrenburg, *Lyudi, gody, zhizn*, vol. III, 246–47.
2. Letter from Beria to Malenkov on July 1, 1953, in O. B. Mozokhina (ed.), *Delo Lavrentiia Berii* (The Case of Lavrenti Beria) (Moscow: Kuchkovo pole, 2015), 25, 32.
3. Ibid., 36, for Beria's letter of July 2, 1953.
4. Central Committee materials, A1046, Reel OO2, *delo* 4, 64, in Widener Library of Harvard University; the letter from Merkulov to Khrushchev is dated July 21, 1953. Andrei Gromyko had a similar experience. Visiting the Kremlin, he heard "Gales of loud laughter . . . coming from inside Khrushchev's office. Who was in there? The Politburo members who the very next day, with heads bent low and melancholy faces, would be burying Stalin"; see Gromyko, *Memoirs*, 357.

For years following Stalin's death there was public speculation that he had been killed. Harrison Salisbury published an article on the front page of the *New York Times* on September 20, 1954, that began with the explicit and provocative claim that "It is by no means impossible that Stalin was murdered on or about March 5, 1953, by the group of his close associates who now run Russia." Fueled by rumors in Moscow, Salisbury pointed to "considerable circumstantial evidence" that the dictator had been slain by his colleagues who acted to protect themselves at a moment of mortal danger to their own lives and well-being.

Such claims persisted. In September 1958, the American television network CBS presented a docudrama called *The Plot to Kill Stalin* in its prestigious Playhouse 90 series. The show depicted Khrushchev, who was now Soviet premier, preventing an aide from giving medicine to Stalin as he lay dying. As the one-time Moscow correspondent Daniel Schorr recalled, "It told an apocryphal story of Khrushchev as an accomplice to Stalin's death. We were told that Khrushchev hit the ceiling when he learned of the program" (see Schorr, *Staying Tuned: A Life in Journalism* (New York: Pocket Books, 2001)). In retaliation the Kremlin closed the CBS bureau in Moscow and did not allow it to re-open until 1960.

5. Central Committee materials, A1046, Reel OO2, *delo* 4, 117; the letter is dated July 12, 1953.

6. Gnedin's letter can be found in V. N. Khaustov (ed.), *Delo Beria: prigovor obzhalavaniyu ne podlezhit* (The Beria Case: Not Subject to Appeal) (Moscow: Mezhdunarodnyi fond "demokratiya," 2012), 98–100. The letter is dated July 16, 1953, just days after Beria's arrest was made public. Stalin's heirs all knew Gnedin quite well, not only from his work at the Ministry of Foreign Affairs, but because his father was Aleksandr Parvus, a close associate of Lenin's. In the 1960s, Gnedin worked closely with Frida Vigdorova who is widely regarded as the "first dissident"; they were together in Leningrad to observe the trial of the poet Joseph Brodsky in March 1964 and compiled a transcript of the proceedings that later embarrassed the regime.

7. Khaustov (ed.), *Delo Beria*, 205–6.

8. *New York Times*, December 20, 1953, E1.

9. Dmitri Volkogonov, *Stalin: Triumph and Tragedy* (New York: Grove Weidenfeld, 1991), 333.

10. Ibid.

11. *New York Times*, December 21, 1953, 3, citing a Tass communiqué.

12. Cited in Knight, *Beria*, 201.

13. Central Committee materials, A1046, Reel OO2, *delo* 4, 127, in Widener Library; the report is dated August 14, 1953.

14. From the diary of Emmet John Hughes, MC073, Box 2, Folder 5, July 13, 1953; Seeley G. Mudd Manuscript Library, Princeton University.

15. Hughes, *The Ordeal of Power*, 360.

16. Hoopes, *The Devil and John Foster Dulles*, 171.

17. Rostow, *Europe After Stalin*, 75.

18. Bohlen, *Witness to History*, 371.

19. Larres, "Eisenhower and the First Forty Days after Stalin's Death," 457.

SELECT BIBLIOGRAPHY

Adams, Sherman. *Firsthand Report: The Story of the Eisenhower Administration*. New York: Harper and Brothers, 1961.

Alliluyeva, Svetlana. *Twenty Letters to a Friend*. Trans. Priscilla Johnson McMillan. New York: Harper & Row, 1967.

Barnes, Steven A. *Death and Redemption: The Gulag and the Shaping of Soviet Society*. Princeton: Princeton University Press, 2011.

Bartoli, Georges. *The Death of Stalin*. Trans. Raymond Rosenthal. New York: Praeger, 1975.

Beam, Jacob. *Multiple Exposure: An American Ambassador's Unique Perspective on East–West Issues*. New York: Norton, 1978.

"Beria Affair, The." *Political Archives of Russia*, Vol. 3, No. 2/3. Commack, New York: Nova Science Publishers, 1992.

Bohlen, Charles. *Witness to History*. New York: Norton, 1973.

Boyle, Peter G. (ed.). *The Churchill–Eisenhower Correspondence, 1953–1955*. Chapel Hill: University of North Carolina Press, 1990.

Brent, Jonathan and Naumov, Vladimir P. *Stalin's Last Crime: The Plot Against the Jewish Doctors, 1948–1953*. New York: HarperCollins, 2003.

Confidential US State Department Central Files. "A Guide to the Soviet Union: Internal Affairs 1950–1954 and Foreign Affairs 1950–1954." Ed. Paul Kesaris, guide compiled by Robert Lester. Frederick, Maryland: A Microfilm Project of University Publications of America, Inc., 1985.

Djilas, Milovan. *Conversations with Stalin*. Trans. Michael B. Petrovich. Harmondsworth: Penguin, 1969.

Documents on Israeli–Soviet Relations 1941–1953, Part II: May 1949–1953. London: Frank Cass, 2000.

Eisenhower, Dwight David. *Mandate for Change 1953–1956: The White House Years, A Personal Account*. Garden City, New York: Doubleday, 1963.

Fitzpatrick, Sheila. *On Stalin's Team: The Years of Living Dangerously in Soviet Politics*. Princeton: Princeton University Press, 2015.

Foreign Relations of the United States, 1952–1954. Vol. VIII: Eastern Europe; Soviet Union; Eastern Mediterranean. Editor in Chief William Z. Slany. Washington: US Government Printing Office, 1984 ("FRUS, VIII").

Frezinsky, Boris. "Ilya Erenburg v gody stalinskogo gosantisemitizma—polemika s g. Kostyrchenko" (Ilya Ehrenburg During the Years of Stalin's Official Antisemitism—An

Argument with Mr. Kostyrchenko). *Pisateli i sovietskie vozhdi* (Writers and Soviet Power). Moscow: Ellis lak, 2008.

Gilboa, Yehoshua A. *The Black Years of Soviet Jewry 1939–1953*. Boston: Little, Brown, 1971.

Gilmore, Eddy. *Me and My Russian Wife*. Garden City, New York: Doubleday, 1954.

Gorlizki, Yoram and Khlevniuk, Oleg. *Cold Peace: Stalin and the Soviet Ruling Circle, 1945–1953*. Oxford: Oxford University Press, 2004.

Gruliow, Leo (ed.). *Current Soviet Policies: The Documentary Record of the Nineteenth Party Congress and the Reorganization after Stalin's Death*. New York: Praeger, 1953.

Hoopes, Townsend. *The Devil and John Foster Dulles*. Boston: Atlantic Monthly Press, 1973.

Hughes, Emmet John. *The Ordeal of Power: A Political Memoir of the Eisenhower Years*. New York: Atheneum, 1963.

Khaustov, V. N. (ed.). *Delo Berii: prigovor obzhalavaniyu ne podlezhit* (The Beria Case: The Sentence is Not Subject to Appeal). Moscow: Mezhdunarodnyi fond "demokratiya," 2012.

Khlevniuk, Oleg. *Master of the House: Stalin and his Inner Circle*. Trans. Nora Seligman Favorov. New Haven: Yale University Press, 2009.

Khrushchev, Nikita. *Khrushchev Remembers*. Trans. and ed. Strobe Talbot. Boston: Little, Brown, 1970.

Khrushchev, Nikita. *Khrushchev Remembers: The Glasnost Tapes*. Trans. and ed. Jerrold L. Schecter and Vyacheslav V. Luchkov. Boston: Little, Brown, 1990.

Khrushchev, Nikita. *Khrushchev Remembers: The Last Testament*. Trans. and ed. Strobe Talbot. Boston: Little, Brown, 1974.

Kostyrchenko, Gennadi. "Deportatsiya—Mistifikatsiya." *Lekhaim*. September 2002.

Kostyrchenko, Gennadi (ed.). *Gosudartsvennyi antisemitizma v SSSR ot nachala do kulminatsii 1938–1953* (Official Antisemitism in the USSR from the Beginning to its Culmination). Moscow: Materik, 2005.

Kostyrchenko, Gennadi. *Out of the Red Shadows: Anti-Semitism in Stalin's Russia*. Trans. from the Russian. Amherst, New York: Prometheus Books, 1995.

Kramer, Mark. "Declassified Materials from CPSU Central Committee Plenums: Sources, context, highlights." *Cahiers du Monde russe*, 40/1–2, janvier–juin 1999.

Kramer, Mark. "The Early Post-Stalin Struggle and Upheavals in East-Central Europe." Part I, *Journal of Cold War Studies*, Vol. 1, No. 1, Winter 1999; Part II, *Journal of Cold War Studies*, Vol. 1, No. 2, Spring 1999; Part III, *Journal of Cold War Studies*, Vol. 1, No. 3, Fall 1999.

Kramer, Mark. "Political Succession and Political Violence in the USSR Following Stalin's Death." *Political Violence: Belief, Behavior, and Legitimation*, ed. Paul Hollander. New York: Palgrave Macmillan, 2008.

Larres, Klaus. *Churchill's Cold War: The Politics of Personal Diplomacy*. New Haven: Yale University Press, 2002.

Larres, Klaus. "Eisenhower and the First Forty Days after Stalin's Death: The Incompatibilty of Détente and Political Warfare." *Diplomacy & Statecraft*, Vol. 6, No. 2, July 1995.

Larres, Klaus and Osgood, Kenneth (eds). *The Cold War After Stalin's Death: A Missed Opportunity for Peace?* Lanham, Maryland: Rowman & Littlefield, 2006.

Leffler, Melvyn P. *For the Soul of Mankind: The United States, the Soviet Union, and the Cold War*. New York: Hill & Wang, 2007.

Leonhard, Wolfgang. *The Kremlin Since Stalin*. Trans. Elizabeth Wiskemann and Marian Jackson. New York: Praeger, 1962.

Mikoyan, Anastas Ivanovich. *Tak bylo: razmyshleniya o minuvshem* (How It Was: Reflections About the Past). Moscow: Vagrius, 1999.

Mozokhina, O. B. (ed.). *Delo Lavrentiia Berii* (The Case of Lavrenti Beria). Moscow: Kuchkovo pole, 2015.

Myasnikov, A. L. (Aleksandr Leonidovich), with the participation of E. I. Chazova. *Ya lechil Stalina* (I Treated Stalin). Moscow: Eksmo, 2011.

Ostermann, Christian F. (ed.). *Uprising in East Germany 1953: The Cold War, the German Question, and the First Major Upheaval Behind the Iron Curtain.* Budapest: Central European University Press, 2001.

Pinkus, Benjamin (ed.). *The Soviet Government and the Jews 1948–1967.* Cambridge: Cambridge University Press, 1984.

Plomper, Jan. *The Stalin Cult: A Study in the Alchemy of Power.* New Haven: Yale University Press, 2012.

Rapoport, Yakov. *The Doctors' Plot of 1953.* Trans. N. A. Persova and R. S. Bobrova. Cambridge: Harvard University Press, 1991.

Resis, Albert (ed.), *Molotov Remembers: Inside Kremlin Politics. Conversations with Felix Chuev.* Chicago: I. R. Dee, 1993.

Rostow, W. W. *Europe After Stalin: Eisenhower's Three Decisions of March 11, 1953.* Austin: University of Texas Press, 1982.

Rybin, A. T. "Ryadom s I. V. Stalinym" (Side by Side with I. V. Stalin). *Sotsiologicheskie issledovaniya* (Sociological Researches), May–June 1988.

Salisbury, Harrison E. *Moscow Journal: The End of Stalin.* Chicago: University of Chicago Press, 1962.

Shepilov, Dmitrii. *The Kremlin's Scholar: A Memoir of Soviet Politics Under Khrushchev.* Ed. Stephen Bittner, trans. Anthony Austin. New Haven: Yale University Press, 2007.

Simonov, Konstantin. *Glazami cheloveka moego pokoleniia* (Through the Eyes of a Man of My Generation). Moscow: Novosti, 1988.

Solzhenitsyn, Aleksandr I. *The Gulag Archipelago 1918–1956: An Experiment in Literary Investigation.* Vol. III, trans. Harry Willetts. New York: Harper & Row, 1978.

Taubman, William. *Khrushchev: The Man and His Era.* New York: Norton, 2003.

Tertz, Abram (Andrei Sinyavsky). *Goodnight!* Trans. Richard Lourie. New York: Penguin, 1989.

Yevtushenko, Yevgeny. *A Precocious Autobiography.* Trans. Andrew R. MacAndrew. New York: Dutton, 1963.

Zubok, Vladislav M. *A Failed Empire: The Soviet Union in the Cold War from Stalin to Gorbachev.* Chapel Hill: University of North Carolina Press, 2009.

LIST OF ILLUSTRATIONS

INDEX

256